GADFLYING CHINA
A Democratic
Perspective

ALSO BY X. DREW LIU

Issues in China's Political Reform (Editor), 1997

Gadflying China
A Democratic Perspective

X. Drew Liu

The China Strategic Institute
Washington, DC

Published in the United States of America in 1999
by The China Strategic Institute
733 15th Street, NW
Suite 700
Washington, DC 20005
Tel: 202.737.0022
Fax: 202.737.0024

Library of Congress Cataloging-in-Publication Data
Liu, X. Drew
    Gadflying China: A Democratic Perspective/by
    X. Drew Liu
1. Democracy-China.   2. China-Politics and
government - 1994-1998. I. Title.

ISBN 0-9660502-1-5

CONTENTS

PART THREE: CHINESE MILITARY IN TRANSITION

PART FOUR: HONG KONG, TAIWAN & GREATER CHINA

PART FIVE: THE UNITED STATES - CHINA RELATIONS

PART SIX: THE MAKING OF JIANG ZEMIN ERA

PREFACE AND ACKNOWLEDGEMENTS

China is like a slow-moving elephant at the crossroads. To avoid collapsing on its own weight, it must move ahead. But to secure its future, it must move in the direction of life-sustaining grasslands, not down a path, which leads to a hopeless desert. As a matter of fact, the image of gadflying an elephant always came to mind when I wrote these essays and papers.

Gadflying China is not always popular among the China-watcher community here in the United States, and perhaps even less so among the Chinese Diaspora. However, I have developed my own rationale for insisting on a critical view of China at each of its turns, i.e., from a democratic perspective. There is perhaps a number of ways to define what democracy is or is about. But to me it is first of all a moral issue. It is impossible to disregard this moral dimension in the wake of the Tiananmen Square massacre in June 1989, when the People's Liberation Army opened fire on unarmed civilians calling for peaceful changes of the government. Here democracy or no democracy is not a question of degree about how much humanity or dignity the nation can assume, but a fundamental choice between choice and no choice, or between enlightened humanism and blind brute force for a great people at a crucial moment of their history.

Indeed, that tragedy in the summer 1989 highlights a defining issue facing the nation: Will China democratize on its way to industrialization and modernity? The stakes are very high, and the answer to that question will, to a great extent, define China's identity and the relationships between China and the rest of the world in the next century. I have the belief that, without democracy, China will pose a threat to the world, including to itself.

This is as much due to its sheer size and superpower potential as it is to its past. The nation is immensely burdened by a sense of pride for its ancient culture and tradition as well as the painful memories of foreign invasions and internal chaos during the last 150 years. Thus, a path-dependent China is mostly likely to become an avenging China, seeking to address the past wrongs with aggressive behavior, reviving the 19th century gunboat diplomacy in the 21st century. The only hope for China to break this vicious, historical cycle is through a democratic framework in which reconciliation and healing may overcome the negative residues from the past. In the summer of 1994, I wrote the mission statement for the newly founded China Strategic Institute as to "bring about a renewal of China in a democratic framework, in which a rediscovery of China's rich history and culture is paralleled by an infusion of new values such as a respect for the rule of law, civil liberties, human rights, and other democratic institutions." Indeed, without democracy China may still be gigantic, but it may be a gigantic mistake, too.

But mere moral and historical arguments are not enough. Democracy is never something inevitable or a settled historical destination for China, or perhaps for any nation. Nor is there such thing called completion of democratization. It is, in a larger sense, an incessant fight and eternal vigil against tyranny, whether by minority or majority. In the case of China, building democracy involves changes in institutions at the highest level to the micro perceptions and behaviors of each individual, in which processes both creative destruction and piece by piece social construction are needed. In short, democratization is a task limited by neither space nor time. It is, therefore, impossible for China to take one or two political shock therapies at the national level to complete the task. Indeed, it is quite probable that efforts are invested by generations of Chinese democrats before the initial fruits of democracy can be seen.

If, as the saying goes, the devils are always in the details, good things cannot be really good merely existing in abstract. Democratization in China, so to speak, must work in concrete and specific terms; it must be a sea change from the bottom up, made possible only by constant reflections and choices of each and every Chinese citizen against the status quo.

But the status quo is surely being reified and mystified by the regime, intentionally or otherwise. Debunking the status quo and moving to democratic alternatives, therefore, are a dual task requiring both critiquing and constructiveness. Metaphorically, I often feel that the Chinese situation is similar to an elephant tied to a pole by a slim and restraining rope. In order to break loose from the rope, the elephant must realize the rope is breakable in the first place and that it has the potential to break it and be free. The ensuing pages reflect my personal journey in finding why the restraining rope is breakable and that China has great potentials to be democratic. Between romancing and demonizing China, I find this to be a sensible thing to do. Besides it is fun, too.

The book is a collection of essays and papers I wrote, mostly between 1996 and 1998, for the China Strategic Institute publications primarily on the then unfolding events and trends related to issues of China's democratization. For the purpose of this book, I grouped the pieces into six parts according to issue and subject, and arrange the pieces in each part in chronological order. Looking over these pieces in retrospect, I cannot fail to see many inadequacies, and wish that the underlying philosophical and historical themes be better developed and made more explicit. But, apart from minor editing, I prefer to let them stand as they were, humbly bearing witness to a great and challenging cause, i.e., China's transformation to democracy. The events and circumstances referred to in these essays occurred in the crucial years when Deng Xiaoping died (February 9, 1997) and the Era of Jiang Zemin was in the making. Personally, those were also memorable years, as my daughter and son were born, and my mother passed away, making me keenly aware of the radicalness of life and death. The Institute provided the perfect occasion and opportunities for me to concentrate on public policy issues regarding China. I had just finished my Ph.D degree from the University of Arizona and had no experience whatsoever in running a think tank in Washington DC. In spite of the difficulties, a lack of funding, differences and frustrations among ourselves, there is always great team work

4

at the Institute with unbeatable spirits and dedication. In particular, I would like to thank Rick Schwartz, Elaine Finkel, Ann Zill, Bob Boisture, Lianchao Han, Heping Shi, Juntao Wang and Xuecan Wu without whose support neither the Institute's work nor my research were possible. My thanks also go to a number of research associates in China, who greatly assisted my research. Throughout the years, the work of many interns volunteering their time and energy at the Institute was indispensable and greatly appreciated. I owe a special debt to a number of friends who offered general support, specific advice or helps over the years, particularly Nancy Pelosi, Bette Bao Lord, Ben Barber, Dan Southerland, Binyan Liu, Louisa Coan, George Lister, John King, and indeed the list can go on. Grants from National Endowment for Democracy are also gratefully acknowledged. Andrew Lai, Mark Chen and Wenhe Lu are appreciated for translating certain Chinese texts into English. Kelly Hearn, Marcia Pope, Will Schroeder, and Steve Valentin have been most helpful in typing and editing the original drafts as well as offering valuable comments on them.

Above all, I feel fortunate for having, and am deeply grateful to, a loving family, particularly my wife, Ruay, without whose emotional support, patience and understanding all this would be impossible to do.

PART ONE

DEMOCRATIC
MANDATE

CHINESE CULTURE AND DEMOCRACY
Issue Brief no. 10 (February 2, 1996)

Among Chinese intellectual circles, a cultural war is going on, the central theme of which is to determine the role of Chinese cultural tradition in reshaping China's 21st century. The Chinese conservatives would like to see Confucianism integrated with the ultra-nationalist sentiment and agenda, forming an ideological core to shore up the authoritarian polity. Conformity and limit on individual expression are framed as the virtue of the Chineseness as against the western democratic institutions based upon individual freedom.

Contrary to the Chinese leadership's wishful thinking, Confucianism will not justify dictatorship. More than two thousand years ago, Confucius taught the basic principles of respecting individuals' rights and dignity: "Do not impose on others things you do no want for yourself" (*ji suo bu yu wu shi yu ren*). The Confucian school insists that the mandate of the heaven is from the commoners: "The heaven beholds through the eyes of the people and hears through the ears of the people" (*tian shi zi wo min shi, tian ting zi wo min ting*). Thus Mencius (372-289 B.C.), the second most recognized Confucian scholar next to Confucius, explicitly said if the rulers fail to respond to the needs of the people, the people have the right to overthrow the rulers. For two thousand years "the People's Supremacy" (*minben sixiang*) became key to dynastic legitimacy. In an alleged Confucianist social order, the constituents came first in importance, the statehood was the next, and the emperors were least important among the three (*min wei gui, sheji ci zhi, jun wei qing*).

Indeed the Chinese communists betrayed the Confucianist principles by reversing the rank order among the three elements. The leadership personnel became the most important in Chinese political order. Mao created the biggest and most flagrant personnel cult in Chinese history. The centrality of the top leaders (Deng Xiaoping and currently

Jiang Zemin) in Chinese political life remains unchanged to this day.

Meanwhile the party-state organizations monopolized political and economic sources of power, eliminating civil liberties of the people. It is often forgotten that in traditional Chinese society government offices never existed below the county level. Most local communities were self-governed where the scholar-gentry presented moral and political leadership. But this social group, buffering between the state power and local communities, was brutally (and in many cases physically) eliminated in the process of the Chinese communist movement in the 1940s and 1950s.

Thus, the current level of the state's interference in family and individual private life would appear outrageous even to the most conservative confucianists in the pre-communist era. With rigid control of information flow (press and even E-mail), the people's eyes and ears were open only to what the dictators have to say. By ruthlessly punishing any voice of dissent, the Chinese leadership has turned the world's most populous country into a nation of dead silence.

The current debate in China on its cultural tradition is not a healthy one. The population are not allowed to explore the true potentials of their tradition for a cultural renaissance in a democratic environment. Instead the public are constantly reminded by the party propaganda machine that democracy and human rights are alien and even contrary to the Chinese values. Those who are not fooled by the government may just look across the Taiwan Strait to contemplate how democracy and Chinese culture have worked together in a Chinese socioeconomic miracle.

Clearly the central question is one of political power rather than culture. And Chinese culture, if allowed to play a role in the process, will reinforce people's demand for their basic human rights and political freedom. Democratic aspirations transcend cultural differences. The Chinese communists should stop abusing Chinese culture and its symbols for the purpose of keeping their political power.

THE NEW MANDATE FOR DEMOCRACY
Issue Brief no. 19 (April 5, 1996)

China's earlier mandate for democracy can be traced back to the Republican Revolution led by Mr. Sun Yat-sen, the founding father of China's Republic. He and his fellow democrats ended the Qing Dynasty and established Asia's first democracy. In the May Fourth Movement (1919), the Chinese public embraced "Mr. Democracy and Mr. Science" depicted as the two distinguished doctors to treat the illness of rapid social disintegration following the downfall of the Qing empire (1911). Though China's first democracy soon collapsed under the foreign colonial policies and war lords politics, the Chinese people's democratic aspiration continued to be a vital political force. Thus before taking power in China, the Chinese communists framed their movement as an effort to "end the political monopoly by one leader, one party and one doctrine". Of course, they betrayed the Chinese people after winning the civil war with the Chinese nationalists, and established a Stalinist regime.

In the unfolding post-Deng era, Sun Yat-sen's ideas are coming back to China, forming a *new democratic mandate* in spite of the changed social and historical circumstances. First, Sun Yat-sen's "Three People's Principles" were fully realized in Taiwan, a source of inspiration and emulation for the Chinese people on the mainland. Taiwan's successful political and economic system is widely recognized among many intellectual and policy circles in China, a fact transcending the differences on the reunification issue across the Strait.

Second, the communist regime is rapidly outgrown by the new social conditions in the reform era. The Leninist Party/State system is no longer viable to govern China's economy and society. Different interests are emerging and undermining the existing governance structure. Such development has forced the central government to reform the current system and gradually adapt to the rule of law. Though organized political opposition is brutally suppressed, the room for dissent in other areas is relentlessly growing, a harbinger for future democratic opposition.

Government's restrictions on civil liberties are becoming more and more unpopular. In fact, many of the restrictions are already broken by people's spontaneous acts. The taboo of criticizing the government, for instance, is significantly undermined as people became bolder in speaking their minds in private and smaller public gatherings. The uncurbed corruption fuels the popular demand for checks and balances in the government, and presses for more accountability of the state officials. The village-level democratic elections are enthusiastically embraced by the rural residents, the rapid spread of which breaks the myth that Chinese do not care for democracy. Even within the communist party, pressures for restoring party's members' democratic rights are increasing. Some of them spontaneously established democratic processes to elect their own branch leaders to represent their own interests. They do not want to be the docile tools for the policies handed down from the Polibureau in Beijing.

Thirdly, the democratic force matured during the years since 1989. They have learned to survive in the harsh political environment, and worked skillfully and effectively in promoting changes in China. Though many of its symbolic leaders were thrown into jail, their members are active in many non-political and professional organizations. Just like it is impossible to kill an idea, the democratic idea is alive and spreading among the new generation of Chinese citizens. In February 1995, Chinese democrats petitioned the National People's Congress (NPC) on fighting corruption and on abolishing the notorious arbitrary detention regulation. Their demand has received wide public support, and over the year NPC has increased its role in supervising the government on anti-corruption measures. The arbitrary detention was also abolished last month by NPC convention. The Chinese government can round up a few dissidents, but it can no longer afford to ignore their demand which has broad public support.

The reason is simple. The new democratic mandate comes from the will of the people, something beyond the control of Jiang Zemin and his colleagues in Beijing. Like in the old Chinese saying, the rulers are the ship on the vast and powerful river formed by the people. When the river is moving, the ship has better to go along with it. China's democratization is like a river moving towards the sea. It may still have a long way to go and a few difficult gorges to pass, but it will arrive at its destination in spite of the ship.

THE MEMORY OF THE JUNE FOURTH
Issue Brief no. 25 (June 4, 1997)

Eight years after the June 4 Massacre (1989) of the pro-democracy demonstrators in the Tiananmen Square and the streets in Beijing, the memory of the tragedy lingers in the minds of all Chinese people, because the foundation of the movement which was crushed lay in popular sentiment. The students who led the movement gave voice to the grievances of the Chinese public, and thus reflected a fundamental principle of democracy — change must come from the people. The pro-democracy demonstration in 1989 embodied the desire of the ordinary citizens to find solutions to the problems of their country.

The movement also arose from the evolution of the Chinese social and economic systems. Although the Chinese economy was increasingly driven by free-market forces, the political system which supported it lagged behind in the form of tyrannical, autocratic and monistic rule. The apparent dichotomy of economic freedom and political repression created an environment which bred bureaucratic corruption and widespread social injustice. Inflation grew, but the working people, sector of society most affected by inflation, found no avenue to express their dissatisfaction with the current state of affairs and economic policies.

The nation's political leadership was not at all restrained by the need for public accountability. The business executives who benefited from the new economic situation had no reason to include the laboring masses in their assessment of economic well-being. Thus, the working men and women were left out of the decision making processes that profoundly impacted their lives. But a country which disregards the ideas of the majority of its citizens cannot move forward. Addressing this problem, the students who protested in Tiananmen Square eight years ago expressed not only specific grievances of the public, but also a grave concern over the general inadequacies of the political establishment in forging national concensus. The students spoke on a much larger and more urgent issue: Chinese modernization could not succeed without political reform.

However, such state of affairs has not changed since 1989. The economy is still developing, but the political structure remains stagnant with the prospect of worsening systemic tensions. Against such backdrop, the lingering memory of the Tiananmen Square massacre serves as a powerful reminder of a job unfinished, because the Chinese government has resisted the changes of the time and refused to change itsself.

Memories of personal tragedies, buried deep in the souls of the relatives and friends of those who were killed in 1989, will persist and become collective memory of a nation for generations. Mothers such as Ding Zilin will not easily allow the memory of their children's deaths at the hands of ruthless tyrants to be forgotten. So the government's attempt to ignore the massacre until the people forget about its significance will fail. The memory of the attack on the people's right to decide their own future will haunt the rulers in Beijing like a ghost until they offer some kind of rectification. Although time can make the incident seem remote to many who did not witness the brutality firsthand, the symbolic value of June 4, 1989 will never depreciate.

It is a mistake for a government to count on its people to forget such an ill-forgotten horror as the Tiananmen Square massacre. The only possible way to make strides towards a rectification of the current situation and to make amends for the tragedies of the past is to move forward toward a government based on democratic institutions. But even this cannot wholly alleviate the pain of those who lost their loved ones, nor can it immediately compensate all who have suffered under Chinese communist tyranny. The fact that we remember it can make the June Fourth Movement a force for positive democratic change in the future so that the deaths of those young people will not have been in vain.

THE TIBET ISSUE AND CHINA'S SOUL
Issue Brief no.31 (August 1, 1997)

Among the overseas Chinese, the Tibet issue gets little if any attention. There is of course the problem of misinformation from the Chinese government. Thus, the condition of the lives of six million Tibetans is almost a taboo, because the issue is primarily framed in terms of whether or not Tibet should gain independence from China. But there seems to be more to it than just political discourse. The Tibetan issue has a human and a moral side of the story significant at both national and individual levels. That story exists at the bottom of the Chinese soul, though it is often suppressed in the subconscious. Many of my Tibetan friends express doubt as to whether Chinese people are willing to or are capable of understanding the sufferings of the Tibetan people. I think the answer is, on the contrary, that Chinese people are quite willing and capable.

The fact is, the Chinese people have suffered a lot from western colonial policies under which foreign intrusions devastated their culture and their communities. The imperial phenomenon is all too familiar to them. They certainly understand what racial discrimination means. At the gate of Waitan, the most popular park in Shanghai, in the 1930s and 1940s there used to hang a sign saying "No Chinese or dogs allowed." The Chinese protested against such racial discrimination on their own soil, but the park's rule remained intact because it was on land leased to the British.

What about foreign military occupation? The Chinese lost about twenty million lives under the Japanese occupation before and during the Second World War. These memories are still fresh in the minds of the elderly Chinese population and have not been forgotten by the younger generation. Because of such memories, the Chinese people recently hailed the end of the colonial era by overwhelmingly supporting Hong Kong's return to China.

The question is, Are the Chinese willing to inflict the same injustice which they have suffered in their own history on the Tibetan people? Historically, there have been cases when the oppressed are liberated only to become oppressive of others, and many nations who have suffered from foreign invasions become expansionist once they are strong. The Dalai Lama himself pointed out that evil always leads to more evil and more suffering, and only true human compassion can stop that vicious cycle. Indeed, for many Chinese, the lesson from their historical experience teaches that nothing matters but raw power and domination.

Thus, aside from the misinformation by the rulers in Beijing, the Tibetan issue is a conflict within the soul of the Chinese nation. It is about who they are and what they are. It may be a touchstone of whether China can transcend its past on the road to a glorious future. And the result depends on which way the Chinese consciousness will turn. Will the Chinese soul be stranded in the mentality of the colonial era where "might makes right" or will it be able to transcend that era and display its tender side of compassion and understanding, qualities which trace back to the teaching of Confucius: "Never impose on another that which you do not want for yourself" (*ji suo bu yu, wu shi yu ren*).

Frankly, I do not know which side of reasoning will win in this soul battle. But the final result will determine to a large extent the identity of China as a nation. The Tibet issue currently is very much suppressed and rarely debated, even in the overseas Chinese community. Perhaps the issue is too disturbing and troubling to the Chinese soul, or perhaps there is a suppressed sense of guilt for having caused the Tibetan people to suffer. But whatever the reasons are, there is no excuse for further avoidance of the issue. And however painful or difficult it may be, the road has to be travelled to achieve the reconciliation with the Tibetan people.

In history, the Chinese and Tibetan peoples lived peacefully side by side, and with intense cultural exchanges to their mutual benefit. Will that day dawn again in the future? I hope so.

THE MOMENT OF TRUTH
Issue Brief no. 35 (August 29, 1997)

A t this moment in China, the 15th Congress of the CCP looms large on the horizon, and so does the party that holds the meeting. But larger than all this is a party member who stands up to speak the truth. Mr. Shang Dewen, an economics professor and veteran CCP member, in an open letter called on Jiang Zemin to push for political reform that would allow the Chinese citizens to directly elect their national leader through multiparty elections.

Indeed, among the fifty million or more Chinese Communist Party members, perhaps few still actually believe in communism. The CCP Constitution stipulates that the first of the five "minimum" requirements (*jiben tiaojian*) for becoming a CCP member is "to serve the people with heart and soul." How many of the CCP members can fulfill this minimal requirement? Perhaps none. Thus, China is a "communist" country which ironically has no communist adherents; and the CCP has more than fifty million members, none of whom meet basic membership requirements.

The tragedy of China is its hypocrisy, enforced by political power and domination. Imagine a scenario of Hans Christian Andersen's *The Emperor's New Clothes*. When the fact that the emperor is naked becomes obvious to all his beholders, who are nonetheless prohibited from mentioning this fact, what will the emperor's subjects do? Perhaps some would look away and ignore the emperor. Indeed, many Chinese citizens choose to ignore politics. It doesn't matter at all to them whether Mr. Jiang has clothes on or not, as long as they can peacefully mind their own business. Others, however, would try to find the right opportunities to speak the truth, which probably would bring them trouble, if not prison terms.

The British poet Shelley wrote that when winter comes, the spring cannot be far behind. His Chinese equivalent would contend: When absurdities abound, can truth be far behind? In Andersen's fable, a child spoke out to end the absurdity. The Chinese absurdity, however, is larger and more powerful than a child could comprehend. But a lie is a lie. When more individuals like Mr. Shang speak the truth, the days will be numbered for those rulers who stand naked in their hypocrisy.

THE MUSCLE AND THE HEART OF CHINA
Issue Brief no. 38 (September 19, 1997)

China is often referred to as a sleeping giant, who is now stirring to wake up. Underlying this metaphor is often a concern about China's future behavior when it is fully industrialized. Will it be an impulsive, hostile, and ultra-nationalist member of the global village in the next century? Or will it be a major engine for the promotion of peace and prosperity in the region and the world? Noticing the growing physique of the giant, people around the world are also watching for signs of a growing heart. As a Jewish proverb says, the heart is half a prophet for the future.

In this light, I cannot help but think that the just concluded 15th Congress of the Chinese Communist Party was a disappointment. On the first day of the meeting, former General Secretary Zhao Ziyang sent a letter to the delegates asking for a revisiting of the Tiananmen Square Incident in order that the regime might regain legitimacy and trust among the Chinese people. But Jiang Zemin and his colleagues were so afraid that they suppressed the voice of conscience within the CCP in every way they could. As a result, the Congress focused completely on China's muscle power, but not at all on the growth of China's heart. The leaders mentioned nothing about China's political reform or an improvement of human rights.

Confucius spent his whole life on the development of a Chinese heart. He said that a people cannot establish itself without a belief (*min wu xin bu li*). But the Chinese leadership seems not to care for nurturing a value system beyond the bankrupt communist ideology. The spirituality of the Chinese nation has never existed at such a low level as it does under the current regime.

Indeed, when the leadership in Beijing views China's future only in terms of GNP or GDP numbers, it is not surprising that money becomes the only fuel that moves things in China. Social justice and human rights do not turn profits, so they continue to be marginalized. And corruption produces profits, so it becomes the standard pattern of behavior whenever opportunities arise. The rule of law cannot be measured in monetary terms, so the leaders feel no urgency to make it into the cornerstone of Chinese social order.

No one can deny the economic progress China made in the last two decades, but nor can one fail to see the decline of moral order, a heavy price to be paid for Deng's rapid economic development without accompanied political reform. Jiang Zemin perhaps does not realize that the world would respect China not just for its muscle, but also for its heart. And without freedom of expression, the Chinese heart will forever be under-developed. The Chinese communist policy of suppressing those liberties will serve the interests of those in power, but at the cost of the Chinese nation as a whole. If China does not want to become a giant with ample muscle and no conscience or heart, democratization is its best regimen.

QUALITY OPPOSITION
Issue Brief no.46 (November 21, 1997)

On November 21, leading Chinese dissident Wei Jingsheng gave his first public speech in New York since his arrival in the United States for medical treatment. Although his health had been threatened during eighteen years of imprisonment, Wei's spirits remain high, and he is still dedicated to the cause of China's democratization. Eighteen years ago, Wei's call for democracy was a weak voice on the Xidan Democracy Wall. But his message was feared by the then paramount leader Deng Xiaoping, who personally gave the directive to punish him with long prison sentences. But during all this time, Wei's message has reached a much larger population in China. His personal courage and persistence in promoting democracy will be sources of inspiration for China's democratic movement.

Today, Wei and his idea remain to be what Jiang Zemin and his ruling clique in Beijing perhaps most fear. Because the regime failed to crush this man's spirit in prison, the leaders in Beijing perhaps hoped to eliminate his influence in China by sending him into exile. But they will fail again because Wei symbolizes the kind of political opposition most threatening to the regime.

First, Wei is a relentless fighter than a mere politician. There has been no ambiguity, no compromise, and no wavering in his vision and principles. During the press conference on Friday, in response to a question about his perceived personal position in China's history, Wei replied curtly that he has no interest in this issue. For the last 18 years, he indeed appears to be moved by a calling rather than by some personal ambition. In the future uphill journey towards his goal, this may turn into a most important cornerstone of his leadership, which could revitalize and make more effective the democratic opposition.

Second, Wei does have the moral authority to command a following and carry the message for democracy to a larger population in China. Through modern communication technologies, he can reach his countrymen much more effectively than he could through the big character posters he used eighteen years ago. Of course, Wei faces the many challenges and dilemmas experienced by all Chinese democratic activists who have been forced into exile. But as he said in the press conference, as long as he can overcome himself, there is nothing that can stop him. There are indeed many obstacles on the road to China's democratization, but judging from the example of this man's personal experience, they can all be overcome.

HOW TO REFORM CHINA'S NATIONAL PEOPLE'S CONGRESS

China Strategic Review, Vol. II, no. 6
(November/December 1997)

In post-Deng China, there are many forces working for China's political reform.   Some activists favor the grassroots approach of mobilizing the masses to seek independent political rights, then forcing the state to recognize such rights. The process of democratization in the Philippines is an example of this approach. In China, many dissidents as well as those whose interests have been sacrificed in the economic reforms (e.g., unemployed workers) favor this grassroots approach. Indeed, without popular participation, political reform in China is impossible to carry through for two reasons. First, the united grassroots democracy forces need to create enough public pressure, due to a shared ideology and popularly perceived common interest, for China to openly embrace democracy, and thereby turn various issues into political opportunities for change. Second, China's new democratic order needs to be substantiated by public participation under the rule of law.

However, there are many political forces that work within the Chinese government apparatus that cannot be neglected in the democratization of China. There is a top down approach to democratize China which differs from the grassroots endeavor in that it takes its departure from vested personal and group interests. This may not sound attractive in ideological and moral terms, but it is still worthy of our attention. As China's economic reform continues, different interest groups are emerging and consolidating. The direction in which the Chinese post-communist political system may evolve will in part depend on the coalition between some of these interest groups which control substantial resources. Since their interests are partially, if not completely, recognized by the current regime, these groups' political reform agendas maintain a conservative nature, i.e., they seek to preserve the order of the current regime. This preference entails that they will hesitate to go forward with the reform of the current political structure as long as there is the potential risk of social disorder.

Thus, whenever there is a grassroots demand for greater political and social rights by the workers and peasants which appears to be disruptive to the current government's order, this group stands in support of the regime's strong-handed policies to contain or even suppress such demands. In a sense, the demand for political reform from within the system represents an effort to advance the political and economic standing of these interest groups within the government, but does not necessary entail an advocation of broad power sharing with the socially, politically, and economically disadvantaged groups.

The irony is that, without some degree of collaboration from these forces, there will be no political reform, but only a bloody revolution at the cost of tens of thousands of human lives, not to mention the additional time to rebuild democratic order. Therefore, the best scenario for democratizing China would be when the forces inside and outside the government work together effectively. The Chinese democrats are challenged to find a point where they can reintegrate the progressive and relatively more liberal forces within the regime and the people's power outside the system. Without some institutional bridges between the top-down and grassroots processes, it is difficult to fully utilize the political opportunities afforded by two decades of economic reform.

This essay considers one such bridging institution, the National People's Congress (NPC), a body that could integrate the progressive wing within the system and the people's power outside the system. The reform of the NPC is less threatening to vested interest groups within the regime. In fact, many factions within the ruling clique have been marginalized since the CCP's Fifteenth Congress, and many hope to use the platform of the NPC to exert their influence. However, the NPC is a platform that also can be regularly utilized by the Chinese public if the reform of its structure is successful, i.e., the reform of its legislative and electoral processes. These opportunities avail themselves as the NPC reaches a position of potentially substantiating constitutional power if the CCP control mechanisms continue to weaken.

Origin and Status Quo

The Chinese constitution stipulates that the NPC is the supreme power of the country. Unlike a Western parliament, which is primarily a legislative branch of the government, the NPC holds a mixture of legislative and executive power. In fact, the idea of forming the NPC drew upon the ideas of the Paris Commune, which was established in 1871 by the citizens of Paris and was highly regarded by Karl Marx. The short-lived Paris Commune emphasized the people's power through the direct election of people's representatives who would simultaneously carry out legislative, executive, and judicial functions. This structure of centralized power is also compatible with the Chinese communist endeavor to win the civil war with the nationalists prior to 1949.

In addition to inspiration from the Paris Commune, the NPC system is strongly influenced by the Soviet model. As the Supreme Soviet was the tool of the Soviet Communist Party, the Chinese NPC also has been dominated by the power of the Chinese Communist Party (CCP), which then became the only significant power in Chinese social, economic, and political matters. A second characteristic of the NPC that draws on the former Soviet model is the elimination of the direct electoral processes as practiced in the Paris Commune. In fact, party control and the absence of open direct elections are two sides of the same coin in the elimination of an effective and authentic voice of the people. Thus, the NPC became the true rubber stamp of the CCP, and its constitutional power remains nominal. In turn, the Chinese constitution became for the most part an ineffective piece of paper.

However, during the last two decades of economic reform, the NPC system has undergone significant changes even though these two characteristics have not fundamentally changed. First, the CCP control over the NPC has been considerably weakened in recent years. Second, experimental direct elections of representatives are being held at county levels. All this has created new opportunities for reforming the NPC and turning this body into a powerful instrument for democratizing China.

Conditions of Further Reform

Within Chinese policy circles, there are two views on why the NPC has been successful in its reform measures over the last two decades. One view, the top-down perspective, holds that the NPC is dependent upon the personnel structure of the CCP elite. The other view, the grassroots perspective looks at the profound changes in the Chinese social structure during the reform era as the root for the reform of the NPC system.

The former view argues that the evolution of the NPC is largely the result of the leadership personalities of Peng Zhen, Wan Li, and Qiao Shi, chairmen of the NPC in the reform era. Peng Zhen was persecuted during the Cultural Revolution. However, when Deng Xiaoping resumed power, Peng's status in the party was rehabilitated, although he failed to enter the inner circle of Deng Xiaoping's ruling clique. Unsatisfied with his marginal position, Peng used the NPC to promote his own base of power within the governing system. Understandably, the NPC, like the People's Political Consultative Committee before the time of reform, was considered a primarily superficial entity. It was labeled a "political flower vase" (*zhengzhi huaping*) because it had no substantial power. Partly for this reason, Peng was given the post of Chairman of the

NPC. It was therefore in his political interest to transform the NPC from a rubber stamp organization into a potentially powerful one.

Peng Zhen's successors, Wan Li and Qiao Shi, perhaps occupy similar periphery positions within the power structure. When Deng Xiaoping appointed the core of the CCP's new generation of leadership, Jiang Zemin became a rising star. Qiao Shi, who is more senior than Jiang, was in an awkward position. In order to pave the way for Jiang's ascendance, many senior leaders were marginalized and appointed chairmen or vice-chairmen of the NPC. Qiao Shi's competitive relationship with Jiang Zemin was common knowledge in China. He utilized the NPC as a bargaining chip to renegotiate post-Deng political order and he promoted the NPC's role in order to promote his own standing. Thus, the reform of the NPC is viewed as conditional to the power struggles within the CCP leadership, which has nothing to do with democratic aspirations.

In contrast to this view, the alternative opinion holds that the NPC's evolution resulted from the profound social changes during the last two decades of reform. During the CCP's Thirteenth Congress, Zhao Ziyang, then general secretary of the CCP, claimed that China was in the primary stage of socialism. According to his political report, China's system of government must reform in order to meet the challenges of the reform era, which included the reform of the NPC. Zhao recognized the necessity of institutionalizing social consultation and dialogue among the different social strata (*jianli shehui ge jieceng de duihua zhidu*.) He also acknowledged that, in the primary stage of Chinese socialism, there were different emerging interests that need to be reconciled. In other words, Zhao indirectly recognized the inevitable social differentiation from a unitary party/state system. In his view, the NPC should provide the institutional support and legal foundation for this dialogue and reconciliation, so he called upon the NPC to strengthen its legislative and supervisory roles. He stressed that the NPC must achieve greater professionalization and reform its legislative and administrative procedures accordingly.

Zhao's remarks were made nearly a decade ago. Since then, more changes have occurred in Chinese society which have required a further overhaul of the system. The control mechanisms of the CCP's system of government are increasingly being weakened by market forces. The CCP grassroots organizations are becoming dysfunctional, especially in the working population. The ideological indoctrination of the CCP has been discarded by most Chinese citizens. The emerging interests or differentiated social strata to which Zhao Ziyang referred have already entrenched themselves in Chinese social life. Following an upsurge of business activities in the private sector, many professionals (e.g., lawyers, doctors, artists, etc.) also have came out of government administrative control.

Indeed, reform has unleashed forces at the grassroots level, such as civic and economic organizations based on private property rights and local interests, that have become increasingly vocal in demanding greater rights and open channels to participation in the decision-making process. The rule of law has become the only alternative to the highly personalized system of Maoist totalitarian government control. Thus, according to these grassroots forces, the reform of the NPC is part and parcel of the larger structural changes currently occurring in Chinese society.

Obviously, both top-down and grassroots views on why the NPC's recent reform measures have succeeded have their own lines of reasoning and emphasize different aspects of the conditions that have allowed for the NPC reforms. But what interests me here is the potential integration of both top-down and grassroots processes. Looking at the fluid nature of the Chinese political situation, the NPC provides a most convenient platform for bridging the grassroots forces and the personal politics in the post-Deng era. This is especially true when we consider the lack of political outlets for the growing number of socially disadvantaged groups such as minorities and unemployed workers from the state sector. The CCP regime is unable to deal effectively with corruption and social justice, and there is no longer a political strongman like Mao Zedong or Deng Xiaoping who can use his personal power to silence differences that exist within the system. In the next section, I will explore the possibility of working out a strategy for utilizing the NPC system as a point of departure for overall political reform aimed at democratizing China.

A Democratic Strategy for Reforming the NPC

It is my personal view that successful political reform towards democratization requires the collaboration of the progressive wing of the ruling apparatus and the popular demand for democratic change. The NPC's reform efforts have offered a golden political opportunity for cooperation between and coordination of the top-down and grassroots reform mind-sets. In addition, the reform of the NPC system presents little if any risk to social order, but on the contrary seems to be the most likely area for social reconciliation and the compromise of group interests. Since this is the case, Chinese democrats should pay particular attention and contribute considerable energy to issues related to the reform of the current NPC system.

As was mentioned previously, the two major obstacles to the NPC's maturity and its democratic role are the Communist Party's traditional tendency to control and the absence of democratic electoral processes. This spring, during the annual NPC conference, Li Peng is scheduled to replace Qiao Shi as the chairman of the NPC. As the number two man in the CCP's ruling clique, Li Peng's political interest lies in the continued strengthening of the NPC, because it will be his only platform. Thus, we should not rule out the possibility that Li Peng will soften his conservative stance after assuming the responsibility of head of the NPC. In fact, for China's third generation of leaders, personal political interests matter more than ideological beliefs. Even Li Peng made an effort to change his conservative image before the Fifteenth Congress of the CCP.

Moreover, the absence of a solitary supreme political figure necessarily results in the emergence of factions. These factions often appear to use their governmental functions to check one another's political power. In the past, Jiang Zemin and Qiao Shi played these roles, and in the future it is also possible for Jiang Zemin and Li Peng to use their respective positions within the party apparatus to check one another's power. Thus, political interests indicate a possibility of continued alienation of the CCP and the NPC systems.

In the present political climate, rampant corruption has led to greater public demand for the strengthening of the NPC's role of supervising government officials. The direct election of NPC county-level representatives will give momentum to the opening up of direct elections of NPC members at various levels. As for the disadvantaged groups, the NPC is increasingly becoming the channel through which they may voice their opinions and actually participate in the decision-making process. Given the chaotic nature of grassroots level regulation of economic and social life, local communities especially consider the NPC as a platform to negotiate a new order. Thus, in the next five years or so, the political opportunity exists to change the status of the NPC fundamentally. I think four areas of reform are key to achieving this end.

First, research should be conducted and public education should be carried out on issues related to the specific steps for returning the NPC's constitutional status as the supreme power of the country. Scholars should write papers to promote the idea of the separation of the party and the government, and the submission of the CCP to the constitution and the rule of law. Without such reforms, it should be pointed out, China will enter into an era of chaos. In the past decade, the NPC has drafted numerous laws and acts, helping China to move into the direction of the rule of law. Now it is high time that the NPC turn its legislative energy towards itself and strengthen itself in order to play a more active role in China's political life.

Second, efforts should be made to promote the direct election of all NPC members. Only in this way will the NPC's true role as a legislative and supervisory body be realized. The direct election at the county level of representatives has already been achieved, but this needs to be expanded to include all NPC members at provincial and national levels. In the areas of competitive open balloting and transparency, there is still much room for improvement.

Third, in terms of rules and procedures, reforms should be made to allow the substantive participation of NPC members in the legislative process. At present, the standing committee of the NPC plays the role of an actual legislative body, while the NPC general assembly only meets once a year for a period of a few weeks. To substantiate the NPC's function, it is necessary to allow the members to conduct meetings throughout the year similar to the conduct of parliaments in other democratic societies. To increase the efficiency of these meetings, the number of NPC representatives should be reduced from the current 3,000 to less than 1,000. Moreover, in each quarter, there should be a designated period when the government officials have to appear before the NPC to report on their work and receive inquiries. Special committees of the NPC should be formed in correspondence with the different government functions so as to increase further the NPC's ability to supervise the government.

Finally, the NPC special committees at various levels should experiment with holding public hearings and calling witnesses to testify on matters concerning public interest. By speaking to the public interest, the NPC may further strengthen its position in Chinese political life. Lobbying should be allowed so that civic and social organizations can contribute their views and expertise. It is certainly in the interest of the proper functioning of the NPC and the rule of law to recruit experts, intellectuals, and scholars to participate in legislative research and issues of concern to Chinese citizens.

In conclusion,   all these measures are necessary to transform the current NPC system into a truly democratic system. Some of these measures require the abandonment of conservative policies of the regime from the top-down, and others, like lobbying and the participation of citizens in a direct election process, can be achieved by citizen initiatives. Fortunately, in the current political climate, the idea of NPC reform is no longer taboo in policy circles. Now is the time for Chinese democrats to begin charting the path for reforming the NPC. Scholars and researchers may seize whatever opportunities they have to debate in the public or private arena the specific methods of reforming the NPC so as to promote social stability, the welfare of the people, and the democratic rights of the citizens.

MAKING ORDER OUT OF CHAOS
Issue Brief no. 50 (January 2, 1998)

L ooking ahead into 1998, the citizens of China have mixed feelings. In the past year, they witnessed the changing of the guard in the CCP's leadership, the return of Hong Kong to China, and the worsening of the corruption problem. Having had a small taste of economic freedom and civil liberty, they certainly do not want to return to the Maoist order where every aspect of life was controlled by an omnipotent party/state system.

Indeed the Chinese people's fear of social chaos and its yearning for order are two sides of the same coin: the nation still lacks an order that people believe to be sustainable. Historically, this social psychology existed in China when the nation faced the prospect of great social transformation.

At this moment of history, sustainable order is indeed absent in China's economic and financial systems, and its cultural status is in great flux, too. As one example, China is currently experiencing the largest relocation and dislocation of its people ever, because over a hundred million people are migrating from their hometowns to seek jobs in major urban centers throughout China.

But deep within the Chinese cultural psychology is a belief that, when a period of disorder plays itself out, a new order will follow, as the phrase *pi ji tai lai* (*I Ching*) indicates. In fact, every culture has a list of myths about the cycle of order and disorder. Greek mythology depicts the beginning as ruled by a goddess named Chaos. The disorder was ended by her son, a god named Eros, who brought to life an order through harmony and love.

A Chinese myth about the beginning describes a powerful male hero named Gonggong, who tried to open a new world, but in the process his head knocked down a pillar of the heavens at Buzhou Mountain. After that, chaos and disorder ruled. Life became possible only after a goddess called Nü Wa who came to the rescue. She made five kinds of colored stone with which she mended the heavens. Hence, the beginning of Chinese civilization.

Today's China is in the beginning of a new era. Economic reform has brought down one of the pillars that sustained the heaven of totalitarian order. Political violence carried out by the regime against its people, the commercial tidal wave that has washed away the roots of the traditional way of life for tens of thousands of people, and moral anomaly — all these call for a modern Nü Wa to establish a new order for an old civilization.

But old mythology cannot replace real change. Thus this new Nü Wa, I think, has to be the Chinese people itself, and one of the five magic color stones to mend the leaking heaven will be freedom and democracy.

POLITICAL SOFT-LANDING
Issue Brief no.51 (January 9, 1998)

For years many in China have complained about one dilemma: China won't be democratized unless the Chinese Communist Party (CCP) is willing to share power, but the CCP won't be willing to share power unless

China is democratic. There is no answer. It's just like the chicken-or-the-egg paradox.

Indeed, like a huge cargo plane, China is taking off economically, but the question is: Where will it land politically? The CCP is like the pilot who knows how to fly a plane but doesn't know the destination, and on the plane sit 1.2 billion passengers. At the moment, the CCP leadership is trying hard to convince the Chinese public that the safest landing for them is the one that never occurs. This may sound very convincing to many, as long as the passengers are not aware that fuel is running out.

And fuel is low. According to one recent study by the Chinese Academy of Social Sciences, there will be 30 million people laid off in 1998 as the result of the forced downsizing and closures of the failing state enterprises. Combined with those who are already unemployed, this means that more than ten percent of the urban population are jobless, something that China has never experienced since the founding of the People's Republic. The CCP can imprison a few thousand dissidents, but it cannot keep millions of workers off the street.

Whether the leaders in Beijing are willing or not, they have to yield to the pressures of the people who seek to provide their children's bread and protect their rights to existence. And the only way to do so would be to allow these people to self-organize under the Chinese law. If President Jiang Zemin and his associates refuse to let the people defend themselves peacefully, they will do so violently because they have no choice. The sharing of power by the CCP will only be possible when it is not a choice but a necessity.

Thus, a solution to the above paradox of democratizing China is simply free information to the people, or to keep the previous metaphor, to let the passengers know that fuel is low and that they cannot afford to sit idly. The recent increase in unemployment has helped many to understand this fact. More and more of them are coming to realize that preparing the nation to land at a democratic destination is a better idea than to continue to circle in the sky, because a soft-landing is better than a crash.

THE STRUGGLE TO DEFINE CHINA'S IDENTITY
Issue Brief no. 51 (April 17, 1998)

Every nation has two sides: that which it exhibits to the rest of the world and that which it exhibits to its own people. The government of China has tried hard to project to the international community an open-minded, tolerant, and progressive image, which is a positive development resulting from two decades of opening up to the outside world. The question is, how much can the international community change China through engagement, trade, and communication? Many people point to increasing economic freedom and growing civil liberties as internal mechanisms that will ultimately join forces with external influences to bring China closer to the international standard reflected in the two UN International covenants. This may be a true prospect, but the key to getting there is the sustained struggle by dissidents inside China.

Indeed, China's future identity can be defined at once by the basic questions the nation asks and by those it does not ask. At the moment, the basic question most people ask is how to get rich quick. To these people, everything else becomes instrumental to a vision of China's wealth and power. But the Chinese dissidents, though they are often silenced and appear weak, pose a larger question of how to pursue equality in life with or without wealth and power. Chinese democrats and liberal intellectuals ask this vital question, without which China will have a dim future.

To the average Chinese citizen, a political dissident looks like a fool who does not know how to care for his personal interests and wellbeing. Indeed, there are hundreds of Chinese dissidents who are paying a daily price for their democratic ideals and for the dignity of humanity. They are the most impoverished minority now in China. Public security has done its utmost to control, suppress, harass, and impoverish these people to try to break their spirit. But so far, these attempts have failed miserably.

I see numerous Chinese apologizers for the government. They say that the Chinese government is changing, so why still oppose it? The fact is, the nature of the government will remain unchanged until the citizens can oppose it without risk. In short, economic reform or economic secularization may gradually diffuse the communist identity of China. But it is the brave democracy activists who will give China a new identity. In a sense, this is a struggle between an identity and a non-identity. To the powerful, it is better that most Chinese citizens remain in the domain of seeking wealth, secularizing their lives until nothing is left but sensual gratification. But China will only realize its true identity when the nation looks back with compassion and understanding at the solitary path taken by Chinese dissidents.

FOUR BUILDING BLOCKS FOR CHINA'S DEMOCRACY
Issue Brief no. 82 (October 2, 1998)

Just as the old Chinese proverb says it takes more than one bite to make a fat man, the growth of democracy in China requires constant nutritious inputs. In spite of the residues of repressive communist policies, democracy is moving forward against all odds, though in a fashion resembling two steps forward and then one step backward. Emerging from a sea of social changes are four mechanisms that sustain and give momentum to China's democratic reform. We may call them the four building blocks for China's future democracy.

The first consists of grassroots elections for rural village officials. In the vast rural areas, the People's Commune or collectivization system faded into history in the 1980s, paralyzing the communist control of the local communities. As time went on, community self-government became the only way for maintaining basic law and order in the rural communities, something the leadership in Beijing was forced to accept. In 1997, the new system was consolidated throughout China's rural areas following nationwide grassroots elections involving 800 million people. Now pressure is building up to expand direct elections to the township and county levels, which may go to even higher levels.

The second democratic building block is the free flow of information. The publishing market has become more open than at any time in the history of the People's Republic. Chinese citizens can watch uncensored programs aired on Hong Kong TV through cable networks. Foreign broadcasts such as Radio Free Asia, VOA, and the BBC play a key role in disseminating timely information to the Chinese public. Furthermore, millions of Chinese now have access to the Internet. The government may be able to crush a demonstration, but it cannot curtail the spread of democratic ideas. The dawning of the information age entails a ground-swelling of democratic aspirations among Chinese citizens.

The third building block is China's legal reform aimed at a greater compatibility with international standards. China has signed the International Covenant on Economic, Social and Cultural Rights, and will soon sign the Convenant on Civil and Political Rights. As these become integrated with the efforts to strengthen the rule of law, civil liberties will gradually expand while repressive mechanisms will fade away. Moreover, these may help nurture a system of checks and balances in the government.

The fourth and often unnoticed one is the growth of civic organizations in China in the last five years. Economic reform has effectively dissolved the Maoist "total institution" where the state takes care of everything. Now Chinese citizens are reclaiming the territories once controlled and dominated by the state. Self-organization and civic activities are increasingly the norm for tackling problems the citizens face in their daily lives. At the present stage, civil society is growing in non-political spheres, but their future political and democratic implications are not to be underestimated.

Needless to say, behind these four developments are the men and women who make them possible. Millions of such

Chinese citizens are engaged in a daily battle to push the envelope. They do it both for their self interest and for their democratic rights. Indeed, the two can no longer be separated.

PART TWO

EVENTS AND ISSUES IN
CHINESE POLITICS

A DEMOCRATIC SOLUTION
TO CHINA'S FAILED RURAL POLICIES
Issue Brief no.1 (October 24, 1994)

Despite brief success in the early 1980's, the rural policies of the Chinese government are proving to be a failure in the long run. Their devastating effects have begun to show in recent years and are bound to persist in the post-Deng era. The rural crises are not only a time bomb for China's social stability but also a cancer to its economic organism. It is high time that the leadership in Beijing fundamentally change its rural policies and resolve the current crises with democratic reform and institutions.

Deepening Problems

China's economic reform has resulted in a hugh social cost to the rural population. In fact, the urban development and industrialization are based upon cruel deprivation of the rural communities. While the state spends one-third of its revenue just to keep the urban state enterprises afloat, it gives numerous IOUs to the peasants for their grain. In addition, the state invests billions of dollars to shore up the showcases of special economic zones while neglecting the basic needs of the rural population. As a result, the urban-rural disparity continues to enlarge in the 1990's. While the urban areas (including some coastal rural townships) prosper, there are 120 million people in the rural population whose annual income is less than 40 U.S. dollars.

To make things worse, much of the small portion allocated by the state for agricultural investment is diverted by local officials to such ventures as land speculation and stock exchanges. Corruption is claiming a heavy toll on rural development. For example, it contributes to the rapid decrease of farm land in China. Corrupt officials abuse their power for selfish economic gains. They sell the land of the peasants to foreign and domestic speculators with hugh kickbacks in the name of industrial development. This land deprivation process is cruel and violent, sometimes not unlike the British Land Enclosures Movement of the 15th century. In 1993, 300,000 hectors of farm land were reportedly taken away from the peasants.

The current price control regimes are primarily based upon considerations of the urban areas. Inflation, therefore, has hit the peasant population the hardest. While agricultural production costs, such as the price of machinery, fertilizer, gas, and electricity, have multiplied in the last few years, the price of grain and other agricultural products is kept low by the state. The state policies have created an impoverished rural population in order to maintain a low wage labor supply — a condition for China's rapid economic growth. The number of economic refugees from rural areas has risen sharply in the 1990's. 100 million such people float about aimlessly in the major cities of the coastal areas. Their living conditions can be compared only to the pre-apartheid black workers of South Africa.

China's rural population accounts for 85 percent of its total population. It is this population which is subject to the most sever suppression by the Chinese government and suffers from the most abhorrent human rights abuses. Although they make up most of the low wage labor supple, they are not allowed to establish residence in the cities in which they work. The current *hukou* (residence registration) system denies the rural population many of the rights enjoyed by city dwellers. They are considered to be second class citizens and so not have any state protection.

The legal system is weakest in the rural areas, leaving peasants to the arbitration of local officials and powerful family clans. The peasants have no channel for expressing their grievances and are cruelly oppressed if they openly challenge the local authorities. The rural communities are increasingly dominated by a coalition between local government officials and powerful family clans. Violent crimes against women and forced child labor are becoming more and more common in rural areas.

Despite the huge sacrifices made by the rural population to help further the nation's economy, the state leadership views them as a burden. Therefore, they are the most targeted segment of the population for population control measures. These measures, such as forced abortions or sterilization, are most prevalent in the rural areas.

Of the 250 million illiterate people in China, almost all are from the rural areas. According to official data, one-fourth of the rural counties in China do not have universal primary education. In the inner provinces, only 30 percent of children enrolled in primary school continue on to junior high. Of these, only 10 per cent continue on to high school. Only a few will ever end up with a college education.

Towards A Democratic Solution

The degradation of the rural areas in recent years has given rise to crisis situations that have the potential to explode in the years ahead. Over the last two years, cases involving peasant rebellion have increased dramatically. According to official reports, the first four months of 1994 witnessed over 720,000 cases involving violence by peasants, an increase of 29 percent over the previous year. In the same period, there were 370 cases of violent civil unrest involving 500 peasants or more. This unrest resulted in 5000 local cadres and peasants being wounded or killed, an increase of 82 percent over the previous year. As expected, the Chinese government raised the level of suppression over the increasingly discontented rural population. Reportedly, 385 military policemen died and 2000 more were injured in 1993 as a result of rural rebellion. The government never publishes similar reports of civilian casualties during such incidents. Clearly, the suppressive policies of the Chinese government, are not working. On the contrary, these policies have led to more bloodshed and violence—a tendency that may cause large scale social unrest in the post-Deng era.

As oppression, violence and social tensions are spreading at an alarming rate in rural China, it is imperative that a social reconciliation be achieved through the framework of democratic institutions. Official oppression must be put to a stop, and the rights of the peasants must be fully recognized and protected. The government must immediately proceed to implement political reforms and push for a peaceful transition to constitutional democracy so that:

- discriminative laws, regulations and policies against peasants be abolished;
- forced abortion and sterilization be abolished; and peasants' rights to life be fully guaranteed;
- peasants' rights to free residence and equal employment opportunities be fully protected;
- peasants be given the full ownership of the land; and their private property rights be fully protected;
- peasants be allowed to organize independent unions and associations;
- open dialogue be conducted between government bodies and independent peasant organizations;
- new laws and policies be adopted through democratic means to promote social reconciliation.

Indeed, the democratic solution is the only solution to end the suffering of the rural population, and to avoid major social unrest in the post-Deng China.

FIGHTING CORRUPTION WITH POLITICAL REFORM
Issue Brief no.5 (March 15, 1995)

On February 25, 1995, twelve prominent intellectuals sent a petition to the plenary session of China's National People's Congress (NPC) regarding the fight on corruption (*New York Times*, 2/25/1995). Rampant corruption, they wrote, has become "a matter of crucial importance that will affect the stability of society and continuation of reform". What are the facts about corruption? How can democratization help curb rampant corruption in China?

Beijing's Bankrupt Policy on Anti-Corruption

The communist government has made efforts to curb corruption, but to no avail. Nation-wide anti-corruption campaigns were launched in 1982, 1986, 1989 and 1993. From 1982, when the two "Resolutions" of cracking down on economic crimes were jointly adopted by the Central Committee of the Communist Party of China (CCCPC), National People's Congress (NPC), and the State Council (SC), until 1993, when CCCPC and SC adopted the anti-corruption "Resolution" and the "Five Rules" which demanded that cadres above the rank of division director exercise resistance against corruption; numerous meetings, speeches, laws and regulations emphasized the importance of fighting corruption. In 1994, "Legal Daily" alone published 134 regulations, provisions, and public statements with an anti-corruption theme. There are now 3,600 "Reporting Centers" throughout China. Law enforcement agencies at every level have established Anti-Corruption Bureau and invited members of the People's Congress and the Chinese People's Political Consultative Conference (CPPCC) to be inspectors. Party and government leaders, both past and present, have stressed that in fighting corruption the future of the party and the nation is at stake.

However, all of these measures have failed miserably. Corruption seems to be a monster that enjoys swimming against the tide: it grows more brazen and powerful with immunity to anti-corruption measures. The amount of money passed as bribes has been steeply rising, the ranks of the cadres involved have been increasing, and the professions involved have become more diversified ---the whole society is steeped in the monster's venom.

According to official statistics in 1982, 6,381 corruption and bribery cases were investigated by public prosecutors. These involved 2 cadres at the prefecture or bureau level, as well as 29 cadres at the county or division level, and the total amount of money retrieved was 21,700,000 yuan. In 1993, public prosecutors took up 13,148 corruption and bribery cases of which 955 were over-1 00,000-yuan cases, 77 were over-500,000-yuan cases, 57 were over-one-million-yuan cases; in addition, there were 208 over-one-million-yuan misappropriation cases. These cases involved 1,037 cadres at the county or division level, 64 cadres at the prefecture or bureau level, and one cadre at the ministerial level. The total amount of money retrieved reached Renminbi 2.2 billion yuan. Compared with 1982, the above figures represent more than a 700% increase in the number of corruption cases, and a 10,000% increase in the amount of money retrieved.

In 1982, the largest amount of money involved in a single corruption case was 69,700 yuan, an amount dwarfed by the numbers from 1993. One case in 1993 reportedly involved 640,000 yuan plus 2,740,000 US dollars. Yet this does not include the following sketchy reports from the official news media:

- In 1992, 100 billion yuan of the nation's public fund was spent on unwarranted feasting. In 1992, a certain prefecture with a revenue of 390 million yuan spent 180 million yuan -- almost half of its revenue -- on gift cigarettes. In 1993, a city in Northeast China spent 14.3 billion yuan of public funds on imported cars during a matter of five month period.

- From January to May, 1993, a certain province sent 9,533 people on overseas trips. On average, each person spent 19,000 yuan, making up a total of 190 million yuan during this period. However, the above average spending was by no means high compared with other cases. There was a city where each person taking an overseas trip reportedly spent an average of 56,700 yuan.

- Astonishing as such visible corruption may be, invisible corruption is even worse. In today's China, the swap of power for money is the order of the day. The so-called spiritual vacuum marked by "an absence of value" and "collapse of faith" has largely been created by poisoning the nation's soul with political corruption whose central theme is "power brings everything."

The Democratic Imperative for Fighting Corruption

Why has corruption escalated despite repeated control measures and campaigns carried out by the ruling party? The cause lies in that the existing anti-corruption policy fails to provide systematic constraints on and supervision of the ruling party itself. In other words, it is impossible to curb corruption by relying exclusively on the intention, words, and unilateral measures of the ruling party; systematic reform measures such as establishment of independent law enforcement institutions and freedom of the media must be implemented. Political reform must be introduced before it is too late.

Short-Term Reform To Curb Rampant Corruption. To reverse the trend of rising corruption, short-term reform measures should be immediately implemented. These include:

- Create mechanisms for NPC to exercise independent supervision of the ruling party and the government; establish an NPC Anti-Corruption Committee to monitor all types of political corruption, with members of the Committee elected among and by NPC delegates through fair elections; delegates elected shall work full-time for the Committee.
- Since corruption in China is not limited to embezzlement, bribery, misappropriation of public funds, and negligence of duty, but also takes the form of willfully squandering and wasting public assets for which there is no punitive legislation, it is necessary that NPC enact a special law to prohibit squandering and wasting public assets so that this form of corruption can be dealt with on a legal basis, rather than relying exclusively on administrative means.
- Immediately institute an examination system and lifetime terms for judges, to gradually reduce, and eventually eliminate, the direct intervention in and control of legal jurisdiction by the ruling party.
- Enact a public servant personal property disclosure law, which would require not only public servants themselves,

but also their family members and adult children, to fully report and make available to the news media their personal properties. If necessary, reference can be made to the relevant laws in Taiwan and South Korea.

- Enact a law which prohibits public servants from engaging in commercial activities while in office; enact existing relevant administrative directives into NPC legislation. Personal businesses of public servants shall be sold or turned over to legally designated agencies for proper management.

- Establish supervision by public opinion, which is the most important measure; the NPC should enact, pursuant to Article 35 of the Constitution, special laws supporting the establishment of public reporting centers and publication of a non-government "Anti-Corruption Journal" to fully safeguard the lawful rights of non-government anti-corruption organizations and news media.

- Begin dismantling the exclusive control of the ruling party over news media (radio stations, TV stations, newspapers, and publishing institutions). Enact, as soon a possible, news media law to gradually transform news media from the exclusive organ the ruling party into the voice of the people across various social strata.

Long-Term Reform To Attack the Root Causes of Corruption. Abuse of political power results in corruption. Absolute political power results in absolute corruption. Therefore, the most effective measure to eradicate the root causes of corruption is to subject political power, particularly the power of the ruling party, to systematic constraint and supervision. Such measures would include:

- Lift the ban on party formation; institute an open, equal, universal and direct election system in which political parties compete for office and allow non-ruling parties to become a political force which effectively constrains the conduct of the ruling party.

- Institute democratic constitutional polity characterized by the separation of power and mutual checks and balances; transform the NPC and CPPCC into legislative bodies, independent of the control of the ruling party, and genuinely separate legislation, jurisdiction, and administration; remove the current control of NPC legislation and domination of judicial system respectively by the ruling party and its Political and Legal Commission.
- Create a constitutional court to examine and supervise the conduct of the ruling Party, NPC, the government, the procuratorate, and the court in terms of constitutionality.
- Lift the ban on newspaper publication to truly guarantee citizens' sacred right to freedom of speech and freedom of expression, which is stipulated by Article 35 of the Constitution; establish the legality of non-government radio stations, TV stations, newspapers, and publishing houses, to turn the news media or public opinion into a fourth power which provides checks and balances against political power,
- Establish the legality of private property in the Constitution to grant equal status to all types of existing business enterprises, be they owned by the state, the collective, or the private citizen, and to implement reform measures aimed at making property ownership more transparent.

HEAVENLY WIND IN CHINA
Issue Brief no. 12 (February 16, 1996)

Along with the visible economic changes, China is undergoing an unparalleled religious renaissance. The rapid increase of the Christian population may soon turn into a political force feared by the leaders in Beijing. On January 14th, the State Council summoned local officials to Beijing for a major strategy meeting to cope with the issue.

There is no doubt that Christianity is sweeping across China like a wild fire, adding roughly a million converts to its ranks each year. According to one estimate, there are at least 25 millions born again Christians in China. The Three Self Patriotic Movement Committee (TSPMC), the state controlled church apparatus, is allowed to print 1.6 million Bibles each year, but this number is unable to meet the demand of the expanding Christian community. As a result, tens of thousands of copies are smuggled into China from abroad or printed underground by local Christian groups.

TSPMC claims that 55 new churches are established every month, but what worries the Beijing leaders the most is the grassroots Christian movement with house churches sprouting up throughout China. The latter are difficult to monitor and therefore exist beyond the control of the state. Early in 1994, Jiang Zeming gave a speech which was later issued as a party directive to its cadres. Jiang called on party members to fight back the Christian influence in "a quiet war" to win the people's heart. However, the rank and file of the Party did not respond to his call. Instead, more party members chose to be baptized by pasters and clergymen.

According one report by the state public security in November 1995, Christians in many areas, especially in south China, now outnumber the communist party members. Guangdong province reportedly now has four million population of Christians, twice the number of communist party members. Late last year the State Council issued an administrative directive stipulating that all church activities must be pre-registered with the county government. Many house-church leaders were arrested and persecuted, but such tactics have virtually no effect on curbing the spread of Christianity.

Moreover, the once well controlled TSPMC is showing signs of distancing itself from state policies. Reverend Ding Guangxun, head of TSPMC and long regarded as a docile follower of party line, appears more intransigent to the party's interference in the Christian community. It is a known fact that many key positions in the TSPMC apparatus are filled by the Party loyalists. Reverend Ding openly advocates proselytizing them, an act very much resented by the communists. Attempts were made to retire and then replace him with a more loyal successor, but these have failed to materialize due to resistance within the TSPMC community. In another act of defiance to the party line, the editorial board of the *Heavenly Wind* (TSPMC's official publication) published an article in its January 1995 issue, arguing that state-banned house churches should be recognized as legitimate Christian institutions. All this shows that the Chinese Christian community is becoming more and more integrated across official and unofficial lines while its distance with the regime is growing wider. The obvious common ground is to protect the constitutional rights of Chinese citizens, and to eliminate religious persecutions by government officials at all levels.

The Beijing Conference on January 14 aimed at strengthening the party's control and monitoring of the Christian and other religious communities. The meeting views the foreign influence and a lack of ideological awareness among the party cadres to be the major causes of the plight. But can the leaders of Beijing turn the clock back to the Mao Era when Stalin-style persecution of religion was the order of the day? It is hardly possible even if the leaders would like to go that far.

But the world needs to remind itself that the Beijing's dictatorship is very much conditioned on the absence of civil society, including religious communities. The revival of Christianity in the East European countries played a significant role in nurturing democratic institutions and in bringing down the former communist regimes. The Chinese Christian movement is as incompatible with the power of the Party as their East European counterparts. In a time when China is facing a historical transition towards social and political pluralism, the international community must be vigilant of renewed religious persecution by the Beijing leaders.

CHINA'S MIGRATING UNREST
Issue Brief no.13 (February 23, 1996)

As most Chinese are still lingering in the mood of celebrating the lunar New Year, which fell on February 19 this year, their leaders are worried about the prospect of post-holiday migration, i.e., tens of millions of peasants who would soon leave the countryside in search of jobs they hope to find in Beijing, Shanghai, Guangzhou and other urban centers. According to Chinese official statistics, the rural labor force, at present, totals 430 million people; 120 million of which work in construction industries, while 50 to 80 million constantly move back and forth between cities and villages in search of employment opportunities. Laborers from this roving work-force do not carry the same papers and documents that a city worker is required to possess. They do not have transfer permits, residence cards or salary cards and are therefor considered "blind" migrants because the government is unable to control their movement.

This year's situation is no exception, the huge crowds of laborers from the inland provinces of Sichuan, Hunan, Guangxi, Guizhou, Anhui, Jiangxi, Henan, Hebei and Gansu are like turbulent waves pouring into big cities like Beijing, Tianjin and Shanghai and into the Pearl River delta, Yangtze River delta and coastal areas of Fujian province. According to the official statistics, out of the twenty to fifty millions of rail passengers in Shanghai and Guangzhou during the Chinese New Year season, half are migrant workers. This monumental "wave of labor" is the combined result of the demand for mobility made by the rural labor force and the creation of a market economy which provides an environment which allows mobility.

Labor migration has had a profound influence on China. On the one hand, it supplies the Chinese cities with needed cheap labor, and therefore stimulates China's urban economic and cultural development. Furthermore, these rural laborers return to their villages with information and skills unavailable to the locals, which may in turn help boost the community development. But what worries the central authorities are the various problems caused by the flow and resettlement of this population. These include the burden on the already over-stretched communications and transportation networks, insufficient resettlement funds and facilities, poor working conditions, unemployment pressures, mismanagement, riots, and increased crime rates.

It is obvious that the Chinese government is not prepared to handle such mass migration, which is unparalleled in the nation's history. Its numbers would be comparable to the scenario in which about half of the U.S. population were constantly on the road searching for employment. A minor mistake in managing this phenomenon may cause huge human tragedy and social unrest. As of yet the Chinese government has turned a "blind" eye to the explosiveness of this problem. Government position remains unchanged as the officials resorts to persuading peasants (sometimes with force) to go back and "retain their countryside resident identity, as if they never left their hometowns." Repressive policy toward this population does not help resolve the problem, but will lead to even greater conflicts, increasing the risk of a major social unrest.

To prevent such desaster down the road, China must hasten her residence registration reform, and quickly establish a extensive united labor market to avoid further chaos and disorder. Legal reform must be implemented to assure the rural unemployed of their rights to minimum wages, decent working conditions, and the due process of resolving their grievances through legal means. A democratic political framework should be established, in which the migrating peasants are encouraged to conduct collective bargaining with their employers. Without such framework, the class actions with ample violence would become the only way of voicing discontent.

As the old Chinese saying goes, it is wise to dredge the waterways in early days than to bank to the impossible inundation later. Any failure to complete fundamental changes will perpetuate the problems, and will lead to the arrival of major social unrest and economic disruptions.

DOUBLE JEOPARDY IN CHINA
Issue Brief no. 29 (July 18, 1997)

This month of July two incidents occur in China without causing a stir, but they may have a long term impact on this nation's future. The first is the annual convening of the Politburo at Beidaihe (a seaside resort northwest of Beijing) to decide on major policy issues as well as personel arrangement for the upcoming 15th Party Congress this fall. Second, the Yellow River (long regarded by the Chinese people as "the cradle" of their civilization) dried up for about twenty days for the first time in China's recorded history. Both are symbolic of the dilemma China faces into the next century.

A dropless Yellow River is as mind-boggling to the Chinese as a warterless Mississippi River would be to the Americans. To many Chinese, deforestration and over-irrigation are to blaim in general, but behind them the failure of the government policies are all too obvious. In fact, no other word than "desaster" can designate the true condition of China's environmental plight. To make things worse, the central government is about to dam the Yangtze River this fall for the Three Gorges Project. In order to create this world biggest dam, 1.5 million people were forced to leave their homeland for relocation. As the rest of world is reflecting on environmental devastations of big-dam projects, the leaders in Beijing are unmoved. The project becomes a show of political will for Chinese premier Li Peng.

This seems unfair. In the land where free expressions are repressed, the will of a political leader can sometimes override everything in the land (including the environment) while the dire consequences are to fall on the entire population. China now has less than one-third of the farmable land as in the United States, though its population is about five times as large. No other country can match China in the scope of desert expansion each year. No sign is in sight to reverse China's exponential growth of industrial polution. Why are the leaders in Beijing so mindless of the hard lessons learned by other nations, and unconcerned of the welfares of their future generation? Look into the crooked political system, and you may have an answer.

There is simply no public accountability on the part of officials who make policies. They respond neither to the public concerns nor to the experts deliberations. Do the Chinese public not know the health problems caused by polution? They certainly do. But the Chinese government has effectively silenced citizens' environmental initiatives for fearing the challenge they may pose to its political monopoly. Under the strict political control, the whole nation is geared to mindless industrialization with no regard to its environmental consequences.

Thus, a surprise indeed if the drying up of the Yellow River would ever register in the mind of the top leaders who are busy with dividing political dividents or power at Beidaihe sea resort. China is facing a double jeopardy of environmental desaster aided by political dictatorship. Enough of the argument that democracy will interrupt China's economic modernization. To me, no democracy is endangering the very livelihood and survival of the Chinese nation.

THE THREAT TO CHINA'S ECONOMIC MODERNIZATION

Issue Brief no. 30 (July 25, 1997)

China faces a formidable problem in its transition to a market economy: urban unemployment. Although reform has spread to many sectors of the economy, the state-owned enterprises and financial institutions basically still practice their old ways. The recent reports on protests by Chinese workers serve as a potent reminder of possible social disintegration if this sector continues to lag behind. But unfortunately, the state's policies prove inadequate in mitigating the plight of the new urban poor. The leadership is still handcuffed to the communist commitment to the state-ownership structure. It fears that letting the private sector take over would loosen the communist grip on power. It may be right.

The state-run sectors are decaying because of poor management, corruption, and official abuse of power. A general lack of funds strains the state's capacity to help the urban poor. But more importantly, the policy makers are still unable to devise an effective safety net to support the unemployed. As a result, workers who have traditionally relied on the state to provide housing, education, and benefits through the state-owned companies and factories are becoming unruly. And rightfully so. While corrupt officials' purses get fatter, the working people are having problems making ends meet. Millions of unemployed laborers in China's urban areas are sinking below the poverty line with little or no help from the government.

Thus, to avert social unrest, the government must do something. It needs to renounce the state's monopoly and public ownership structure while allowing the private sector to take over the state's ailing enterprises. The leaders should recognize that injecting capital into state enterprises is not a solution to the problems. The current system favors or gives special treatment to financial institutions that solely deal with the state enterprises and lose money. These institutions have a range of mechanisms to provide capital to the state sector, which finds its way to the bank accounts of corrupt officials. The banking system and the corrupt officials together manage to issue bonds and force other banks to buy them, issue currency, and make short term loans, all to their own benefit. However, bonds cannot be cashed, loans have a tendency of not being repaid, and the issuance of currency has great potential to cause inflation.

There also needs to be a support system for the urban unemployed. Their economic rights must be respected and protected by democratic insititutions. Otherwise, toppling state enterprises will only lead to massive unrest in China's urban areas. In fact, worker uprisings have been occurring far more frequently than the media report and the Chinese authorities admit. Large scale protests are exactly what the government fears the most, although the government does not seem to care nor do much for the economic underclass. The leaders in Beijing seem set on avoiding rather than squarely facing this issue. This policy posture, if not corrected, could throw China off the track of economic modernization.

Disillusion of urban workers leads to demonstrations, which lead to police intervention and more political control. This can only escalate workers' grievances. Following this pattern, the world should know what may happen next under a regime which quashed violently the peaceful student movement in Tiananmen just eight years ago.

THE MIDDLE CLASS AND DEMOCRACY
Issue Brief no. 33 (August 15, 1997)

In academic circles, the relationship between democracy and the existence of a middle class is thought to be well documented. Indeed, a growing middle class could aid China's democratization. But it is wrong to say that because China has not yet developed a middle class it is thus ineligible for democracy. In fact, this argument has somewhat become a tactical excuse used by President Jiang Zemin to forestall democratic reform. According to one of his recent speeches, only when the economy has developed to a sufficient degree can democratic reforms be implemented; otherwise reform will bring about total chaos and disorder (*Shijie Ribao* [world journal], July 5, 1997). Mr. Jiang did not specify, however, what level of economic development would qualify China for democracy.

It is true that China's economic level is currently not as high as the levels of many developed countries, but in relative terms it already exceeds the levels of Britiain and the United States when they developed democratic institutions. There are some regions in China, such as Shanghai and Guangdong,

where the level of economic development and GDP per capita
have already caught up with those of some newly
industrialized countries that enjoy full democracy. According
to China's official press, Shanghai's GDP per capita will
surpass 3,000 dollars, which is higher than in many
democratic countries. But if Shanghai is still not up to par in
the eyes of Jiang Zemin, then what about the 600 million
Chinese farmers who are able to elect their own village
officials and practice democracy with perfect success already?
Does Mr. Jiang know that the GDP per capita in many of these
areas now averages lower than 300 dollars? Truth is that the
level of economic development should not be confused with
the form of political governance. Nor can political domination
be explained away by economic conditions of a country.

A sound and visionary policy should promote both
political and economic reforms simultaneously. Economic
reform so far has brought about great social development as
well as social stability in China, but a point has already been
reached where the lack of political reform means more
tensions and social conflict. Corruption and social injustice
have become explosive issues in China solely because of the
chasm between economic and political reforms. Economic
reform that keeps out development of democratic institutions
can hardly succeed in the end.

In fact, a viable middle class has already begun to emerge
during the last two decades in China. However, this newly-
risen middle class cannot grow smoothly or take on more
political responsibilities with the political arrangement now in
place. The political power of the Chinese communists erodes
and dampens the spirit and effectiveness of a new generation
of business leaders. Official corruption has become a great
hindrance to the healthy growth of the new generation of
Chinese entrepreneurs and the private sector.

Furthermore, if a middle class and democracy are related,
and if both require incremental processes to develop, then
why shouldn't the growth of the middle class go hand in hand
with incremental steps of political liberalization?

WHEN THE FISH IS IN THE FISHBOWL
Issue Brief no. 37 (September 12, 1997)

This week the Chinese leadership becomes the fish in the bowl in a limited sense. The world sets its eyes on the 15th congress of the Communist Party. President Jiang Zemin and his colleagues are keenly aware of this scrutinizing gaze and will perform as if all were well. Thus, contrary to the opinions of many China watchers, the 15th congress is more ritualistic than a real decision making event on important policy and personnel issues. The substantive changes in Chinese politics always take place in the backroom away from the public's view. The really nasty factional infights occur only at times when the fish is out of the fishbowl or when there is no party congress in session.

Indeed, there have been many crucial moments when the tide has changed within Chinese leadership circles, moments such as the Anti-rightist Campaign (1957), the Great Leap Forward (1958), the launch of the Cultural Revolution (1966), the overthrow of the Gang of Four (1976), the repositioning of Deng Xiaoping (1978), the overthrow of Hu Yaobang and Zhao Ziyang (1986 and 1989), and the appointment of Jiang Zemin as the party's boss (1989). These events are often regarded as watershed moments in China's political development. But none were tied to party congresses.

The reason for this is quite simple. The decision-making process is highly concentrated in the hands of a few at the top, while the rank and file of the party have no influence on important policy issues and personnel changes. A well-known editorial in the *People's Daily* in 1957 carried the title "The Party Members Should Be the Docile Tools of the Party" (*gong chan dang yuan ying zuo dang de xun fu gong ju*) . Perhaps Jiang would not repeat such an opinion in his daily directives, but he certainly treats his party members that way in reality. His power and legitimacy come more from the informal Beidaihe gatherings of politburo members than from the party congresses.

To make the party congress more than a public relations gimmick for the ruling clique, the party must be democratized (and it has a long way to go before this can be achieved). But when the party is democratic, can it still be communist? In the former USSR and in Eastern European countries, true democracy within the communist party was the beginning of the end for the communist political system. In those countries, the communist elite was often voted out of office by its own party members once the members had the liberty to do so.

To most Chinese citizens, the CCP is not only an abbreviation for the Chinese Communist Party, but also for the Chinese Corruption Party. Many CCP members have come to see that only in a fully democratic environment could the CCP be saved from corruption. Some also argue that China's political reform should start with true democratic reform within the CCP. They probably agree that their common goal is to end the dictatorship within the party and force the elite always to exist in a fishbowl.

STRUCTURAL UNCERTAINTY AFTER THE FIFTEENTH CONGRESS OF THE CCP

China Strategic Review, Vol. II, no. 5
(September/October 1997)

The death of Deng Xiaoping leaves China with a series of uncertainties, among which are a temporary vacuum in the succession of power. With the conclusion of the Fifteenth Congress in September, the power succession was complete with Jiang Zemin prevailing over all other factions. But in spite of propaganda's claim that a new era was born under the Jiang leadership, the Chinese political system remains basically the same, which is unlikely to be stable unless it returns to strongman politics or advances to democracy.

The regime now has a structural power vacuum that Jiang Zemin cannot fill even though he desires to be a new strongman in China. Deng left the Chinese government with a structure and political culture catering to one person rule, but ironically it is no longer possible for the system to produce such a new strong figure to sustain or to keep it stable. Although Deng Xiaoping was outstandig in pushing through liberal reform policies for the economy, he failed to construct a good system to ensure long term development. On the one hand, establishing other entities within the unitary party system is neither legal nor possible. On the other hand, this mononistic power structure exists only nominally, and there is no way to achieve unity without a paramount leader. In such a situation, if the "Jiang core" is overly aggressive, it will anger other factions; if it retreats, it will lure other aggressive politicians to challenge it and attempt to take its place.

There are no effective mechanisms to allow factions or different interest groups to negotiate a balanced or compromised order of power distribution. A lawless struggle for power is inevitably ruthless, and opportunities for compromise are extremely small. In the past, everything depended on one dominant person's charisma or personal prestige to affect compromise or balance of power.

Mao and Deng had played that role in the past, because their power in the party, the government, and the military had firm foundations which were laid during a long period of war. In recent peaceful times, however, skilled bureaucrats like Jiang Zemin have no way to retrace the paths of Mao and Deng and monopolize all these power sources.

Unless China moves towards greater democracy to allow for greater power-sharing among different interests and for their participation in the decision making processes of the government, Jiang's position cannot be stabilized. This is especially so when we take into consideration the growing social differentiation accumulated in the last two decades. Even Jiang Zemin himself has repeatedly admitted that the economic reform has given rise to new contradictions and conflicts that were unseen in the previous period.

However, with the conservative Jiang-Li alliance dominating the Chinese political landscape, it is difficult to imagine a prospect where checks and balance and the division of government would come into being. Jiang's demise might be caused by his desire to be a strongman without the necessary qualifications. His legitimacy is much weaker than perhaps he himself would like to admit. Thus, looking at the not-too-distant future, this is not such a stable structure.

This structural uncertainty in the power distribution could cause problems for the elite in the Chinese government. Its imprecise nature might lead to constant challenges to the Jiang core from the conflicting factions that are aligned with different interest groups in Chinese society.

Naturally, the masses bear the brunt of the damage. Turbulence in the government doubtless will affect the process of modernizing the economy. The economic system lacks merit and effective control or regulatary mechanisms due to the absence of the rule of law. Regarding this, the structural uncertainty of the system of government after Deng's death could very well promote anxiety about China's development and stability in the future.

Because of this, all Chinese should strive to repair the flaws in the governance system by actively promoting democracy and rule of law. Specifically stated, there should be three steps:

1) Promoting CCP reform that make internal party factions transparent to the public so as to pave the way for a pluralistic government;

2) Reforming and implementing the constitutional role of the NPC and introducing true checks and balances into the current system of government in order to prepare for a smooth transition to a democratic, constitutional system.

3) Reevaluating the Tiananmen Incident, and promoting the freedom of press and expressions by Chinese citizens.

In short, post-Deng China is in a period of change, in which Jiang's regime is nothing but a transitory one. If Jiang continues to resist the call of history for democratization, but attempts to monopolize political power in terms of strongman politics as was the case in the Mao and Deng eras, China will definitely fall into chaos. To prevent such a consequence, China has to turn to democracy for a political salvation of the nation. There is simply no other alternative.

THE CLAY FEET OF A TEMPLE GOD
Issue Brief no. 47 (December 5, 1997)

The melting down of the East Asian financial markets is a big deal to China in spite of the calculated confidence expressed by Chinese economic czar Zhu Rongji that China's economy will not be affected by troubles in its neighboring countries. Chinese officials even uttered that, unlike its neighbors, China faces the pressure of currency appreciation, not devaluation.

Indeed, China's RMB is not freely convertible to the US dollar (a deterrence to foreign speculators). But this will not save China from East Asia's economic fall off. First, the engine of China's economy is geared toward export markets in the West, but with the devaluation of the East Asian currencies, Chinese goods will face competitive pressure from cheaper goods from other East Asian nations. Second, contrary to the optimistic prediction by the Chinese leadership, the financial troubles in the region will cause sources of foreign investment into China to dry up. In fact, there are already signs of a slow-down of foreign investment in China. The big money supply machines in Hong Kong, Taiwan, and Japan are facing serious financial contraction.

But what is more threatening to the Chinese economy is the combination of external difficulties and internal ills. Without the security of the foreign export market and foreign investment, President Jiang Zemin's bold initiative during the 15th CCP Congress to reform the state sector appears hollow and unachievable. But Jiang is already half-way out with the state sector reforms, because the local governments, upon receiving the political signal, began to throw off the burden of such enterprises. As a result, a large number of former workers in the state sector was made to join the population of the unemployed, the social impact of which began to be felt only recently. Thus, at the moment, in order to absorb the increasing population of the unemployed for the sake of basic social stability, China's economy must maintain a high growth rate of eight percent. But the achievement of this goal becomes questionable with the downfall of the Asian tigers.

Thus, Jiang Zemin is caught in a dilemma of state sector reform. Rolling back such reform is politically unfeasible, but pushing it forward is economically unachievable. To make the situation even worse, the US trade imbalance due to the currency devaluation crisis in East Asia will likely focus Congress's eye on the huge trade deficit that already exists with China. Any trade pressure from Washington on Beijing will translate into chilly political winds in Jiang Zemin's house. According to a Chinese fable, even a huge and seemingly powerful image of a temple's god whose feet are made of clay will topple over after floodwaters wash his feet away. Just like this giant god standing in the old Chinese temple, Mr. Jiang may appear dominating, but his feet are made of clay. Leaking water on the floor may well threaten his standing.

LAW AND DISORDER IN CHINA
Issue Brief no. 49 (December 19, 1997)

In the past decade or so, the policy clichés mouthed by the Chinese leadership are : "The need to maintain stability outweighs all issues" (*wen ding ya dao yi qie*), and "Eliminate sources of instability at an initial stage." To protect against possible rebellions, the Chinese government drastically increased the number of the Chinese Armed Police Force (*wu zhuang jing cha*) by changing the clothes of some divisions of the People's Liberation Army and then making them go through anti-riot training. The size of this force is now much larger than the American National Guard.

The regime also invested heavily to upgrade the equipment of the State Security Ministry, the Chinese KGB. All this was done in addition to the already huge existing police force, the Chinese Public Security Ministry (*gong an bu*).

It seems that the leaders in Beijing have no sense of security and hope to do everything they can to promote the law-enforcement establishment. But contrary to their expectations, the effort to police the Chinese people has led to more disorder. First, there is no clear division of duties among these three police forces, and their work often overlaps to create tension among them. At the grassroots level, each force's attention to guarding its own turf and out-competing the others often takes precedent over the real job of fighting crimes. Recently, there have been several incidents reported of open gun fire between the different forces.

Moreover, all three police forces are corrupt, especially at the lower levels. Many in these forces are more friendly to the local mafia and crime organizations than to the victims of crime who need their protection. Their participation in the illegal pornography industry and the underground world is well known to the Chinese public. They work for money and power, not the people or the law. Like the corrupt officials, their souls are for sale in the nationwide craze to get rich.

It is true that social order is important to the Chinese people's livelihood, but without democratic institutions to make law-enforcement accountable to the public, police forces can bring about more victimization and disorder in Chinese society, not to mention that they squander huge amounts of public wealth. Indeed, as China's public order continues to deteriorate, the police forces may even, like Frankenstein, turn around to threaten those who created them for the purpose of controlling the powerless.

THE WRONG DIRECTION
FOR CHINA'S FINANCIAL SYSTEM
Issue Brief no. 52 (January 16, 1998)

During the past few days, the Chinese government has been having an important conference on China's financial reform. All the managers of the local banks throughout China participated in the meeting. Chinese financial czar Zhu Rongji gave a speech emphasizing reform with stability for the current system with regard to the turmoil of the financial market in East Asian countries. However, many of the control mechanisms stressed in the conference have origins in the old economic structure based on state planning and administrative controls. This is a step backwards in the reform of China's ailing financial system.

There are lessons to be learned from the problems in East Asia's financial systems, which include weak institutions for curbing corruption and a financial system embedded in corrupt bureaucracy. Influence peddling, lack of transparency, weakness in regulation, and a weakness in the rule of law account for the setback of the East Asian tigers, and China should learn from this experience. But the Chinese leadership has drawn the wrong conclusions by assuming that China has been saved from the trouble by doing the opposite of liberalizing its financial system. Indeed, the non-convertible renminbi may have prevented international speculators from attacking the Chinese currency, but that does not mean the Chinese financial system is safe. Going back to the old administrative controls will not solve Chinese financial problems, but will make them even worse.

The right direction for China's financial reform would be toward an increase in transparency, the rule of law, and curbing the meddling of officials in the financial market. Only in this way can the Chinese financial system become a stabilizing factor in China. To go in such a direction, China must implement reforms that put an end to official corruption and the state's monopoly in China's economic life. To fight evil with evil will only result in more evil.

Like clams at the bottom of the sea, the leaders in Beijing open their shells to test the environment, but as soon as a stir in the environment can be felt, they tend to retreat into their shells to hide. These shells are both the psychological and the institutional systems based on the old rules of the game — the old administrative control mechanisms for monopolizing social, economic, and political power in China. Indeed, if the leaders in Beijing do not have the courage to embrace the new global environment, they will never come out of their shells. In the end, they will be swept away by the current.

PANEGYRIC AND PANIC FOR CHINESE PROPAGANDISTS

Issue Brief no. 53 (January 23, 1998)

In China, the people most fearful of the free flow of ideas are those who are cogs and screws in the Chinese propaganda machine. Indeed, they are like this for a reason. If Chinese citizens enjoy a free press, are exposed to the ideas of freedom, democracy, human rights, and other issues of concern to them, there will be an end to the occupation of several thousands of propogandists. As China is moving in the direction of greater openness and civil liberties, the propagandists may become panicked about their job security in the future, because the Chinese public is apparently growing impatient of the lies they churn out each day.

Ironically, their job security is intimately related to the job security of President Jiang Zemin and his colleagues. So, to promote their mutual interest, a conference was convened last week by thousands of Chinese propagandists in Beijing to discuss a strategy for their future. Dressed in his Mao suit, which is perfect for this occasion of CCP political ritual, Jiang Zemin gave a speech to this crowd, urging them to carry on with "this difficult work" (*jianju de gongzuo*). They were urged, in particular, to turn out more laudation for the communist party and its policies and to fight against "Western bourgeois ideas" (ideas of freedom and democracy in their lexicon), which tend to undermine the CCP leadership.

Of course, the Chinese propogandists want to control what goes through people's minds, but they know they have failed miserably. No one in China now buys their indoctrination any more. However, if the propaganda machine believes it can still control the media outlets in order to contain the spread of the ideas of freedom and democracy, it will fail in the end, too. Perhaps, because the propagandists realize this inevitable failure, they delivered a scathing attack on Radio Free Asia (RFA), accusing the station of harming China's stability (*China Daily*, 1/21/98). After reading the piece, I said to myself that they have a right to their expressed indignation and deep fear for the information transmitted to China on RFA wave lengths. I only hope that they dare to publish the attack in the Chinese language in the *People's Daily*. (The *China Daily* is an English publication). Then, I think, the Chinese people will have a chance to reply: "Why don't you get an honest job?"

THE RISING CONSCIOUSNESS OF THE PEOPLE
Issue Brief no. 54 (January 30, 1998)

Within the leadership compound of Zhongnanhai, the biggest issue of concern is stability. Surrounded by threats from all sides, the leadership has a reason for fearing the loss of political control in China. According to President Jiang Zemin's recent speeches, the two most significant threats are rampant corruption and the plight of the working population.

Indeed, the disease of corruption has eaten into the heart of the regime, and no one seems to be able to cure it. The reason is simple: if the regime gets serious about cracking down on corruption, it will lose the support of a group most loyal to the regime, namely, the corrupt officials in the party and government organizations. Thus Jiang Zemin depends paradoxically on corruption in the form of vested interests to maintain the regime's stability.

On the lower end of the social spectrum, there are 10 million urban unemployed and 100 million rural unemployed. Their protests and demonstrations for economic rights occurred throughout China in 1997. If these spontaneous movements become organized and strive for coalitions across different localities, they may topple the regime. Because the regime perceives this as such a great threat to its stability, security forces have used "extreme measures" [*fei chang shou duan*], such as staged automobile accidents, to thwart the workers' movement from developing into a Chinese *Solidarity*.

The sharp contrast in treatment of corrupt officials and the working population exposes the nature of the regime that has evolved from a Leninist party into a more fascist-styled dictatorship. The difference between the two is that the former relies on ideological control, deceit, and mass movements to control dissent, while the latter depends on raw violence and murder to deter rebellion. Thus, the present regime must rely on public callousness to carry out its dark deeds under the cover of night.

This means that the Achilles heel of Jiang Zemin is the consciousness of the public, including those working within the system, of the plight of the working poor as compared with the corruption of some officials. Recent news indicates that there is a growing awakening of consciousness within the system, which is reflected by a proposal by a group of officials represented by the former official Fang Jue (*Washington Post*, "Former Chinese Official Advocates Democracy," Steven Mufson, 1/12/98). When the public conscience is troubled, the days of the regime will be numbered. Then the question is: How can the leaders in Zhongnanhai effectively prevent the awakening of the Chinese consciousness and the Chinese conscience? Jiang Zemin's job in this respect is indeed not an easy one.

BEHIND THE BIG, EMPTY CHINESE PRESS
Issue Brief no. 55 (February 6, 1998)

As China enters the Year of the Tiger, one big challenge to the leadership of Zhongnanhai is to make people feel good about themselves at a time when things around them are getting worse. To achieve this, and through this to gain the legitimacy to rule, President Jiang Zemin's rhetoric in the Chinese press is gravitating in three directions, possibly guided by three notorious propaganda strategies: fake it, exaggerate it, or make it empty. Let me explain.

First, make false statements to the public. This is when you hear something like this in the official CCTV: "Great achievements are being made in the banking industry and the Bank of China has made more profit than it did last year." The people in their right minds should think that the banks are really in trouble. Similarly, when Jiang Zemin and Li Peng claim repeatedly in the press that China's political situation is well and stable, what they mean to say is that there are many troubles and a lack of stability.

Another of Jiang Zemin's strategies is to say big things in the abstract and ignore concrete problems faced by the Chinese citizens. Thus, Jiang Zemin recently has tended to speak more of the destiny and the glory of the Chinese nation in the 21st century because he wants to draw attention away from the meager food at the dinner tables of the people. Similarly, the regime always uses macro statistics to gloss over the micro problems of state enterprises and other economic areas. Of course, people are not allowed to ask the question, "If China is doing so well, why am I doing so poorly?"

The third strategy is one of emptiness — empty slogans, empty promises, empty concepts, and empty words. When Jiang Zemin speaks of China's spiritual civilization and self-reliance and hard struggle, his rhetoric is repeated thousands of times in the Chinese press. However, people really don't know what he is talking about. Indeed, for Jiang Zemin, the point is not what he has to say, but his capacity to talk and keep talking. If Mark Twain were in China today, he probably would have noticed that the big weatherman is free to talk anything about the weather, because nobody can do anything about it. But nobody is allowed to talk about the weatherman because the weatherman is afraid that somebody can do something about his talking.

For thousands of frustrated journalists, the golden rule set by the regime is: if a condition is true, do not report it, but try to make it disappear by using aggregate statistics (use false statistics if necessary) or by making it abstract. Even in fiction, the hero often appears pretentiously big and empty. Too much specific reference to real life is risky to the writers, who therefore take the safer route and write about personalities who resemble the big and empty like Jiang Zemin himself.

BUREAUCRATIC CAPITALISM
Issue Brief no. 57 (February 20, 1998)

A year has passed since Deng Xiaoping died, and it is time to take a close look at what Jiang's era will mean. I would argue that Jiang's China does not practice either communism or pure capitalism, but a kind of capitalism of the bureaucracy. This new system rests on two pillars.

The first pillar is corruption, through which officials join forces with both foreign and domestic capitalists to make a killing. The game is not played by the rule of law, and there is no sense of transparency in the system. Rather, this is a game of networking and contacts between business and government. Now China's bureaucratic capitalism is taking the audacious step of getting rid of tens of millions of urban workers in the state sector. It uses the pretense of realizing the market economy to justify this move, but in reality its reasoning disregards the interests of the Chinese working class. As a result, the property the state has accumulated through the sweat of the working class over the last few decades has quickly ended up in the pockets of these bureaucratic capitalists.

The second pillar of bureaucratic capitalism is the expansion of government organs. According to one statistic, by the end of 1996, sixty percent of government revenue went to pay for the wages of officials at various levels. Since 1993, about one million new officials have been added each year to the government machine. Thus, twenty years ago, there was a ratio of fifty people on average to one official. Now there are only thirty people per one official.[1] An ever-increasing officialdom has resulted in heavier and heavier burdens on the Chinese people. The government is getting bigger because

---

[1] Source of statistics: *World Journal*, 2/12/98, p. D4

it needs more official staff to execute control. In fact, without strict official control, bureaucratic capitalism would be no more. With such control, the bureaucratic capitalists can promote their vested interests through corruption and continue to protect themselves against the political dissatisfaction of the working class.

The Chinese economic czar Zhu Rongji may want to reduce the size of the government, but hopefully he is aware of what he is really running up against. If in spite of such opposition he wishes to follow his conscience and alleviate the burden and plight of the Chinese people, he should recognize that popular support and democratic reform are the only medicine that can help cure this diseases of the Chinese system.

A MOVE AGAINST THE RULE OF LAW
Issue Brief no. 58 (Febuary 27, 1998)

During a number of recent meetings with Western dignitaries, President Jiang Zemin repeatedly mentioned that the rule of law is the direction of China's system of government in the future. Of course, he said this to please his foreign guests, when in reality he is trying to undermine the process. Indeed, the National People's Congress (NPC), the legislative body of China, has been showing signs of greater independence in recent years. All the democratic-minded people think that this trend is key to the ultimate success of establishing the rule of law in China. This prospect must have scared Jiang, because he recently gave instructions that the rule of law must be subject to the authority and apparatus of the Chinese Communist Party (CCP). Specifically, he ordered that a new bureau be set up under the CCP Central Administration to control legal and legislative affairs. Ironically, the new bureau bears the name of the Bureau of the Rule of Law. This organ is designed to rein in the NPC and put everything about the rule of law under the control of the CCP.

Jiang's strategy is clear. Within the circle of the communist elite, he has tried to consolidate his "Jiang Core" position [*Jiang hexin*], and within the CCP apparatus he has emphasized that the localities must submit to the center. Throughout China he has emphasized the party's leadership. But in truth, this approach only enlarges his personal power and control over the nation. He pays only lip service to building the rule of law; what he wants is the "rule of Jiang."

Indeed, the very purpose of the rule of law is to put a limit on the presently unlimited power of the CCP and to put the brakes on the personal ambitions of the highest leadership. It protects civil liberties. Therefore, the party must submit itself to the rule of law, rather than the rule of law submitting itself to the needs of the party.

This move of Jiang's reminds me of the tactic *fu di chou xin*, which is one of the well known *Thirty-six Strategies*. It means that to prevent water from boiling in the cauldron, one must first remove the firewood from beneath. Perhaps Jiang Zemin hopes that by removing the independence of the legislative process he can end China's evolution towards greater rule of law. The bottom line is, he doesn't want to see the law rule, he wants to see himself rule as a paramount leader, even though he may use the term "rule of law" to cover up his true intentions. Jiang says he is a big promoter of the rule of law, but in reality he is a big obstructor, if not its biggest enemy. If continuing down this path, he will get burned for trying to remove the firewood.

THE BUREAUCRATS VERSUS
THE WORKING PEOPLE

Issue Brief no. 59 (March 6, 1998)

Recently, the Chinese government announced that it would cut four million bureaucratic jobs from the current 33 million. Behind the news is little indication of how these 33 million bureaucrats live upon the Chinese working class. After all, in a country where the per capita income is less than 500 dollars a year, sustaining this stratum of 33 million bureaucrats is not a slight burden, especially for the Chinese working population. According to the old Chinese saying, bad politics is worse than a [man-eating] tiger [*ke zheng meng yu hu*]. Here is how this tiger eats the population in China.

In the urban areas, there are around 30 million working class citizens who are unemployed, struggling below the poverty line. For the rest of the urban working population, the tiger gets to them in the form of stocks. In many state enterprises, the government has forced the employees of the enterprises either to become unemployed or to buy stock in the enterprise with their life's savings. This is not a method for privatizing the state enterprises, but for raising money to sustain the same government-appointed bureaucrats. In addition, these bureaucrats are able to use the loopholes of the poorly regulated system of capital market to make a killing. Moreover, the corrupt officials devour a large proportion of the profits of the private sector through corrupt activities and forced bribery.

In the rural areas, the tiger eats the peasants through a new form of land management called "dual plot management" [*liang tian zhi*]. In this system, the government divides the land into "food producing plot" [*kou liang tian*] and "responsibility plot" [*ze ren tian*]. The food producing land is for the basic food needs of the farmers themselves, and the responsibility land, which is far larger in many communities than the former, becomes land leased to the peasants who are then required to contribute the yield from this land directly to the state. In China's vast rural areas, many local governments arbitrarily appropriate land for "responsibility" purposes, forcing the rural population to hand out part of its yield in the form of both money and produce.

Premier Zhu Rongji may want to reduce four million government jobs—which is a step forward—but the larger problem remains unchanged. The bureaucrats get richer and the working class gets poorer. The very nature of the Chinese government is an integrated function or system of political domination and economic exploitation of the Chinese working men and women. Indeed, nothing but full democratization can resolve China's worsening political and economic injustices.

THE POLITICAL SHOW SEASON
Issue Brief no. 60 (March 13, 1998)

N̲o one denies the importance of the National People's Congress (NPC) Convention and the Chinese People's Political Consultative Committee (CPPCC) Convention each spring, especially this year when the representatives voted to change the leadership of the Chinese government. But this is also the primary occasion for political show. Indeed, members of the third generation of leadership, with Jiang Zemin at its core, are competing with each other to show the thousands of representatives from all parts of China their open-minded and democratic qualities. This has become Chinese political ritual, in which the highest leadership condescends to listen to opinions from the people. The reality, however, is that they pose to listen because they want the votes of the people's representatives, and they probably never mean to hear because they cannot be held accountable in the current political system.

This reminds me of the way the Monkey King of the well-known Chinese classic tries to fool the Gold-Horned Monster and Silver-Horned Monster. Before fighting the monsters, the Monkey King must change into another person in order to get into their lair. Once inside, he can then become the Monkey King again to wreak havoc there. I think the Chinese leaders are trying to fool the people's representatives like this in order to get them later. When the representatives' votes are cast and they return home after the meetings, then the leaders will turn back into their true selves, domineering and arrogant in the face of their subjects.

This uniquely Chinese political ritual seems to have created a Chinese political cycle. In the spring, at the time of the two meetings of the NPC and the CPPCC, the opinions and criticisms from the masses and from the lower levels of the government are tolerated as if a political thawing were occurring. But right after the meetings, as the natural summer begins, the political winter descends on China, during which the leadership emphasizes discipline and conformity with the communist Politburo. Indeed, the season of political show is the season of hypocrisy. The only way to eradicate such hypocrisy is by full democratization, where all officials are held accountable all the time through democratic institutions.

THE GREAT LEADER COMPLEX
Issue Brief no. 61 (March 20, 1998)

With the death of Deng Xiaoping, China's strongman politics ended. But that did not mean that China got over its "great leader complex," a psychosis that still permeates the Chinese elite circles, including officials at all levels of government. This complex compels them to expect a great leader who can solve China's social, political, and economic problems. It is like a mirage on the Chinese political horizon, which confuses China's search for democracy. In fact, the present popularity of Premier Zhu Rongji among many Chinese is part and parcel of this complex.

China's political system is highly centralized in terms of decision-making power. No one can do anything without someone at the top giving consent. This system has remained unchanged since the founding of the People's Republic of China in 1949. Over the years, it has cultivated sycophantism, double-speak, hypocrisy, and mediocrity in the Chinese government apparatus. Ironically, the more incompetent the officials are, the more likely they are to seek the patronage of the top. And the more that patronage is passed down from the top, the less creative the patronized officials are and the more they lack initiative. Thus, the great leader complex is a disease that has handicapped Chinese officialdom. It is also the root cause of its incompetence and mediocrity. In a sense, the great leader complex and the one-party dictatorship are two sides of the same coin.

Indeed, the continuation of the Chinese communist system depends in a way on a collective illusion or expectation that a great leader is capable of having everything under control and thereby keeping basic order. Obviously, Jiang Zemin is no great leader. Nor is Zhu Rongji. In fact no one, not even a great leader, can save the communist system down the road.

A true leader can only exist in a democratic system, in which he is held accountable for his actions by the public. The reason Zhu Rongji has proven capable of being an above-average leader in China so far is because he respects fact. In other words, he is less likely to get carried away by lies or illusions of great leader complex. We must wait and see whether he will continue to practice what the Chinese call "seeking truth from fact" [*shi shi qiu shi*]. However, as a technocrat, Zhu can never provide the Chinese nation with a vision that will transcend the present difficulties and embrace the endless opportunities for the next century. This is the kind of leadership that China needs, and will only emerge from a liberal democratic system that realizes the potential of its people.

DOWNSIZING THE PARTY APPARATUS
Issue Brief no. 62 (March 27, 1998)

In China, the single most powerful and populous organization is the Communist Party. It is a parasite on all levels of government. In Premier Zhu Rongji's recently released "New Deal," the government will be reduced both in the number of officials and the number of government organs. But Zhu Rongji's efforts are mainly to make the division of labor in government more efficient, which is a welcome step. However, the biggest contradiction in China is not between one government function and another, or between the central government and the local governments. Rather, the biggest conflict is potentially between the government and the governed. In other words, the problem of division between the different branches of government is a minor one compared to the huge problem of legitimacy in the Chinese political life and system.

The first obstacle to tackling this larger political problem is the omnipotent and omnipresent party machine that dominates all aspects of Chinese life and all levels of Chinese government. Thus, in addition to cutting the size of the government, it is more important for the regime to cut the size of the party apparatus. It is simply immoral for the Chinese Communist Party to directly spend tax revenue for its own interests, especially to pay the salaries of the millions of CCP operatives.

President Jiang Zemin always says that the CCP provides necessary and indispensable leadership for China's economic development and modernization. But in reality the party constitutes a huge waste of resources. For instance, Jiang Zemin recently attended a celebration at a certain military academy where he said that the party must continue to exert leadership within the military system. The fact is, the party machine proves to be a heavy burden on the military modernization effort. Over half of the military officers in the People's Liberation Army are not professional military personnel, but are political commissars and directors. Simply by dismissing these non-professionals in the Chinese military system, the number of military officers could be reduced by half, which would save tens of millions of dollars. The same goes for the party cadres who populate all governmental and non-governmental organizations.

Chairman Mao used to call on party leaders to serve the people. The best thing they can do to serve the people now is get a real job in the marketplace.

EL NIÑO IN BEIJING

Issue Brief no. 63 (April 3, 1998)

Recently, there have been mixed reports about Beijing's handling of the subject of political reform. On some university campuses students and scholars are talking about democracy more openly. Much of this discussion, through books and conferences on the subject, is currently tolerated, as long as it continues to exist in the domain of words rather than actions. The Western media has generally welcomed what the *Far Eastern Economic Review* calls the "Beijing spring." But no one knows how long the regime will tolerate liberal intellectuals and their deliberations on democratic reform. Contrarily, harsh treatment of Chinese political dissidents still occurs. On Friday morning, Xu Wenli was arrested and his apartment was thoroughly searched. Yang Qingheng, a well-known Shanghai dissident, was sentenced to three years in prison for his bold call for workers to organize themselves. There are no signs that the regime will relent in its efforts to silence political dissidents.

So the question then is why the regime imprisons political dissidents but allows some intellectuals to talk about democracy, even though the two groups are saying basically the same thing. It is as if one is treated by the regime not by what one says, but by what the regime perceives one to be. The regime regards political dissidents and former prisoners of conscience as political enemies, which is residual thinking leftover from the Mao-era mentality of class struggle. Indeed, in the regime's political logic, being labeled as a class enemy or counterrevolutionary means that in Chinese society you will naturally be classified as subhuman. And in the collective subconscious of Chinese officials, class enemies and the like do not deserve human rights. Thus the greatest inhumanity of the regime is not the denial of rights, but the denial of humanity, especially of those who dare to differ politically.

In this regard what is happening in Beijing now is not a true political thawing, but rather the result of a "political El Niño." President Jiang Zemin will tolerate some democratic talk for the sake of his public image and for warming up US-China relations before President Clinton's visit. However, the real political thawing—the beginning of the democratic process—depends on institutional change rather than talk. And the touchstone of such change is the way the regime treats political dissidents. It must put an end to political discrimination of dissidents and begin to regard them as ordinary and lawful citizens of China. Without this type of change, the euphoria in the Western media will not last, and those who romanticize China's political prospects will soon face another big disappointment.

THE STALLING ENGINES OF THE CHINESE ECONOMY
Issue Brief no. 74 (July 10, 1998)

No matter how hard President Jiang Zemin tried to impress the world with China's economic success during the Clinton-Jiang summit, serious problems are beginning to emerge at an unprecedented scale and scope since China launched economic reforms twenty years ago. Since that time, the three powerful engines (i.e. exports, domestic consumption, and foreign investment) of China's economy are showing signs of severe fatigue, threatening to slow down, if not completely stall, its economy.

First, exports are dwindling fast due to the Asian financial crisis. For the first time since the early 1990s, Chinese exports decreased in the first quarter of this year, and there are no signs of improvement in the second. Some Chinese experts estimate that the export slowdown alone will probably cut China's GDP growth rate by two percent this year.

Second, domestic consumption is more sluggish than ever. Housing projects, which Clinton visited in Shanghai, are part of the one sector in which the Chinese government hopes to create a strong demand to propel the entire economy. But that is not working. Now with 15 million people added to the unemployment pool in Chinese urban areas, who have the money to buy those new homes? Besides, the underdeveloped financial institutions and home mortgage facilities make it impossible for average Chinese to buy homes. In response to this, Zhu Rongji has tried recently to inject a huge amount of investment into infrastructure building, such as railways and big construction projects, in hopes of achieving a nearly twenty percent jump of such investment over the last year. But the effectiveness of such measures on the economy are yet to be seen, though pressures to stimulate growth are mounting.

Third, the rate of foreign investment is slowing down, too. During the first five months of 1998, the rate of foreign investment in China decreased by about 1.49 percent from the same period last year. Zhu Rongji set the goal of this year's actualized foreign investment in China at 30 billion dollars, but economic figures so far are less optimistic for achieving this goal. Bureaucratic red tape and a weak rule of law make foreigners think twice about investing in China.

Then there is the biggest flood of the century, which is still devastating China's southern and northeastern provinces. The damage inflicted on grain production and agricultural income will add to the inflationary pressures stemming from an aggressive monetary policy (which ranges from lowered interest rates to drastic credit expansion). These will also add to the ills of the Chinese banking system in terms of non-performing loans and bad debt. All this shows that China must overhaul its economic institutions, a task unachievable without initiating serious political reforms.

THE END OF ZHU RONGJI'S NEW DEAL
Issue Brief no. 77 (August 14, 1998)

Premier Zhu Rongji, also known as China's economic czar, shed tears during an inspection tour on the rising Yangtze River — the first time he did so in public. No one can tell what went through his mind at the moment, but Mr. Zhu is in trouble at the most crucial juncture of the Chinese reform era. Only half a year ago in his debut press conference as premier, Zhu expressed confidence in achieving broad-ranging goals: 8 percent of GDP growth, downsizing government by firing 4 million officials, rescuing the state sector by firing 30 million workers, privatizing the housing sector, etc. But Zhu did not foresee two unexpected events: the rising waters in China and the falling currency in Japan and other Asian nations. These may have caused his new deal to end sooner than most people could have expected.

The "flood of the century" inundated millions of Chinese homes and vast reaches of agricultural land. The Chinese authorities admitted it has impacted the lives of 240 million people, roughly one-fifth of China's total population. To make things worse, the flood occurred in the most economically vital regions (Yangtze and Nenjiang valleys), accounting for more than half of China's industrial capacities. Some Chinese scholars recently estimated that the flood will slow down Chinese economic growth by at least 0.5 percent this year. But the real consequence should be much worse. The flood damage will take years to repair and the agricultural loss will have ripple effects in both regional and national economies.

Unfortunately, Zhu's ability to fight the problems caused by the floods has already been undermined by another confounding problem: the deepening Asian financial crisis. The falling Japanese yen signals that the crisis is far from over, and the leadership in Beijing seems to have underestimated the serious nature and implication of this crisis. As exports continue to fall, the Chinese economy has slowed down and the unemployment rate has risen drastically. So Zhu's plan for reforming the state enterprises has been stalled. The housing sector reform has been postponed indefinitely, and the downsizing of the government has been partly suspended. Indeed, for the first time since Jiang Zemin took power, the regime's policies seem to be in disarray.

But the regime cannot afford such policy drift because economic woes are turning political. This is a highly centralized and tightly controlled system, in which any minor problem may translate into major political crisis. Thus natural disasters always have political consequences, and economic difficulties always lead to political instability. Faced by both domestic and foreign woes, China is forced to reconsider its reform plans. Crucial decisions may be made in the ongoing meeting by the Politburo members at the Beidaihe Resort. And the most crucial decision will be whether China's reform should go forward or backward. Turning the wheel back will definitely lead to chaos because of the expected deepening of conflicts and contradictions within the current governance system. But to push forward such reforms, political change will become increasingly indispensable.

A LESSON FROM THE ENVIRONMENT
Issue Brief no. 78 (August 21, 1998)

The rainfall and flood damage done in China are two separate things, though the official media in China are trying to confuse them. They do so to cover up one of the most notorious public policy failures — China's environmental fiasco. True, China is now experiencing the biggest flood damage it has seen since the founding of the People's Republic in 1949, but the quantity of water flows are still less than some historical flood records from the 1950s and 1960s.

Chairman Mao used to frame the process of socialist construction as a battle between man and nature. His philosophy was that man must triumph over nature (*ren ding sheng tian*) in order to achieve economic development. Thus in designing economic policies, the Chinese communists ignored the Chinese traditional wisdom of seeking harmony between man and nature. Hence the total disregard for environmental needs.

As a result, deforestation became a state policy for making more farm land, especially in the mid and lower reaches of the Chinese river systems. In the upper reaches, however, the state encouraged over-logging to increase its revenue. In the Yangtze system, for example, forestation has been reduced by about 75% percent since the early 1950s. The natural system to resist the flood was also devastated by the effort to turn lakes of the river systems into farmland. In Hubei, one of the most devastated provinces in this year's flood, the lake area was reduced by nearly 80%. If these lakes were saved, the provincial government would have been saved the trouble of flooding vast rural regions to save the metropolitan cities.

The deforestation led to the erosion of river banks in the upper reaches and silt-accumulation in the lower reaches. Indeed, the last four decades witnessed fast accumulation of silt in all China's river systems. As a result, the Yangtze and Yellow Rivers, the two biggest in China, flow above the ground level in some heavily populated areas by as much as ten to twenty feet. Curiously, the Chinese public often see reports about the historic records of the water levels at various sites, but are not informed of the fact that the accumulated silt is the cause of the high water levels. The official media did not mention that the cubic meter per minute level of the water flows this year remains below some flood records of the 1950s and 1960s.

Before, forests constituted a strong protection against flood, but deforestation has made rainfall more likely to turn into floods. According to the estimate, the loss of a hectare of forest means that the same land has lost its flood holding capacity by 2,500 cubic meters of water. Hence, smaller rainfall can translate into bigger floods now as compared to a few decades ago. Decades of environmental devastation has led to this year's loss of life and property, a lesson the Chinese government is still refusing to learn. Even though the Chinese media has framed this year's flood as a natural disaster, it is in fact as much the fault of the failed government policies.

THE OLIGARCHIES IN
LOCAL CHINESE COMMUNITIES
Issue Brief no. 79 (September 4, 1998)

As the Russian financial turmoil spreads across its borders, the western media has begun to turn its attention to Russian oligopolies and their role in the current crisis. Both Russia and China have a weak rule of law coupled by ample rule of oligopoly. The main difference perhaps is that Russia's oligopolies rule from Moscow, while China's oligopolies exist outside the nation's capital in a sea of somewhat compartmentalized local communities.

This difference may be a reflection of the divergent paths through which they attempt to exit the failing system of communism. The Soviet system was swept away by a top-down political process, but Chinese communism has been chipped away by market processes from bottom-up. In either case, at the moment of transition and power vacuum, weak institutions allow a few to achieve astronomical wealth overnight through legal or illegal means. China' s road to capitalism has given rise to thousands of local oligopolies that control both the political and economic life of the respective local communities. They often use violence to intimidate the locals.

Like in Russia, the Chinese oligopolistic powers are fed by corruption and weakness in the rule of law. They thrive on three factors that may or may not be unique in Chinese society. First, the local oligopolies are formed through a close integration of local economic business interests and political power. Privatization of the public sector is marred by a series of scandalous incidents where officials award public property to their friends and relatives. According to the estimate of some Chinese scholars, the annual loss of the public property to local officials and their alliances through legal or illegal means may now stand at between 60 and 80 billion dollars, a process that becomes a hotbed for an oligopolistic structure.

Second, the new local oligopolies draw strength from the revival of clan organizations in the local communities. They ride the coattails of the old religious revival and clan activities, and provide resources and political support for them. Third, local oligopolies reap huge profits by relying on illegal or underground economic activities. Tax evasion and lowering wages are standard practices of the enterprises controlled by the local oligopolies.

The emergence of a local oligopolistic structure may have serious consequences. On the one hand, they may undermine the Leninist party/state system through which Beijing maintains its political monopoly, a development which is not necessarily a bad thing. But on the other hand, such oligopolies may also pose a threat to China's democratization, as being witnessed in Russia. For instance, many of the rural elections became less credible due to their bribery and intimidating practices on the voters. It is indeed shocking to see the powerful political and economic clout local Chinese oligopolies wield as the country moves toward a market economy. The Chinese people need to liberate themselves from the domination of the oligopolies in their local communities, and they can only achieve this through advocating sweeping reform aimed at guaranteeing citizen's human rights and the rule of law.

CHINA'S AGRICULTURAL SUMMIT
Issue Brief no. 83 (October 9, 1998)

On October 12th, the Central Committee of the Chinese Communist Party (CCP) will hold a plenary session in Beijing, a major political event since Jiang Zemin consolidated his power at the 15th Party Congress a year ago. Those who have expected Jiang to use this event to initiate major reforms on China's political system will be disappointed, for the meeting will focus on China's agricultural sector.

But for many Chinese who do not expect a political watershed to result, the meeting is still off the mark. Why not an environmental summit? The environmental plight (pollution, floods and water shortage) is threatening the lives of tens of millions of citizens. Or a financial summit? Bad debts and non-performing loans in the Chinese banking system are ten times as worse than the Japanese banks. What about a summit to help some thirty million unemployed urbanites who are struggling without adequate social security protection? The reform of the ailing state sector has lost its steam, which qualifies it to be a candidate for a summit. How about a summit on crime and corruption?

Indeed, the agenda reflects Jiang Zemin's typical approach to dealing with pressing issues in Chinese society. First, he picks an easier and less controversial issue, or one experiencing the least resistance. It is therefore not surprising that agricultural reform entails the least, or even, no policy controversy within the ruling elite. Any other reform agenda would likely create a policy storm and even a showdown between the liberal and conservative wings, a scenario that would force Jiang to choose sides. Thus, even though more assertive in foreign policy issues, Jiang remains a weak leader in domestic policy issues.

Second, enveloped in the policy thinking deeply rooted in the communist tradition, Jiang regards economic conditions as the key to upholding the communist political order. And according to this tradition, agriculture, among others, serves as the basis of the economic order, even though it produces less then 20% of the GDP. Compared to the urban unemployed, the rural population presents a lesser threat to the regime. Although China is ushering swiftly into the information age, some of the thinking behind policy still lingers in the age of a planned economy.

Third, in spite of the professed achievement, grain production in 1997 fell by 12 million tons as compared to the previous year, and this was blamed on the drought in 1997. This year, of course, they can blame the flood were there a sharp drop in grain production. But the real problem of the agricultural stagnation is due to a human rather than natural factor. The reforms have claimed a heavy toll on the rural population, who are victimized daily by local officials' abuse of power. For instance, the illegal taxation on the peasants have become unbearable, causing numerous violent incidents to erupt in the last two years. Unless the regime allows grassroots democratic elections to expand to the township and county levels, there will be no reversal of this disturbing and destabilizing trend.

Jiang Zemin may still think of ways to tinker with the outdated governance structure, but the fact is the communist political system is so corrupt and wasteful that anything short of true democratic reform will only scratch the surface. The rural sector is no exception.

WHY CHINA'S TRICKLE-DOWN POLITICAL REFORM WILL FAIL

Issue Brief no. 85 (October 23, 1998)

Among the Chinese political elite and intellectuals, democratic transition is no longer a taboo issue. It is instead a hot topic that has been forced onto the agenda of the top leadership by three emerging circumstances. First, years of western pressure from both public condemnation and private persuasion on human rights issues have come to bear fruit. Following the high-profiled summit meetings between President Jiang Zemin and western leaders, the cause of human rights and democracy has become increasingly tied to China's relationship with the western countries, culminating in China's signing of the Covenant on Civil and Political Rights earlier this month. Now the game is to "trust and verify", making it difficult for the regime to dodge the issue of political reform.

Second, the resumption of dialogues between Taiwan and China highlights the issue of China's democratization. If Beijing wants Taiwan to accept a unification arrangement, democratic reform is an unavoidable step. This became a major point of contention during Koo Chen-fu's recent visit to China. Third and most importantly, rampant corruption and the Chinese public demand for political reform have had a ground-swelling effect on China's political scene.

Thus, the debate on political reform has gone beyond the stage of "should it or should it not", and has become "how to implement a peaceful and smooth democratic transition". However, Jiang Zemin is still hesitating or playing a non-committal game. He speaks in favor of democratic reform in general terms, but acts slowly, if at all, with any policy measures to implement such reform. The regime has shown limited tolerance over some liberal intellectuals calling for democratic transition, but has blocked any political processes from the bottom up to implement the reform. The recently concluded plenary meeting of the CCP central committee ruled out the expansion of grassroots elections to township and county levels in the rural areas.

It seems that Jiang is doing again what he is best at: performing a balancing act between the different political camps. This however may be based upon a false conception that China's democratic transition can be prolonged into a trickle-down process from elite groups to the rest of the population. Clearly, Jiang hopes to release a chained 'genie' out of the bottle, an impossible prospect. The Chinese public which is disillusioned with the present political arrangements would not have the patience to wait for a trickle-down strategy initiated by the top. To protect their interests, they would want in the first place their rights to free speech and press and the right to choose their leaders immediately restored according to Chinese laws. This will make Jiang's cautious edging towards elite democracy look somewhat like playing with fire on dry land. The changing political landscape is forcing Jiang and his successors to choose one of two options: lead the tide of political reform, or resist it and then risk being swept away by it. The clock has long run out for a trickle-down approach.

PART   THREE

CHINESE MILITARY IN

TRANSITION

INVITING WOLF INTO THE HOUSE
Issue Brief no. 14 (March 1, 1996)

Chinese president Jiang Zemin recently spoke out, on several occasions, on the need to "talk politics". Jiang's words imply that he wishes to rekindle the ideological struggle and purge pro-western influences in China. The military leaders, smelling the change of the political wind, initiated a campaign to indoctrinate the military rank and file with communist dogma and the Party line. Jiang's move is apparently related to the high level power struggle which has intensified with the deterioration of Deng's health. Although Jiang is primarily concerned with securing his own political clout, his current policy bears the possible consequence of increasing the power of the military and hence reversing Deng Xiaoping's policy of keeping the generals out of the political center stage. Despite Deng's earlier efforts, China's military is becoming an increasingly important player. Through numerous military controlled business enterprises, the military has already carved out a niche for itself in China's economy. Their political capital has been rising as the public becomes more and more disillusioned by the rampant corruption of civilian officials. In fact Jiang may soon discover that he helped create his greatest rival.

During the Dengist era, political power rested on the three most important branches of China's political structure: the Party, the military, and the civilian government. However, economic modernization requires that the polity and economy be effectively separated in the domain of decision making, thereby giving technical bureaucrats more weight in deciding on matters of reform and economic development. During the past 17 years of reform, Deng successfully prevented the military and Party ideologues from interfering in the reform process. He adopted the policies of "taking the economic development as the central task", "separating the Party and the government", and "promoting the professionalization of the military". But these Dengist tenets are subject to change as Jiang tries to exercise his own political muscles. The recent move is but one step to re-politicize the military and thereby involving the generals in the central government's decision making processes. This may be necessary for Jiang to consolidate his power base in the succession struggle, but in the long run it will pave the way for the generals to usurp power in China. This will have serious consequences for China's modernization programs.

First, with the rise of the military in the political arena, civilian control of the government will be seriously undermined, giving rise to more irrational state policies. This will lead China away from the "East Asian Model" of development, where domestic power struggles do not impend the formulation of rational economic policy. Instead China's economic policies will become hostage to infighting between factions that are drawn along different political and ideological lines. Second, nationalism would be further strengthened as the military prioritizes the issues of reunification with Taiwan and reclamation of the Spratly Islands, thus impacting China's overall relations with the West. If this tendency toward ultra-nationalism is to become more mainstream, it may effectively put a stop to China's reforms and open door policy. Thirdly, under the premise of nationalism, Cold War politics will be revived, possibly leading to an ideological struggle between those that are in favor of creating a liberal democracy and those that support market communism.

There is an old Chinese story about a man "inviting the wolf into the house", and finally being killed by the wolf. As of yet Jiang's alignment with the military is based upon mutual needs, but his conduct opens the door for the military strongmen, some of whom have aspirations of assuming the supreme power in China. For now the military leaders wait on the sidelines watching the succession struggle, but their turn will come as Jiang and other civilian officials are further weakened in the process. There does not seem to be any candidate able to fill the seat of paramount leader after Deng Xiaoping dies. The vacuum of power that will follow Deng's departure will stimulate severe competition. Jiang Zemin would have grossly misjudged the situation if he were to assert himself as China's next political strongman.

Mao said that political power comes from the barrel of a gun, and this dictum remains true for a country lacking the rule of law or strong institutions for leadership transition. But the barrel of a gun cannot produce a modern economy. Jiang Zemin is playing a dangerous political game, of which he himself may end up a victim. But the biggest tragedy would be the suffering of the Chinese people, and their aborted effort to modernize their own country. It will also thrust the region and world into great instability in the next century.

To avoid this grave consequence, the leaders of the world should pressure Beijing into immediately starting political reform that promotes rule of law and prevents military strongmen from taking power in China. Such reform should insist on the principles of free press and public accountability based on checks and balances within the government. The independence of the judiciary system should be enforced along with greater transparency and due process of the law.

LIBERATING THE LIBERATION ARMY
Issue Brief no. 48 (December 12, 1997)

Upcoming meetings between Chinese and American top military officers disguise the two armies in the costume of cozy engagement, but in reality the natures of the two armed forces are quite polar. Regardless of any agreement on issues of global security and defense strategies, the fact that the two forces occupy different positions in their domestic political structures would abort any meaningful exchange from the beginning, not say any positive results.

The US military is a professional force which exists in the framework of a constitutional democracy. As such, the US military is non-political, and thereby safe from any domestic turmoil or politics of the civilian government. The military can never serve the interest of any particular political group or faction. At the very least, the military in this country cannot be used as a tool for the promotion of any one individual or interest group in the country's government structure; rather, it exists solely for the defense of the nation itself. China's military is, of course, a mechanism for national defense, but it is also a political tool of the Communist Party. The People's Liberation Army (PLA) was in fact created during the emergence of the Chinese communist revolution in 1920s. Ever since then the PLA remains a running dog of the political elite.

The exchange between the Chinese Lt. General Xiong Guangkai and the American Under-Secretary of Defense Walter Slocombe proceeds, then, from very different perspectives. There is little, if at all, common language for the two parties. The US should take this opportunity for dialogue to promote the professionalization, nationalization (*guojiahua*), and neutralization (in terms of internal politics) of the Chinese military, especially at the time when the call for ending the Communist Party's use of the PLA as its tool begins to be heard in Chinese society and in the Chinese military itself. The US participants in this exchange must stress to their Chinese counterparts the immense importance of a professional army in the scheme of military modernization. This delinking of the PLA from the Communist Party is an inalienable part of China's democratization process.

Of course, the oppressive and dictatorial Chinese regime and many in the PLA would like to use the contact with the US military to modernize China's weaponry. But for the sake of stability and peace in the region and the world, the US must continually tout this professionalization of the military as the *only* means to the modernization of the Chinese army. It is the Chinese military institution, not Chinese military technology, which needs to be rebuilt in the first place.

The Pentagon can play a major role in the true modernization of the PLA in a democratic framework. In an era when democratization is inevitable for the People's Republic of China, the US military can and should contribute to the liberation of the PLA from the yoke of the CCP.

NOW, WHERE DOES THE BARREL OF THE GUN POINT?
DEMOCRATIZATION AND MILITARY MODERNIZATION
China Strategic Review, Vol. II, no. 6
(November/December 1997)

In Western democratic countries, military and civilian functions are well defined, and their roles are so independent of each other that people pay little attention to the connection between the military and democratic institutions. Indeed, in the post-War era, the military is rarely seen interferencing in the civilian democratic processes. Even in the Eastern European countries and the former USSR, the military played a minor role in the democratic transformation, i.e., it neither significantly hindered nor promoted the democratic processes.

But things look quite different in China, where the military has never been a passive witness in the country's political life. In 1989, for instance, the Chinese military quickly stepped into the political crisis and helped the regime carry out a bloody crackdown on the democratic movement. This incident shows that the Chinese military, lacking the kind of professionalization of its counterparts in other communist regimes, is far from a modern force designed for national defense. Because the Chinese military was highly integrated with the Chinese Communist Party (CCP) in the early history of the force's development, it historically was subordinate to the needs of the party for taking power in China. At peace time, its political role in Chinese civilian life remained strong.

But in the 1990s, things are beginning to change, when the Chinese military evolves rapidly towards its goal of being a professional armed force. The questions are: Given the trend, will the PLA be able to remain neutral in China's domestic political changes? What will be the specific role, if any, of the Chinese military in nation's future transition to democracy? If a political crisis, similar to the one in 1989, occurs in the future, how will the Chinese military react? More importantly, what is the best strategy for the Chinese democrats to prepare the People's Liberation Army (PLA) for a peaceful democratic transition?

The Party Directs the Gun

The notion that "The party directs the gun" (*dang zhi hui qiang*) was first uttered by Mao Zedong during the civil war with the Chinese nationalists in the 1920s. Specifically, it denotes that the party controls the military not only at the upper levels of the military's hierarchy, but extensively at every level. Mao developed a consistent policy by which he subjected military forces to the leadership of the party.

The communist movement in the pre-1949 years was conducted primarily through military and political campaigns to defeat the Japanese and Chinese nationalists in an effort to take power in China. Thus, throughout the revolutionary years, the CCP and the PLA were regarded as one united entity rather than as two separate organizations. According to Mao's policy, in addition to its military function, the PLA must serve as the CCP's organization team and propaganda team among the masses. Moreover, the PLA played a prominent role in establishing and managing the revolutionary governments in the red areas during the civil war.

To guarantee these multiple roles of the party-military machine, CCP committees were instituted at all levels above the company level in the Chinese military force. In war time, this dual leadership system (one military commander and one political commissar in each unit) insured the absolute loyalty of the army to the CCP leadership.

At the same time, the military operations were forced to "fight" political campaigns to eliminate the landed class (through land reform) and establish new governments in the newly liberated areas. This historical experience throughout the Chinese communist revolution created a highly integrated system of personnel, ideology, and organization across the CCP and the PLA, the legacy of which continued into the contemporary era.

The Tendency of the PLA to Become Non-Political

Mao once said that wherever a force exists, there will be a counterforce. Indeed, within the military ranks, there seems to be a consistent effort at getting out of the political yoke of the CCP and becoming a more professional, less political force. This tendency existed in the war years, but became much more obvious when the country was at peace. In the post-1949 era, there have been two major movements towards professionalizing the Chinese military, when the military focused its energy on its national defense capabilities.

The first such reform occurred soon after the CCP took power in 1949 when the military leadership emphasized the formalization (*zheng gui hua*) of the force, an act seen in retrospect as aimed at transforming the PLA from a guerrilla-styled armed force to a national defense force. Peng Dehuai and Luo Ruiqing, the generals who were in charge of the reform, tried to emphasize the military role of the army, while playing down its political role. In many ways, they worked to reform the military after the Soviet model. They instituted, for instance, the ranking of officers and introduced the Soviet system of command and control as well as a system of training and management of the force. Even though the Soviet military differed in many aspects with the militaries of the Western democracies, the Soviet military model was still a professional military. Throughout this period, Mao was uncomfortable with the direction of the reform, which he regarded as deviating from his idea of the people's army.

Indeed, the reform was unable to go very far before the Cultural Revolution began in 1966, when Mao ousted the reform-minded generals and put an end to their efforts. Moreover, during the Cultural Revolution (1966-1976) the Chinese military system reverted to the earlier war-time system, and the ranking system was completely abolished. Under Mao's direction, the PLA resumed a strong and high-profile political role, literally becoming "a great school of Mao Zedong Thought" (*mao zedong sixiang da xue xiao*). When the Cultural Revolution created turmoil throughout China, Mao ordered the PLA to support the leftists (*zhi zuo*). Tens of thousands of the military officers were placed directly in civilian government organizations throughout China to take charge and supervise the reorganization of the government at all levels below the central government. The Chinese military once again became a tool of internal politics and further deviated from its goal of professionalization as a force for national defense.

Soon after Mao died, Deng Xiaoping took control of the PLA, the government, and the CCP. In 1981, Deng ordered the Chinese military to fight a war with the Vietnamese in which the Chinese forces suffered huge causalities. The embarrassing weakness of the PLA in matters of both training and weaponry was thrown in the face of the military and CCP leaders. This war convinced Deng Xiaoping and his followers in the military of the urgent need to initiate reforms to professionalize the PLA. Hence, the second wave of modernizing and professionalizing the Chinese military began. In the late 1980s, the ranking system for military officers was reinstituted. Military training was given precedent over political study sessions for the soldiers. Professional military academies were established throughout China to train the new generation of officers. The old Maoist strategy to manage the military through political indoctrination was gradually abandoned. The once-popular idea that "politics is in command" (*zheng zhi gua shuai*) was replaced by a new slogan of "building the army through modernization" (*xiandai hua jian jun*), symbolizing a new drive to rebuild a professional Chinese national defense force.

Then, in 1991, the Persian Gulf War sent another shock through the ranks of the PLA. The war, studied closely by the Chinese military, made the military leaders fully aware of the vulnerabilities of the Chinese national defense. The state of Chinese weaponry, including the absence of high tech warfare capabilities, could be fatal to the Chinese military in modern warfare. In a sense, the American military operations in the Persian Gulf, apart from destroying much of the Iraqi military apparatus, also dealt a fatal blow to the PLA's long treasured military strategy and tradition based on the concept of "the people's war" (*renmin zhanzheng*) which traditionally downplayed the importance of weaponry. Both the civilian and military leadership reached the conclusion that the future of the Chinese military was professionalization. Then the question remains: under the condition of greater professionalization, what would be the best strategy for preparing the Chinese military for a possible democratic transition?

Preparing the Chinese Military for a Democratic Transition

The attitude of the Chinese military will be one of the decisive factors in China's democratic transition in the next century. It is high time, therefore, for Chinese democrats to think about a strategy for preparing the military both ideologically and institutionally for a possible democratic transition. Even though the military may not lead the democratic movement, it is at least necessary to achieve political neutrality in the military so it will not object to democratic changes in the future.

There are at least five areas in which the Chinese military system is undergoing changes that may affect the military attitude to China's democratization. First, the introduction of the rule of law into the military structure is a primary step towards the further depoliticization of the PLA. Recently, Jiang Zemin, chairman of both the state and CCP military commissions, expressed the new course of governing the military as *yi fa zhi jun* (governing the military in accordance with laws).

However, this policy needs to be upgraded if it is to bring the military under the general order of the rule of law. Numerous legislative and institutional measures need to be taken to establish a legal system for the PLA. The military structure needs a new system of commands and controls, in which the party's line of control through political commissars should be abandoned. An extensive military court system, which functions under explicit laws and regulations, should replace this secondary-line of control. These suggested conditions are taken for granted in many other countries, but in China the military has a long history of being ruled along political lines and under political policy initiatives. This concept of rule of law within the military will require great efforts to succeed.

Externally, the military should be restored to its constitutional position, which places it under the jurisdiction of the National People's Congress and not directly under the leadership of the CCP. This constitutional position of the PLA should be a primary condition for the Chinese military reform aimed at being a true national defense force. Under such conditions, the civilian leadership of the military needs to be instituted.

The second area for reforming the military is gradually ending the political role and presence of the CCP in the military. Currently, party organizations exist at every level of the military, a negative factor for its greater professionalization. Under the general rule of law, there is no legitimate ground for insisting on the CCP control of the military (*dang zhi hui qiang*). In fact, the real threat to the new generation of party leadership is just the reverse, namely, the gun directing the party (*qiang zhi hui dang*). To prevent this outcome, Jiang Zemin and his colleagues should be wise enough to realize that depoliticization of the PLA is also in their interests.

Recently, the CCP leadership has given the green light for a greater separation of party and government within government organizations. It also has promoted the separation of the party and enterprises in order to modernize China's economy. For very similar reasons, it is also necessary to separate the party and the military. I think that at the present stage, Jiang Zemin is not ready to take this step. Jiang needs his association with the military to enhance his personal power status as his base of power is still weak But, in time it is probably in his best interest to push the Chinese military to focus on matters of national defense and completely remove itself from internal politics. His expressed policy of ruling the military by law indicates a inclination in this direction, but more action need to be taken to substantiate such a development.

Third, the Chinese military needs to develop a professional self-image as a legitimate national defense force. Since the founding of the PRC, the Chinese military has been indoctrinated with a political mission for following the CCP's party line. Unfortunately, this political mission has sometimes taken precedent over its professional goal of defending the country against external invasions. The Tiananmen Massacre of 1989 is an example of the military's politicization. Deng Xiaoping ordered the army to play the role of CCP stooge in suppressing the democratic movement in Beijing. This incident certainly tarnished the army's image among the people, causing many members of the military to reconsider its role. Consequently, it will be more difficult in the future for the CCP elite to persuade the PLA to shoot civilians for a designated political purpose. The military officers would also have to have a greater incentive to resist being used as political tools in China's domestic politics.

Moreover, as the Chinese military widens avenues for conducting exchanges with Western military forces, the negative image of the PLA caused by the Tiananmen Massacre of 1989 has become more palpable in its exchange activities. Eight years after the event, more of the PLA top brass have come to the conclusion that the crackdown should not be the military's responsibility. In the post-Tiananmen era, more and more military personnel are certain to protest a situation where the army is called in to shoot civilians. Interestingly, the negative image of the PLA as the result of its participation in Tiananmen in 1989 has made many PLA officers wary of meddling in Chinese domestic politics. In recent years, PLA officers largely distanced themselves from the political processes, as can be seen in their absence in the succession power struggle among the Chinese civilian leadership. The new generation of PLA officers seem more concerned about external factors that threaten China's territorial integrity and national defense. The crisis of the Taiwan Straits, the geo-military power balance, and China's territorial conflict with other countries in the South China Sea seem to have absorbed the top brass's attention rather than domestic politics.

It is certainly worth encouraging the Chinese military to heighten its awareness of its professional role in national defense, especially through public education and military exchange programs. Already such exchanges have opened the eyes of the Chinese military to its institutional weaknesses resulting from the CCP control. The more exposed to the Western professional military institutions, the less likely the Chinese military is to return to the traditional role of political tool of the CCP.

Fourth, the changes that have occurred among the cadets at the military academies are producing a new generation of military officers, who may be more sympathetic to China's democratization. In the past, officers were selected according to the soldier's loyalty to the party in political matters. None of these officers had much professional military training or education. Beginning in the 1980s, the Chinese military established its own system of military academies, which have produced larger numbers of military officers. Now most middle- and low-ranking officers came from this population of educated professional soldiers.

The importance of this shift cannot be underestimated. Unlike the previous generation of military officers who, illiterate or semi-literate, were servile to the CCP, the new officers are educated professionals who come primarily from urban areas. They are more autonomous and far more knowledgeable about advanced military institutions in other countries. More importantly, they understand that a democratic system is in the long-term interest of their professional development. Though they have not climbed to the top-brass level, the powerful networks they formed among themselves as cadets in the military academies may still render them a powerful force in the military ranks. The support of these officers for a transition to democracy could grow out of these networks if most of them favor democracy over authoritarianism in the future.

For similar reasons, this new generation of officers is very difficult for the CCP to control. This generation did not go through the CCP indoctrination that its elders underwent, nor has it served in the PLA in a time of war. Politically, they are also alienated from the CCP's orthodox ideology. They are more inclined to find pride in their role as professional military officers rather than in a political role under CCP. Perhaps they hold greater admiration for the famous Western military commanders like Montgomery, Hyden, and Hamil than for their party boss Jiang Zemin.

However, this generation of military officers is not averse to power. In many developing countries where political institutions are weakened, the military elite tend to take the opportunity to seize the political power of the country. In a similar vein, the new generation of the Chinese military officers may desire supreme political power if such conditions prevail. At the moment, they prefer to be depoliticized or be professionalized because of the burden created by the CCP control. Things will be quite different if political power is easy for them to grasp. Whether these officers with political ambitions have the opportunity to become politically active depends upon China's overall political situation. If China's economic reform was aborted or the economy failed, it could lead to large-scale social unrest, and it is very likely that the Chinese military in various localities would extend its power to restore stability and gain a lion's share of political power in the process.

Fifth, the military's increasing participation in China's economic life has produced mixed results regarding the future role of the military. The business involvement of the PLA stems partly from a lack of funds for improving the living standards of the military rank and file, and from the existence of prolific opportunities to earn extra income. As a result,

many military installations have business outlets which allow
them to turn a profit in the marketplace. This practice may
entangle military interests in a complex web of local interests,
distracting it from its interest in the national defense.
Moreover, many productive units within the military
establishment are forced to produce goods for the civilian
marketplace in order to survive. These economic activities
tend to be a new source of corruption, especially in the present
time when the general rule of law is rather weak. The
tendency of the military to acquire economic power may
further weaken some of the CCP control mechanisms in the
military ranks, but it may also risk the prospect of effective
civilian control of the military after China's democratization.

Conclusion

In sum, the most crucial aspect in the fundamental reform of
the Chinese military involves changing the CCP's presence in
the PLA. In fact, beyond the party-military relationship, the
party itself is in the process of disintegration. In both the
urban and rural areas, the grassroots functions of the party are
not functioning. Most grassroots party branches have
difficulty organizing even a meeting of party members. It is
not rash to think that the CCP organizations gradually will
become ineffective at the grassroots level and gradually
become a defunct mechanism for controlling society. In fact,
there seems to be a large spontaneous movement to
dismember the CCP from the bottom up. Such disinterest in
and decreased loyalty to the party are also obvious in the
military ranks as the influence of the party steadily decreases
in the PLA.

At the present, however, the Chinese military is being
depoliticized through programs of professionalization, though
the end seems still unclear. However, if the trend identified in
the above five areas can be sustained through the next decade
or so, one can reasonably hope that the Chinese military will
not pose a threat to China's transition to democracy in the
next century. Chinese democrats should remain clearheaded

about the long history of the party-military relationship. Perhaps a pro-democracy military will emerge only at the time when a pro-democracy force in the CCP begins to appear. It is possible that the CCP can be changed from within as exhibited in the former eastern European countries and USSR. But regardless of the specific processes in which China is democratized, the role of the military remains a decisive factor.

SECRETARY COHEN'S BALANCING ACT

Issue Brief no. 80 (September 18, 1998)

As the storm gathered in Washington over independent counsel Ken Starr's report, President Jiang Zemin may have watched from the other side of the Pacific with some anxiety. Jiang worries that Clinton's weakened leadership may cause a loss of momentum on a number of bilateral initiatives achieved during the Clinton-Jiang summit two month ago. But this week, Jiang may feel greatly relieved.

China's top military commander, Zhang Wannian, is completing an unprecedented visit to Washington. General Zhang is Jiang's chosen man to head the world's largest armed forces, and is the highest ranking officer of the People's Liberation Army (PLA) to visit the United States. Shuttling between the White House and the Pentagon, General Zhang has been well received by both the President and his defense secretary, William Cohen.

To Jiang, the US-China military tie is one of the pillars needed to sustain the strategic partnership between the two countries. Jiang would like to use this relationship to serve two important purposes: to help modernize Chinese defense forces and put pressure on Taiwan. General Zhang reportedly described   US-China military ties as moving forward with "good momentum", and his meetings with Secretary Cohen as "positive, constructive and productive". These words made me feel uncomfortable since the PLA remains the most powerful institution to shore up the Chinese communist dictatorship. This is the same army that opened fire on unarmed civilians who demanded democracy ten years ago.

So in addition to the "positive, constructive and productive", there ought to be some factors designed to balance the equation. First, Secretary Cohen should give a thumbs-down to General Zhang to express his dismay with the shameful and cowardly massacre of civilians in 1989. Secretary Cohen needs to say it frankly and as it is: the PLA's role in that incident was unprofessional, degrading and unacceptable.

Secondly, Cohen needs to remind Zhang that the Pentagon cannot expand its ties with the PLA unless the latter sheds its image as a political tool of the communist party. The ties must be built on a professional basis, a view also embraced by the Chinese military. But the Chinese top brass must make good on their words with deeds, i.e., getting the Party out of its ranks. Now half of the military officers are still political operatives (political commissars) whose job is to ensure the direct Party control of the military.

Thus, the bottom line in this relationship is not "3 NOs to Taiwan" nor accident prevention between the two forces nor "transparency", but the question of how to change a Red Army into an institution that can fit into a modern and democratic China. Expanded US-China military contacts should reflect the dimension of the PLA's institutional reform in this direction.

PART FOUR

HONG KONG, TAIWAN
AND GREATER CHINA

THE WINDS OF WAR IN THE TAIWAN STRAIT
Issue Brief no. 11 (February 9, 1996)

With missiles fired and tension mounting, the Taiwan Strait is filled with the winds of war. The situation has never been so alarming since the American Pacific Fleet was deployed there more than forty years ago. Clearly both China and Taiwan will enjoy enormous gains by keeping the waters calm between them. During the reform era, Taiwan businessmen invested tens of billion dollars, and cross-strait trade stood at an impressive 15.1 billion dollars in 1993, growing at about 30 percent annual rate.

But that status quo is made obsolete by changes in both China and Taiwan. A democratic and newly industrialized Taiwan seeks more international recognition than being absorbed into the periphery of Beijing's dictatorship. The mainland China, with newly gained economic and military muscle, is quietly ushering in the post-Deng era with a rapid ascendance of nationalism. The new generation of Chinese generals are the pinnacle of this emerging political force. They reportedly told Mr. Freeman, former State Department official and China scholar, that a plan had been completed to conduct a 30 day missile attack on Taiwan, and that the U.S. should think twice of its Los Angeles before helping Taiwan's war effort.

The question to President Jiang Zemin is not "attack or not attack Taiwan", but how to save face and be reconciled with the ultra-nationalist political force, a monster created by the Chinese leaders themselves. Jiang Zemin is a mediocre opportunist, but aspires to be a paramount leader like his predecessor Deng Xiaoping. Now he has at stake his legitimacy and support among the generals. Captured by his own ambition and cornered by the extreme forces he himself helped to unleash, Jiang has no other choice than going along, even though this may bring the Chinese nation closer to another civil war. The prospect of huge human and property costs is never a deterrent to someone aspiring to be a dictator.

The middle ground is rapidly disappearing, and a military showdown is looming on the horizon. But a military option is really not an option, and the stakes are too high. To prepare such a war would cost Taiwan's prosperity and would lead China into self destruction, not to mention the prospect of regional arms race and global economic disruption. Before it is too late to prevent that undesirable outcome, the western nations should move fast to prevent it.

Between backing down (being aloof is one form of backing down) or facing up to China's military hard-liners, the United States has no easy solution. But it would be a grave mistake to allow the Chinese military hard-liners to win credit for this crisis. The United States government needs to send a clear warning to the Chinese conservatives of the grave consequences of launching a war. Strategic ambiguity should rest on ample deterrence to the Chinese military hard-liners. Appeasement at this time would only feed into their ambition and consolidation. Instead of soft-pedaling the hard-liners, the west should seek to frustrate the hard-liners and set back their ambitions.

All dictators throughout history overestimate their own military capacity, and have a tendency to use it when they under-estimate the other's determination to face up the challenge. It is high time for the rest of the world to say: "Enough is enough." That strong and united stand by western countries and Japan would cool many ultra-nationalist "hot heads" in the Chinese military rank. The Pentagon should indicate to their military counterparts that such maneuvering will lead to an end to the bilateral military dialogue and cooperation. Beijing's leaders should be likewise told without ambiguity that if they cannot curb their general's aggressive words and deeds, China will suffer economically in its relations with the West and Japan. In short, the Chinese conservatives should be defeated before they lock the country into a major confrontation with the rest of the world. Only international pressures can split Chinese leadership ranks, and allow moderate factions to exert more influence.

On the other hand, Taiwan's security rests on China's peaceful transition to constitutional democracy. The people on both sides of the Taiwan Strait have a common destiny, and they should join forces in the historical task of ending dictatorship in Beijing. It is wrong and irresponsible for the leaders of Taiwan not to keep this in mind while making foreign and domestic policies. In seeking international recognition, Taiwan should first have a China policy, which is understood and supported by the majority of the Chinese people.

THE US SHOULD BRING TAIWAN AND CHINA TOGETHER UNDER DEMOCRACY
Issue Brief no. 15 (March 8, 1996)

With M-9 and M-11 missiles landing provocatively close to Keelung and Kaoshiung, two of Taiwan's biggest ports, Beijing has declared to the world that it is determined to achieve unification with Taiwan, even if this requires the use of brutal force. But the democratic Taiwan is unlikely to submit to the terms of "one country, two systems", the formula used in the reunification of Hong Kong with China. The people of Taiwan are particularly resentful of being forced into a marriage with the chauvinistic mainland where freedom and human rights are not respected. The two sides seem to be rapidly heading toward military confrontation, and the world community seems unable to respond fast enough to diffuse the situation.

Before it is too late to prevent further escalation, the Clinton Administration should act quickly to bring the two sides back to the negotiation table. Only quiet US diplomacy is capable of reversing the current dangerous trend. Similar to the role it played in the Middle East peace process, the US should act as mediator between Taiwan and China, initiating a peace process that will end in one China under one democratic system. Exposure to Taiwan's thriving democracy ought to have its effects on China's political structure. If open trade has moved China closer to a free market economy, then we could expect the process of peaceful reunification between China and Taiwan would liberalize China's political system.

China should immediately cease its military threats to Taiwan and negotiate with Taiwan for a settlement that fully guarantees Taiwan's security and its rights to participating in regional and international organizations. The threat of using force will not bring the two sides together, but will drive them further apart.

The people of Taiwan, for good reason, wish to safeguard their democratic freedoms and are wary of immediate unification with an autocratic state. We can interpret the independence movement as being a reflection of Taiwan's wish to embrace democracy and to distance itself from totalitarianism. The proponents of the independence movement seem to believe that only the creation of a sovereign state can protect Taiwan's maturing democracy from the autocratic whims of the Chinese state. However, in light of the recent saber rattling from Beijing, it is apparent that the exact opposite is true. The push for independence only serves to provoke an ultra-nationalistic response from the mainland, increasing the chances that Beijing will unilaterally impose its authoritarian regime on the Taiwanese people. The pursuit of international recognition without Beijing's consent is only causing tension and instability across the Strait. The potential consequences of Taiwan's bid for independence would pose a major setback for the mainland's budding liberal forces and moderate wings in the government. State propaganda depicts Taiwan as a rouge province, its defiant declarations of independence only play into the hands of the ultra-nationalist forces in Beijing. Taiwan should not allow the Chinese government to depict it as seeking for independence by ducking the reunification issue.

In short, Taiwan simply cannot divorce itself from China without risking a war, now or in the future, and its greatest hope in preserving its freedoms is to help China to democratize itself in the peaceful process of reunification. China's democratization is the ultimate guarantor of Taiwan's security and economic interest. Immediately after the election, the president of Taiwan should open negotiations with China which would herald in an era of close cooperation and exchange, paving the way for reunification with China. At the negotiating table Taiwan can state its own terms on the unification issue. The negotiations should be comprehensive, including in particular the demand for China's concession on liberalizing its political system, and allowing democratic institutions (e.g., the rule of law, respect for human rights, civil liberties and a free press) to take roots in China. Taiwan would be wise to use its political and economic progress to induce China back on track toward a peaceful transition to a constitutional democracy.

THE IMPLICATIONS OF TAIWAN'S DEMOCRACY FOR MAINLAND CHINA
Issue Brief no. 17 (March 23, 1996)

March 23, 1996 will be recorded in Chinese history as one of the greatest and most memorable day to the ordinary Chinese people. On this day and for the first time in China's five thousand year history, constitutional democracy was completely realized by the 21 million people on Taiwan. It is also a resounding defeat to Beijing's intimidation and anti-democrat policy. Taiwan's democratic achievement broke the myth that Chinese culture and tradition are unlikely for developing democracy. For the first time Confucianist ideal that "people are the essence of state politics" (*min wei bang ben*) came into reality. This not only brings pride to the people of Taiwan, but also to the Chinese people throughout the world.

However, Taiwan's milestone is not the end of history, but a first step in a long march to bring the rest of China under the same democratic institutions. In fact Taiwan's security and stability of new democracy are closely related to the process of China's democratization. Without such a process, Taiwan's freedom and democratic institutions are built upon sands, and this is so in spite of the expanding international

111

wan. This is no time for euphoria. The tension
it is still high and uncertain. Now is the time
n people join forces with 1.2 billion people to
achi͟e͟ ͟ ͟ ͟ ͟a's peaceful democratization, which is to the
economic and political benefits of both China and Taiwan as
well as to regional stability.

Perhaps the quasi-hostage situation which the mainland
China has put Taiwan into has fed into the separatist
sentiment of the island's residents. As a mainlander I
personally understand and share the Taiwan people's "tragic
feeling" as often referred to, but the historical reality is that
Chinese people whether living in Hong Kong, Taiwan or on
the mainland share a common fate and destiny. We are not
free unless all of us are free. The dictatorship from Beijing is
like a mountain, and our common historical task is to move
the mountain. As the old Chinese fable tells, moving the
mountain is not easy, but joint and sustained efforts by all are
capable of overcoming difficulties.

To achieve this, the new democratic leaders in Taiwan
need to formally negotiate with Beijing for ending the current
tension and usher into an era of full political and economic
exchanges with China. The final reunification between the
two sides should be the final goal while allowing the time that
China transforms itself peacefully to constitutional democracy
during such exchanges. And it is only through such
exchanges that Taiwan's democratic achievement is identified
by the majority of the Chinese people. Winning the
recognition of the 1.2 billion people on the mainland should
take precedence of seeking international recognition. Only
when democracy takes roots in China can Taiwan's
democracy sustains its blossom.

The international community should continue to pressure
Beijing to the negotiation table to settle the issue peacefully.
Intimidation and use of force should not be allowed to work,
but Taiwan should not waste such international support by
evading its responsibility for promoting one China, and one
democratic China.

HOW TO DIFFUSE CHINA'S MILITANT NATIONALISM
Issue Brief no. 18 (March 29, 1996)

Along with the rapid growth of Chinese economy and disappearance of Marxist ideology, the rise of nationalist sentiment among the Chinese public is but a natural course of development. The current tension over the Taiwan Strait has raised many eyebrows in the west and led people to question the prospect of China's rising nationalism. However, it would be simplistic and harmful to equate this rising sentiment in China to military adventurism. To defuse the dangers posed by the militant nationalism, it is necessary to analyze and understand the roots of the Chinese nationalistic sentiment. There are in fact two kinds of nationalism, the origin of which had quite different historical background.

The first genre of nationalism originates from the shared identity among the Chinese in their culture and tradition. It is basically an inward-looking attitude rather than outward expansionism. In most of Chinese history, this genre was the mainstream, and did relatively little harm to its neighbors. Confucianism served as the core values and institutions, which did not take a hostile attitude to other ethnic or racial groups. Such historically rooted nationalist sentiment has nothing to do with the mentality of military glory and conquests as seen in the history of the Roman empire and modern colonialism. On the contrary, it was infused with free cultural exchanges with other nations based upon equality and mutual learning. Indeed, the root-seeking efforts by the Chinese should be encouraged, and this may in time bring about further mutations of China's sociopolitical system towards greater integration with the mainstream of the international community. No civilization can afford to be stagnant and unresponsive to the changing world environment. Chinese culture is changing over the last two thousand years, and is capable of a renaissance by embracing many western values and institutions, in particular, human rights and democratic institutions.

The other genre of nationalism was fairly recent in Chinese history. It was born out of a series of humiliating defeats by the western powers and Japan in the past. Under the colonial policies, Chinese people suffered invasions, humiliations and lack of respect due to its economic and political backwardness. Such sentiment resulted in the Boxers Rebellion in 1900, and directly contributed to the rise of communism in China. Though western colonialism and Japanese expansionism ended half a century ago, the historical wound went deep and still needs time to heal. Under the communist rule in the Cold War era, Chinese people were not given the opportunities to engage in a healing process until fairly recently when China was opened to the outside world. Thus the second genre of nationalism has much hatred and xenophobia in its making, and tends toward violence and revenge of the past humiliations. Clearly this is the kind of militant nationalism that is destructive and outright dangerous to regional stability and world peace. The current military show of force in the Taiwan Strait is deeply rooted in this genre of nationalism. If this nationalism were allowed to grow and then dominate China's political landscape in the next century as the military hard-liners would like to see, it would have grave consequences for the region and world, not to say the nightmare it may create to the people of Taiwan and mainland.

Therefore the international community and Chinese democrats have a shared responsibility to defuse the militant nationalism. First, it is correct for the U.S. to show a hard-line policy on Chinese military's aptitude to use force as a means to resolve differences. They must be taught a lesson that such a tactic is useless and counter-productive in the modern world. But victory over such militant nationalism also requires that the Administration implement its China policy free from the perceived shadows of the colonial past. On the Taiwan issue, peaceful reunification rather than peaceful separation should therefore be the cornerstone in handling the current crisis. The Administration's engagement policy needs to continue, though such engagement must have clearly spelt principles and bottom-lines.

Second, the world should encourage Chinese people to aspire for a cultural renaissance and economic development through peaceful exchanges with the rest of the world, thus creating valves to defuse xenophobia or militant nationalism. In due process, the Chinese people will regain their confidence in the world through their hard work and creativeness rather than through 19th century's gun politics. To achieve this, it is particularly important to keep the Chinese public exposed to the western culture and current world events. Voice of America, Radio Free Asia, various contacts and academic exchanges are a precious window for the Chinese public to the outside world, and therefore need to be strengthened. In addition to diplomacy at governmental levels, multi-tracked and people's diplomacy is needed to keep the communication and information flow live and effective.

In fact, one result of the last 17 years of exposure to the outside world is the emergence of a large group of intellectuals who have a quite up-to-date world view. Since 1978, three hundred thousand Chinese nationals have studied abroad, and over seventy thousand have returned to China to work at key positions throughout the Chinese society. In spite of current setbacks in the democratic movement in general, ultimate democratization remains the final goal among most Chinese citizens. Even the neo-conservatives are unsuccessful in challenging this mainstream consensus. To most intellectuals, the dividing arguments are not on whether China should democratize, but on how and to what extent China should democratize. In such light, the western support for Chinese democrats not only needs to be strengthened both morally and substantially, but must also include a dimension of patience and perseverance.

In its history, Chinese culture showed strong ability to absorb foreign cultures and institutions when challenged by them. The introduction and absorption of Buddhism in the 5th through 11th centuries were an example in point.

Taiwan's democratization is another and more recent one. In current events, Taiwan should be made both a stronghold and bridge: a stronghold in the sense that its democracy must be prevented from military intimidation, and a bridge in the sense that its economic and democratic achievement be a source of inspiration and emulation for the Chinese people in a long and peaceful process of reunification with the mainland.

BEIJING'S STRATEGY ON CONTAINING HONG KONG'S DEMOCRACY
Issue Brief no. 21 (April 19, 1996)

A recently disclosed Chinese internal report (World Journal, 4/16/96) estimates that Hong Kong's democrats will be effectively forced out of the territory after its return to China on July 1, 1997. Indeed, while still committed to keeping Hong Kong's economic prosperity, Beijing has exhibited a systematic strategy to contain and then root out Hong Kong's democratic forces.

First and as a first step, Beijing has declared that Hong Kong's democratically elected legislators will be formally replaced by a pro-Beijing group at the time of transition. Through a well controlled selection process, Beijing will appoint some coopted businessmen and professionals to rule Hong Kong. There is no solid legal basis in current arrangement to protect Hong Kong people's political rights, and Hong Kong's rule of law will be at the mercy of, and conditional upon, Beijing's changeable mood.

Second, Beijing has quietly put its big paw in Hong Kong's free media, one of the last defenses for the freedom and human rights of Hong Kong residents. The control of the media is being achieved through Beijing's aggressive purchase of Hong Kong's major media companies, and through forcing independent-minded journalists into a self-censorship. Beijing has consistently made the point that those who dare to criticize China's policy will be squeezed out of the profession.

Third, isolating Hong Kong's democrats is a current policy carried out by Beijing heavy-handedly. Those who show solidarity with the Democratic Party are either made to suffer in their business dealings with China or ostracized from Hong Kong's political processes. Clearly the leadership in Beijing hopes that a marginalized democratic opposition, with no media attention and no role in Hong Kong's political process, will be left to die in public spheres.

Moreover, Beijing is also attempting to split and further weaken the democratic coalition in Hong Kong. Great pressures are put on its moderate wings to soften their political stand to Beijing. There are already signs of division within the coalition, which will seriously undermine the effectiveness of Hong Kong's democratic opposition in the post-transition era. In addition, Beijing has been working hard to undercut the financial resources of the democrats in order to weaken their organizational capacity.

As of today, Beijing seems to be quite successful in implementing these measures. But the dictators in Beijing may still miscalculate on the democratic aspiration of the Hong Kong people. Human rights and democracy are deeply rooted in people's heart as shown in the democrats' overwhelming victory in the last election. In spite of the current setbacks, Hong Kong people will continue to push for democracy, and the return of the territory to China will not alter this fact. Beijing's hope that the Hong Kong residents will give up their democratic aspiration for keeping the economic status quo is doomed to failure.

Hong Kong's colonial status, a last sign of the western colonial policy, should and must be ended. So should be its undemocratic system. The British government has shamefully betrayed the 5 million residents of Hong Kong by failing to institute democracy earlier for its selfish interest. It has repeatedly sold out these people for the sake of its economic gains from Beijing. Now that they are fighting a uphill battle for their democratic rights, the world has a strong obligation to support them. A strong moral support from the international community should boost their morale, and more importantly make them feel that they are not alone in fighting for freedom and democracy.

THE HONG KONG CLOCK OF COUNTING DOWN
Issue Brief no. 26 (June 27, 1997)

After the First Opium War in 1840, Hong Kong was seized by the Great Britain as a first step toward the colonization of China. The ensuing imperialistic invasions by Japan and Western powers inflicted on China enormous humiliation and human suffering, which greatly hindered China's modernization. In a sense, China's modern history started from Hong Kong, an era dominated by an interplay of imperialism, nationalism and communism.

The Chinese communists rose on the tide of Chinese nationalism as against imperialism. They promised to the Chinese people a just and democratic society free from the kind of sufferings they experienced during the colonial invasions. Mao'a vision of a China standing on its own feet grips the imagination of many. But as soon as the communists consolidated their power after 1949, they went back on their word and began to persecute the very people who had supported them. As a result, China did not stand up; nor its people. The domination of the communist elite began another cycle of suffering, devastation, and humiliation for the people and country. In 1957, about 550,000 Chinese intellectuals were labeled rightists by the government because they voiced criticisms of the Chinese Communist Party. In 1958, the government designed its Great Leap Forward. As a result of this collectivization movement, tens of millions of people died of starvation, and the Chinese economy was devastated. In the '60s and '70s, the so-called Great Proletarian Cultural Revolution inspired a wave of persecution under which the lives of more than 100 million people were shattered.

It is a sad story that communists replaced the colonialists in repressing the population. The Chinese people have hardly had the time to breathe freely without the burden of harassment and domination by the powerful, foreign or domestic. By the end of the Cold War, communism was ended in the hearts of the Chinese people. They expressed their frustrations at the betrayal by the communists in the 1989 Democratic Movement, from which the cries for freedom reverberated all the way to the countries of Eastern Europe and the Soviet Union, contributing to the downfall of communism there.

After the Second World War, the West loosened its colonial grip on developing nations, and many nations experienced comprehensive modernization through free-market economics and democracy. But because of the communist policies, China remained under-developed. The post-Cold War era is for many countries the beginning of greater cooperation among nations and of the full recognition of human dignity based on the political and economic rights of the individual.

Nations embracing human rights, civil liberties, and economic freedom under the rule of law serve as a bright contrast to the failure of the communist experiment in mainland China. Indeed, China needs to completely shed its unhappy past dominated by the twin brothers: imperialism and communism. Therefore, the ticking of the count-down clock for Hong Kong's return to China not only signals the end of colonialism in China, but also counts down to the end of communist rule and institutions in China. The day will come when all Chinese people in Hong Kong, Taiwan, and mainland China will truly stand up, living with dignity under democracy, liberty, and human rights.

THE HONG KONG MODEL
Implications for China's Government Reform
China Strategic Review, Vol. II, no. 3 (May/June 1997)

Hong Kong returns to China under the formula of "one country, two systems," which was laid down by the late paramount leader Deng Xiaoping. After June 30, 1997, the more interesting issue is whether under one country the two systems can finally evolve into one democratic system for all of China.

Limited Windows for Political Reform

China's current mission, according to the leadership in Beijing, is to arduously develop the economy without changing the highly centralized power system or the sovereignty of the Chinese Communist Party. All economic and political reforms will proceed in accordance with this principle. Economically, China will conduct its market reform with the aim of making the economy more flexible, thus allowing China to participate in the economic activities of the international community.

Politically, reforms will be limited to improving the administrative system, thus ensuring the efficient working conditions that rapid economic development requires. China does not plan to establish a Western-style democracy, but only wants to improve two areas: the efficiency of its administrative system and its ability to listen to — not follow — various viewpoints and opinions. These improvements are meant to strengthen the government's central power and, at the same time, avoid mistakes in decision-making. The realization of these objectives would be a system with features similar to Hong Kong's political system, that is, an administration-oriented system incorporating many perspectives into all the administrative levels.

If this system can be considered democratic at all, one must label it a "consulting democracy" (*zixun minzhu*) or democracy of the elite (*jingying minzhu*) like that of Hong Kong. Among China's objectives for its political system, similarities to Hong Kong's political system exist. Both involve centralized political power and the implementation of very relaxed and free economic policies. This is the same model used by the successful "Four Little Dragons," namely Taiwan, Singapore, South Korea, and Hong Kong.

The Hong Kong Model Reinterpreted

Neo-conservatism, the most recent political trend in China, also promotes this model. Therefore, Hong Kong's political system and the systems of the other "Little Dragons" may well be the models that China will imitate in its future political reform. However, among all of the "Little Dragon" countries, Hong Kong could be the least influential in China's political reform because of its former colonial status.

Since the Chinese government began to adopt reforms and its open-door development policy in 1978, great achievements in economic development have been made, but at the same time, alongside this rapid growth, political instability has developed. This instability came to a head in the June 4th crackdown in 1989, after which China's leaders regarded political stability as one of their top priorities.

Economic development and the consolidation and perpetuation of the authoritarian power system became the two main objectives of the Chinese communists. In this regard, the "Four Little Dragons" certainly provide experiences from which China may learn. In other words, many in China will try to look at Hong Kong's rule of law as an alternative to China's corrupt and unstable political system.

Starting with a Democracy of the Elite?

In the past decade, China's governmental organs have experienced a down-sizing in the number of government personnel, which alleviated the problem of oversized bureaucracy. Meanwhile, a recruiting system has been gradually implemented, based on the recruitment examination and the meritocracy model, which will ensure greater efficiency in the government.

In order to make the decision-making process a more reasonable and rational one, some government functions have begun to pay attention to outside consultants, taking advantage of the various consulting agencies consisting of a diverse set of experts and researchers. This represents a natural process of system differentiation due to the increased complexity of modern social and economic life.

For instance, the People's Congress and the People's Political Consultative Committee are becoming more and more dependent on professional assistance in their routine work. Beyond their legislative role and role in general state policies, their daily work is more professional than political, and related primarily to service-oriented consultation and representation of systemic channels of expression for different social interests. At the same time, the government policy-making process will inevitably rely on direct consultation with civil organizations or NGOs.

Here Hong Kong's system has a lot to offer the Chinese policy makers. The British worked well with this system to solicit support from business and professional communities. Though falling short of a full democracy, this system, if adopted in China, may pave the way for China's transition to democracy.

Less Control, More Freedom

A new set of objectives for China's reform and open-door development is to increase the role of the market in regulating much of economic and social life. The government will turn away from its usual all-inclusive role which takes charge of every social affair in the highly centralized administrative system. Transferring its trivial economic, administrative, and managerial powers to enterprises and corresponding sectors of society, the government will close down some of its administrative organs in specialized industries. New and future economic entities will have less direct obligations to fulfill the central administrative duties of the government.

At least according to the claimed reform plans, the government will no longer interfere as much with economic activities, except in the large- and medium-sized state-owned enterprises, so that businesses and manufacturers will become autonomous economic entities responsible for their own losses or gains. At the same time, the government will also strengthen the services of its administrative agencies in finance, pricing, commerce, and industry.

In order to develop and improve the market economy, more and more legal and economic means will be employed to consolidate the government's ability to adjust development at a macro-economic level. Hainan, Shenzhen, Zhuhai, and other special economic zones adjacent to Hong Kong have already established a preliminary system featuring less government control and more economic freedom (*xiao zhengfu, da shehui*). It seems likely that such reform measures will be adopted in more areas.

Taking on Government Corruption

Since the beginning of China's reforms, corruption in the government has been a serious problem, but in recent years corruption has grown extreme. After the reform policies were carried out in the transition of state-owned enterprises to modern businesses, a process troubled by social injustice and public resentment, the state lost a large amount of capital to corrupt officials and their family members.

Although the Chinese government has taken some measures to punish corrupt officials, few results have been achieved. Since 1989, the government has to some extent reinforced its self-supervision system, taking measures to check and control bribery, venality, and other forms of corruption among government officials. However, corruption is still a serious problem which poses a threat to the legitimacy of the government as well as basic social stability. In order to effectively eradicate corruption in the government, some politicians and scholars in mainland China propose imitating Hong Kong by establishing an anti-corruption organ within the State Council.

There are numerous instances of official police and government involvement in criminal acts and corruption, and the forms of corruption are many. But actual laws and economic regulations fall short of reinforcement, giving rise to all kinds of corruption, which severely threatens the legitimacy of the communist leadership in China. Although it is faced with a serious corruption problem, the government cannot find any effective measures to cope with it. If the problem continues to exacerbate unchecked, the danger of a political crisis will be just around the corner.

It is under theses circumstances that many people propose to imitate Hong Kong's *Lianzheng* Office, the previously mentioned anti-corruption organ, by establishing an anti-corruption unit directly under the State Council's supervision in order to harshly punish corruption. This kind of proposition has been brought forward in both the People's Congress and the People's Political Consultative Committee. Hong Kong's *Lianzheng* Office has a very good reputation among the people in the mainland, which points to the anger that the Chinese people have towards the corruption of their government. In addition, the political and administrative systems of the Hong Kong government are characterized by their effectiveness in governing a modern metropolis rather than a nation. Therefore, it is worthwhile for many big cities in the mainland to regard Hong Kong's experience as a teaching tool.

Conclusion

Because of the current political control, most policy researchers in mainland China are still reluctant to discuss the political factors contributing to Hong Kong's economic success. If this persists, only a slight possibility exists that Hong Kong's political system would serve as a model for political reform in mainland China. But in spite of this problem, Hong Kong's model still lingers in people's minds, which influences their thinking without their acknowledgment.

Under the current circumstances, there is little chance that China will soon make efforts in establishing a democratic system; instead, the tendency will be to develop a consulting mechanism which will ensure that the government is able to listen to the opinions of different social classes and groups.

Coupled with some of the "freedom" granted to the media, the government can use many extant consulting organizations for consultation, such as the People's Political Consultative Committee and non-government policy groups. The pattern of development in these areas forecasts the probable orientation of China's political development in the next few years. In this regard, Hong Kong provides good experience from which China can benefit. Its role is limited but vital in the process of democratizing China.

HONG KONG'S DAY AFTER
Issue Brief no. 27 (July 3, 1997)

Hong Kong has been handed over to Chinese rule, an event much celebrated by Chinese people world wide, and looked upon positively by other nations who would like to see an end to colonialism. But to end colonial rule does not mean a through train to freedom and democracy for the people. As Hong Kong's transition settles down into history, the issue of individual liberty and government domination still remains. But the divide now is not between Hong Kong and China, but between Chinese people and their rulers.

Now is the time when the world will see whether or not the rulers in Beijing keep their word. The people of Hong Kong seem to have demonstrated already that it will not easily relinquish its democratic ideals. Tung Chee-hwa still faces the test of standing for his people or siding with the new rulers against the people. On the fundamental issues regarding civil liberties and the rule of law, we hope Mr. Tung will not, as he reportedly said on his second day in office, "accommodate or humor" the Chinese leaders.

"One country two systems" is a legitimate policy to facilitate Hong Kong's return to the motherland, but it cannot be a legitimate excuse for treating the people of Hong Kong and China as first- and second-class citizens. The rulers in Beijing have to respond to the question why Chinese mainlanders and Hong Kongers should have differentiated treatments and unequal rights. If civil liberties are what can be enjoyed in Hong Kong, then why not in China? Though it is natural for the Chinese and Hong Kong people to desire those same human rights, the rulers may still find this shocking.

It is therefore important for the international community to protect political liberties in Hong Kong and its rule of law not only for the sake of 6.3 million Hong Kong residents but also for 1.2 billion Chinese people. Whether like it or not, Hong Kong becomes a lighthouse to a great nation at a great historical moment of transformation. Hong Kong's system provides an alternative to Beijing's political system dead-ended by rampant corruption, and the gradual implementation of the Hong Kong's way is in the interest of the Chinese nation as well as the peace and prosperity of the world.

The leadership in Beijing should recognize Hong Kong's merits, and start to catch up on its learning curve. Thus, Hong Kong's day after is a time for a wake-up call to the leaders in Beijing: China is moving into a new era, and if can't lead, get out of its way!

THE GHOST AND THE DARKNESS FROM INDONESIA
Issue Brief no. 76 (July 31, 1998)

This week the sleeping lion of China has been poked---a lion Napoleon described as sleeping peacefully for centuries. The title of the essay came from the name of a movie I recently saw, which tells the story of a African railway project being stalked by a man-killing African lion. Unfortunately, the same madness and terror are not completely foreign to the contemporary human societies.

To many Asian leaders, victimizing ethnic Chinese is not a new strategy for the racially dominant groups to vent their frustrations. Indeed, from Suharto's killing of an estimated 300,000 ethnic Chinese in 1960s to the vast exodus of ethnic Chinese boat people from Vietnam in the 1980s, the racially motivated assault and cleansing never stopped. But this time, the Indonesian savagery in May 1998 against ethnic Chinese women and children may have turned the tide among one-fifth of the human race.

Ironically, the difference was made by modern communications, like televisions and the internet. Graphic pictures began to arrive in people's living room of the rape, torture, and killing of ethnic Chinese women and children. Horrible stories were reported in the Chinese media of gang rape and the fatal stabbing of small children in front of family members. Watching these in the headlines of the Chinese media throughout the world for days and weeks proved too much for a people who are still with a collective memory of injustice and humiliation during the last 150 years.

This is a memory of the Opium War (1840-1842), a war the British fought to gain Hong Kong and the rights to push addictive drugs to China from British East India. This is also a memory of the Rape of Nanking when Japanese soldiers indiscriminately killed about 300,000 Chinese men, women and children. In short, a memory full of suffering, destruction and deaths. Curiously, the Chinese communities in mainland China, Hong Kong, Taiwan, Singapore and elsewhere bear little resemblance in social system and ideology except for this common memory of victimization.

Indeed, the Chinese communities throughout the world are witnessing a rare solidarity among themselves over this incident, something unseen since the end of the Second World War. Even Beijing changed its original hands-off tactics. It allowed the public to watch the Indonesian atrocities through an uncensored Hong Kong cable TV channel, and the Chinese Central TV network showed footage of the Chinese foreign minister pressing his Indonesian counterpart to address the issue during their recent Manila meeting.

Today most Chinese see the Indonesian atrocities as human rights violations, and rightly so. This perception may deepen their commitment to human rights principles. For the Habibi government, a public apology, thorough investigation, and swift justice are the right things to do. However, that government seems callous and slow to react, apparently hopeful that the event will die down like previous ones in the past. But it will not. And by failing to act forcefully, the Indonesians let an alternative and dangerous force emerge from the ghost and the darkness of the past memory, a force of hatred and vengeance--such as militant Chinese nationalism-- that will someday bring destruction to both China and its neighbors.

ENGAGING THE CROSS-STRAIT ENGAGEMENT
Issue Brief no. 81 (September 25, 1998)

In about three weeks, China and Taiwan will resume their high-level talks in Beijing. The meeting between Wang Daohan and Koo Chen-fu will supposedly continue from their previous dialogue in Singapore in 1993, but the circumstances have drastically changed since that historic event. Though the Clinton Administration still adheres to a policy of having no role in the cross-strait talks or negotiation, the changing circumstances and vital US interest in the region may make such a standing-on-the-side posture increasingly outdated, if not more self-contradictory.

First and foremost, Taiwan has become a full democracy, something that makes it impossible for the US to stand on the side if the communist mainland tries to take the island over by force. On the other hand, Taiwan's democratization has accelerated its independence aspirations. The polls in the last five years reflect a steady increase of its citizens who support Taiwan's ultimate independence from China. Taiwan's pro-independence party (DPP) now controls most of the county level governments as a result of a major 1997 election. This puts enormous pressure on Beijing to take actions, for better or for worse, to resolve the cross-strait issue.

Indeed, the task of taking Taiwan back now seems to be Jiang Zemin's main preoccupation aside from continuing economic modernization initiatives. The 1996 episode of the missile firing around Taiwan indicates that China is willing to risk war to achieve its goal. In response to Beijing's military intimidation that year, President Clinton sent two US carrier battle groups to the region to support Taiwan, which brought the two nuclear powers dangerously close to a confrontation. In China, the episode was followed by a sudden rise in ultra-nationalistic sentiment, poisoning the atmosphere for both US-China relations and the political process edging towards democratization. Since then, however, Jiang Zemin seems to have learned the lesson that unification with Taiwan must be achieved via Washington's understanding, if not cooperation.

Indeed, the recent Clinton-Jiang summit has set a new stage for both China and Taiwan on the reunification issue. Clinton's three NOs are a major concession to Jiang Zemin, and in return, Jiang must show greater flexibility to resolve the unification issue through peaceful means, and must make progress in the areas of human rights and political reform in order to improve the atmosphere for the US-China-Taiwan triangle. Seen in such a light, Taiwan has emerged as the biggest leverage to induce China to evolve towards a constitutional democracy, a task Clinton Administration officials have referred to as the biggest challenge to post-Cold War US diplomacy. For this reason, the Administration should actively engage the cross-strait engagement just as it did in Middle East and Northern Ireland. To gain progress on reunification, Beijing may have to accept Washington's participation in the process. Taipei may need Washington to balance the overwhelming size and influence of China in order to protect its own interests. The negotiation process may be long and arduous, but the US participation is key to a peaceful settlement that may ensure Taiwan's security and China's commitment to democratization, both of which are vital to the American interest.

A COMMON DESTINY FOR CHINA AND TAIWAN
Issue Brief no. 84 (October 16, 1998)

In spite of the cozy atmosphere reported in the second round of Koo-Wang talks, many Taiwanese still regard China as a big bully next door determined to take over their home. To many Chinese, however, Taiwan is like a rebel forgetting its own Chinese roots. Both are right, albeit for a shared and unfortunate reason---they both lost a sense of "Chineseness" that used to empower them. Historically, China was not unlike Europe. It consisted of distinct ethnic groups with diverse vernaculars. But they did not build separate nation-states as the Europeans did. Rather, for centuries, the people intermingled to build a common destiny based on common culture and mutual tolerance. Such Chineseness was revered as higher than either the emperor or the differences among them.

Indeed, it was not the ruling empire (sometimes with an ethnic minority as the ruler) that held China together for centuries, but rather the succeeding dynasties that were instrumental in embodying this Chineseness. But that common destiny was shaken first by the European and Japanese imperial invasions, and then completely shattered by the Chinese communist movement. The gentry or community scholars were all wiped out, and so were the traditional human ecological systems of self-governance where the "mountains are high and the emperor far away".

Since 1949 when the communists took power, the state organization gradually penetrated every aspect of Chinese social life. Subsequently, the people were brain-washed in never-ending political movements; their culture and traditions were systematically destroyed for the adoption of official communist ideology. The mutual tolerance among them was gone, too. Incessant class struggles tore the fabric of families and communities until violence, brutality, and political domination became the order of the day. This was the kind of China ushering into the reform era twenty years ago. What else can one expect to result other than a bully? But the bullying behavior of China (remember the missile firings?) has also alienated the people of Taiwan who have since become increasingly assertive in claiming their own separate identity. Some therefore look for an exit from China. But they are wrong, too.

Regardless of the present political situation, Taiwan and China are inseparable in their shared history and cultural tradition. They need each other for the prosperity and well-being of their people. Both can either strive for a common destiny, in which their rich history and culture are rediscovered, or they can engage in mutual destruction. To facilitate this common destiny, China must change, democratization being the first and most essential step. It must stop bullying Taiwan and relearn the Chineseness of its culture and tolerance in which unwilling reunification would be an unknown term. It should allow Taiwan to develop its own legitimate international status. Only by doing so can it regain the confidence of the Taiwan people. On the other hand, Taiwan should seek to help China rediscover itself in a democratic framework.

PART FIVE

U. S. - CHINA
RELATIONS

MANAGING THE EMERGING CHINA:
New Structure And Old Problems in Us-China Relations

China Strategic Review, Vol. I, no. 9 (December 5, 1996)

China policy poses one of the biggest challenges to American foreign relations, and perhaps the single most difficult one for President Clinton's second term in office. Indeed, as Assistant Secretary of State Winston Lord has pointed out, Beijing will be the most difficult regime to deal with in the next two decades. During the first term of Clinton's presidency, US-China relations were caught in a series of disputes over human rights, trade and arms proliferation. Though these issues remain as sticky as ever, the bilateral relationship seems to be on a new course based on an improved atmosphere and sustained by a series of expected high-level contacts. The emerging new structure of US-China relations is organized around a more general theme of how to integrate China into the international community in political, economic and security areas. It is high time to think strategically about this monumental task and to give a fresh assessment of this integrative process which lies at the core of Sino-US. relations.

First , the emergence of this new structure is central to both American and Chinese national interests. On the Chinese side, a stable and positive Sino-American relationship is a precondition for China's modernization. Beijing has long recognized the leadership position of the United States in the western world. Without improving ties with the latter, it is impossible for China to maintain a constructive relationship with Europe and Japan. Moreover, without western and Japanese technology and investment, China's economic reform will come to a halt.

At the present stage, roughly one third of all Chinese exports end up in the American market, a situation that allows China to maintain a near double digit growth rate. According to a recently published report, nearly fifty percent of the China's GDP in 1995 was churned out by exports (China Times Daily, 11/13/96). The dependence of the Chinese economy on foreign trade is unusual for a country with a large internal market, and is much higher than in the United States (17 percent) and Japan (13 percent). This indirectly reflects the fundamental illness of the Chinese economy, namely, the ailing state sector. The same report argues that China's economy is entering into a stage where the potential of labor intensive and low tech products has reached its limit. Most firms in these low-end categories have already moved from Taiwan and Hong Kong into mainland China. Therefore, to sustain growth, China will have to turn to the west and Japan for more capital and technological intensive investment. Clearly, without American support, China may not be able to achieve this end.

Besides economic necessity, China also needs the United States on the issue of Taiwan-China reunification, which is also high on the agenda of the Chinese leadership. The prospect of Taiwan gaining independent status remains a touchy issue in China both in its internal politics and foreign diplomacy. Thus, without improved Sino-US relations, the crisis in the Taiwan Strait may erupt again at any time. And the tacit support of American leaders is perceived by Beijing as a necessary condition to lure or force Taiwan back to the negotiation table to settle the reunification issue with mainland China.

With respect to foreign diplomacy and security issues, what Beijing fears most is the rise of a perceived "China threat" and potential western containment policies that may follow such a perception. After the Chinese missile test near Taiwan in March 1996, alarm over China's future military role in the region has increased significantly among nations. Japan has shifted to a much more defensive gear in security matters regarding China, moving US-Japanese security relations to a new level. If the traditional US-Japanese strategic ties were grounded in a Cold War desire to contain the Soviets, a similar arrangement would send a chilling signal to Chinese leaders. Thus, to prevent a rising tide against China, it is imperative for Beijing to take steps to improve relations with

Washington. In short, the leaders in Beijing have always wanted to say "no" to Washington, but their national objectives and their limited resources prevent them from doing so. That is why the Chinese have been vocal about improving Sino-US ties. At least in the perceivable future, China will still need the United States more than the US needs China.

On the other hand, the west, particularly the United States, also has an interest in integrating China into the international system. First, the United States needs the unprecedented economic opportunities provided by China's growth and its huge market potential. Secondly, the United States needs China's cooperation in maintaining regional stability, especially on the Korean subcontinent. Third, China's cooperation is desired in the UN and on arms proliferation issues. However, judging from the overall conditions of US-China relations, American needs tend to fade into long term geopolitics or to lie in future economic opportunities. China's needs are more immediate, tangible and are likely to have a short term impact on China's political and economic development. In other words, China falls into the category of "potential superpower," and currently has little if any substantive means (political, economic or military) to directly challenge US national interests.

This certainly gives the United States substantial leverage when trying to facilitate China's integration into the existing international order in economic, security and political areas. However, it is no small challenge to accomplish such a task. The three substantive areas are littered with pitfalls. The first and foremost question is the relative sequence of undertaking the task, or how to prioritize the work in the three areas in an overall strategy.

It is certainly a mistake to wait for a later time to initiate the process, for this will feed into China's ultra-nationalist rhetoric and its political ascendance. It should be recognized that it takes both sides (the west and China) to accomplish the task of integrating China. In other words, it is a game based on interaction between China and the west, particularly the United States. The most likely starting point would be in the economic arena and would focus on China's formal entry into the World Trade Organization (WTO). Recently there have been indications that both sides are willing to move WTO negotiations forward. But it would be a mistake if the United States focused narrowly on the issue of market access. It is strategically more important to use the WTO platform to change China's economic system. Though China has made impressive progress towards a market economy, residual forces from the former communist system impede a thorough, full-scale transition. The state still controls most of the key sectors in the economy, and private property rights have yet to be fully installed. The leaders in Beijing are still reluctant to privatize state-owned enterprises, whether for political or ideological reasons. Therefore the WTO platform should be a leverage to ensure that the privatization process continues. China should be urged not only to end its state monopoly in trade and other key sectors, but also to embrace true private property rights based on the rule of law. Lowering China's tariffs and eliminating trade barriers are two ways to achieve this, but they should not be considered ends in themselves.

Chinese leaders should be convinced that the plight of the ailing state sector can only be resolved by reforms that end state ownership and the planned economy. Therefore, the time table should be set to phase out state control while allowing the private sector to take over. The overarching strategy is to force the visible hand of the state out of the market while strengthening the invisible hand of the market. If this can be achieved, it will remove one fundamental barrier to China's economic integration with the rest of the world. If, on the other hand, this cannot be achieved, China will forever play under a different set of rules, even if trade barriers are reduced to acceptable levels. More importantly, the absence of direct state control over the economy will be a precondition for China to seriously establish and enforce the rule of law as the only viable alternative to control. Another important task is for China to reduce official corruption and initiate political reform. In the short run, such reforms may prove difficult both ideologically and politically, but it is the only way China's economy will keep growing and modernizing while maintaining basic social order. Therefore, they are good for China as well as for the world.

In security areas, the Taiwan issue lies at the core in spite of Beijing's claim that it is an internal affair. As long as there are tensions across the Taiwan Strait, regional stability is always at risk. And as long as the reunification issue remains unsettled, China's integration into regional or world security arrangements will remain elusive. No matter who is in power after Deng Xiaoping dies, pressure for Taiwan to unify with China will likely increase, especially as China continues to gain economic and military might in the coming years. After China takes back Hong Kong in July 1997, the Taiwan issue will be a prominent one in bilateral security dialogue. Indeed, Beijing is demanding to link the issue of Chinese arms proliferation with American arms sales to Taiwan. Though the Taiwan issue is not as urgent or as easy to settle as economic matters are in bilateral relations, its importance is not to be underestimated. It is right for the United States to maintain its current "one-China" policy and to strive for cross-strait stability, but the effect such a policy may have will decrease as China approaches superpower status. This is especially so if Hong Kong's return to China proves uneventful after 1997. Then the impatience of Beijing is likely to grow, threatening the current peace and fragile balance across the Taiwan Strait.

While a secure and democratic Taiwan is in America's interest, an independent Taiwan is not. Taiwan carries the gene of democracy, and if it is unified peacefully with China, rather than being annexed by the latter, it will play a pivotal role in moving China towards democracy. Thus Taiwan should be thought of not only as a stronghold of democracy in the Far East, but also as a bridge to bring China more fully into the world community as a responsible nation that respects human rights and democratic institutions. Therefore, instead of staying clear of cross-strait quarrels, the United States should play a more active role in promoting a peaceful settlement between China and Taiwan after July 1997, just as it has tried to do in the Middle East. For as time passes on, the strategic importance of this area will be equal to, if not surpass that of the Middle East. While paying attention to Taiwan's security, the United States should also encourage Taipei to conduct open political dialogue with Beijing. Ultimately, unification will depend on the people and the governments on both sides of the Taiwan Strait, and a successful unification scheme will bring China closer to democracy and make it a more responsible member of the world community. Now the major barrier to reunification is the political and economic differences between the two sides. And China should initiate meaningful political reforms to bridge such gaps. Unification should not be enforced by power and might, but by popular will. Therefore unification will not and should not end in dictatorship in Beijing, but in freedom and democracy for all the Chinese. Here the United States has tremendous diplomatic leverage, and should fully utilize it to change Beijing's security perception and behavior.

Perhaps the most difficult and challenging task is to ensure China's democratization, the fundamental aspect of politically integrating China with the rest of the world. Though apparently untenable at the moment, constitutional democracy is, after all, the only viable, peaceful and orderly framework to resolve China's political problems. The existing political structures are unable to meet tomorrow's challenges. The existing control and mobilization mechanisms are rapidly outpaced by the emerging forces unleashed by economic reform. The conditions in Chinese society are nearing a threshold where political change is essential if basic social order is to be preserved. This may be less obvious when viewed from the outside, but it is not difficult to reach such a conclusion if one considers the rapid growth of the private sector and civil society, along with the differentiation of interest in China. Thus, in the process of integrating China with the rest of the world, the vision of moving China towards a constitutional democracy should never be lost. Without such a vision and efforts to realize it, it is unlikely that China will remain politically stable down the road. Of course, no one expects China to be modeled exactly after American democracy or other democratic models, but a process of infusing into the system concepts such as checks and balances, rule of law, civil liberties and a greater respect for human rights is still achievable. Thus the United States should never stop pressuring China on the issue of human rights abuses. In addition, the US-China bilateral dialogue and engagement should be broadened to cover the difficulties and differences resulting from the incompatibility in ideology and political structures between the two countries.

In short, the emerging new structure of the US-China relationship should be encouraged, though the problems of trade, Taiwan, security and human rights are as difficult to overcome. However, if the new structure consists of mere formal high-level contacts while lacking substance, the task of managing China's global integration will fail, causing grave consequences for the region and the world. The China policy of Clinton's second term seems hopeful, but it needs to be based less on protocol and more on substance. Above all, the Clinton administration must implement a China policy with persistence and with a vision to change China's economic and political systems while integrating it in political, economic and security areas. In such a process, the United States should apply primarily a positive strategy to encourage both Chinese leaders and institutions to integrate comprehensively with the world, and produce a stable pattern of positive interactions in US-China bilateral relations. The engagement, therefore, should not be limited to high level meetings per se, but more importantly should actively involve open, substantive and comprehensive contacts of all social and civic institutions between the two countries. It is only through such contacts that China may have an opportunity to outgrow its

communist past and embrace a new future desired both by the
Chinese and by the rest of the world.

REFOCUSING CHINA POLICY
Issue Brief no. 9 (August 21, 1995)

R ecent events in U.S.-China relations are not only a test
on a China policy adopted by four presidents from
Carter to Clinton, but also represent a growing pattern
that may end up in a major confrontation between two
powerful nations in the next century. China's identity crisis
as it gains more power and status underlies the current
instability in bilateral relations. Should China elect to proceed
down its traditional road of empire building embracing a
"central kingdom" mentality, it will inevitably challenge the
existing world order, not to mention norms or standards of
life shared by democratic nations. Conversely, China can
become a major contributor to world peace and prosperity in
the next century. However, such a role as envisioned by many
Chinese requires that the rule of law, civil liberties, human
rights and other democratic institutions be introduced into
China's current system of governance. In short, China as a
nation is at a crossroads, undecided as to their future course,
yet on the verge of a decision that will have long-standing
consequences for the region and the world.

China is a nuclear power, home to one-fifth of the human
race, harbors one of the fastest-growing economies and
exhibits advancing military capabilities. Perhaps for these
reasons the Chinese leadership expects special treatment or
respect from other nations. But such status comes with special
obligations, among which is to assure the rest of the world of
its peaceful identity and commitment to developing
democratic values and institutions. However, there is no sign
that China is nurturing democratic institutions while
modernizing its economy and military. This fact should not
be reduced to simple defenses of a leadership transition crisis
or obscure cultural arguments. It is much more insidious.
Consequently, as the Chinese government increasingly fans

the flames of ultra-conservatism and ultra-nationalism among its citizenry, the time is ripe for the international community to fire a warning shot across their bow. Timely intervention now may prevent major confrontations at a later time.

Given its sheer size and resultant potential to impact the community of nations, China's democratization is not merely an "internal affair" but of great consequence to the world. Until the government is accountable to its citizens and individual voices can be heard without fear of reprisal, China will remain a threatening giant with ample muscles but no heart and conscience. Consequently, while democratizing China is ultimately the task of the Chinese people, the world has a responsibility to reinforce the efforts of its citizens seeking an open and free system, unshackled from dictatorship. As China enters a period of uncertainty and transition, such support may make a huge difference.

To accomplish this, the United States must play a leadership role that transcends both containment and appeasement policies toward China. Containing China did not work in the cold war and will not work in the post-cold war era. Pursuit of this policy may undesirably feed into the dangerous xenophobia fanned by the current leaders in China, thereby jeopardizing any chance of peaceful transition to democracy in the post-Deng era. Moreover, containment cannot work because the economic links fostered between China and the world in the last 16 years make such a policy unimplementable. A worst scenario, following the containment policy, would be the rise of the military and ultra-nationalist groups trapping China to expansionism, with the world left to continually face choices between armed intervention and concessions.

Likewise, appeasement or "doing nothing" about China's internal development is equally dangerous. The nature of the regime cannot be changed simply through trade as there is no guarantee that economic liberalization will necessarily lead to democratization. In fact, market economies have corroborated many dictators or aggressors in history. For now, the community of nations is comfortable with the status quo, unalarmed by apparent incompatibility between China's economic liberalization and continued dictatorship.

However, the unfolding succession struggle holds consequences for China's relations with the world, making it important for the US policy makers to focus upon *what* social forces are on the rise rather than *who* will come on top in the end. Clearly, the growing strength of ultra-conservatives and ultra-nationalists is alarming. It is not inconceivable for new leaders to reverse many of Deng's policies in order to shore up the Leninist governing structure. It would therefore be a big mistake for the West to wait for the dust to settle and then deal with whomever is in power. To wait on the sidelines is perhaps the worst kind of appeasement.

Rejecting the use of containment and appeasement measures, the United States should launch a multidimensional initiative aimed at supporting China's democratization, contributing to China's internal political changes, if necessary. While the U.S. should not seek confrontation with China, neither should it refrain from combining cooperation with constructive conflict to weaken the conservative elements of the regime. Engagement is not appeasement if pressures are added to it. A host of measures could be adopted that aims at isolating the ultra-conservative elements in the regime, while openly and discretely encouraging more liberal elements to exert their influence.

First, an overall policy review is needed to lay the ground for an integrated and long term China policy based upon new paradigms. During the recent ASEAN meeting in Brunei, US. Secretary of State Warren Christopher reportedly told his Chinese counterpart that it is in the interests of the United States to maintain constructive relations with a strong, open and prosperous China. Such a policy statement has unresolved paradoxes, which will inevitably be read as hypocritical by the Chinese leaders. If China is locked to the path of empire building, such "constructive relations" would seem impossible. Instead, Mr. Christopher should tell Chinese leaders that the mutual interests of both nations lie in China's economic prosperity paralleled by democratic institutions. American security and economic concerns are directly linked to such parallel reform in China. Indeed, given the potential impact and influence of China upon the world scene, the rest of the world has an obligation to ensure that China chooses the road to peace, which can only be guaranteed through development of democratic institutions at home.

The United States, while continuing to expand trade with China, should give stronger and more explicit support to those fighting for freedom and democracy in China. Senior officials of the Administration should regularly consult with leaders of China's democratic movement, and meet dissidents who push for political reform within the framework of the Chinese law. The United States should also provide moral as well as material support for the growth of civil society and independent organizations in China. In the short run, Radio Free Asia should be immediately established to provide the Chinese public with needed information and analysis of China's political situation and to promote democratic alternatives for China.

In economic area, the U.S. should also use its leverage at the World Trade Organization and the International Monetary Fund to press China on legal reforms, including enforcing the rule of law, respect for private property rights, transparency and due process.

Moreover, the U.S. government needs to change its strategy of engagement with China. In addition to dealing with Beijing, the U.S. should also communicate with local and provincial leaders in China. The importance of identifying moderate wings in the government and other sociopolitical forces in China cannot be underestimated. Forging cooperative relationships with the liberal element will facilitate firm yet fair challenges to the conservative element in the Chinese government, thus causing them to loose face and credit in the eyes of the Chinese people.

To accomplish such goals, broad coordination needs to be achieved through diplomatic cooperation with other democratic countries and non-government organizations throughout the world. In the U.S., it is important that such a policy be bipartisan and not event-driven so that a consensus between branches of government can once again be cultivated. Only through such efforts can China be spurred to a productive course in Asia.

CHINA RESTRUCTURES ITS POLICY ON THE U.S.
Issue Brief no. 20 (April 12, 1996)

Out of the apparent deadlock with the U.S. on Taiwan, arms proliferation, trade and human rights issues, China is quietly restructuring its U.S. policy, and gets prepared for the worst that may occur to the relations between the two countries since the Nixon era. This policy shift may signal an end to Deng Xiaoping's earlier policy emphasizing "developing cooperation with the U.S." The new policy, which is endorsed by Jiang Zemin and his colleagues, will translate into more of China's "struggling with the U.S." on selected fronts. Though short of any intention for a showdown or military hostility, such policy inclination will add new complexity and tensions to the already strained relations between Beijing and Washington.

The policy shift was deeply rooted in Beijing's belief in Washington's intention to "contain" China. On September 28, 1995, Chinese president Jiang Zemin spoke to the Fifth Plenary Session of the 14th Party Congress, accusing the U.S. of leading a campaign to "xihua" (i.e., westernizing through democratization) and "fenhua" (i.e., splitting Taiwan and Tibet from) China. He also told the session that America will not give up a "containment" policy to prevent China's economic takeoff. Earlier this year, he repeatedly called on the high-ranking officials to "talk politics", which is a move aimed at preparing the cadres for the "coming of complex international struggles".

Indeed in the past year or so, China has gradually changed strategy of dealing with the Clinton Administration. Instead of responding to its high level engagement, Beijing chose to position itself for more confrontation with the U.S. On the one hand, Beijing has applied more strengths to resist the U.S. pressures, and hardened its positions on Taiwan, arms proliferation, trade and human rights issues.

On the other hand, it has sought to divide the western alliance in order to minimize cost for confronting the U.S head on. Beijing has literally given up its hope to enter the World Trade Organization in the near future, and quietly prepares itself for a limited trade war with the U.S. (short of losing its MFN status).

Under this general strategy, playing the European card against Washington was used for dual purposes. First, it warned the Europeans to stay on the side in Beijing-Washington conflicts. Second, it put pressures on Washington by shifting lucrative contracts from American businesses to their European counterparts. The recent visit by Li Peng to France with 1.5 billion dollar purchase of airbus clearly corroborated this approach. On this front, the Chinese have already scored partial victory with France and Germany.

Stabilizing Sino-Japanese relations was also on the top agenda of Chinese diplomats in an effort to isolate Washington. Immediately after the military exercises in the Taiwan Strait, Chinese foreign minister Qian Qichen went to Tokyo to reassure the Japanese of mainland China's intention on peaceful unification with Taiwan. With President Clinton's impending visit to Japan, it is noticeable that Tokyo has become the key vote in swinging the balance of power in the west Pacific against China. Whether Japan will go along with the gradual expansion of the U.S.-Japanese security arrangement in the region remains to be seen. The Japanese have danced cautiously on a thin line to avoid either antagonizing Beijing or disappointing Washington.

As part of its diplomatic initiatives against Washington, Beijing is increasing its cooperation with Russia and other states in former Soviet Union. How much Beijing can score on this one will be scrutinized when President Yeltzen visited Beijing later this month. With Russian's June election coming close, this development may have grave consequences in the global geopolitics if the Russian communists regain power in Moscow. To control the spillover of the Taiwan crisis, throngs of Beijing leaders have made their way to countries in Asia, South America and Africa.

As a result of Beijing's aggressive maneuvers, the Clinton Administration's China policy faces most difficult challenges since the end of the Cold War. Instead of passively waiting for the fallout, the Administration should take actions to reverse the trend.

First, it is high time that the event-driven and reactive measures on China were replaced by a clearly defined, comprehensive and long term China policy. Such a policy should be built upon the perception that China's prosperity and peaceful democratization are in the long term interest of both nations, and the leaders in Beijing should be brought to share this common ground. Second, the Administration should aggressively market this policy to its allies, and seek multilateralism on China policy.

Third, it is wrong to make the dictators in Beijing feel too sure about the renewal of its MFN status, especially at a time when there are fundamental problems in the bilateral relations. Delinking trade and human rights is a tactic decision to encourage China's economic and legal reform, and therefore should not be counted as a guarantee that MFN is to be renewed each year regardless of what the leadership in Beijing does.

The Administration's engagement policy should be encouraged, but such engagement would be meaningless if it does not include solid advice on Beijing as how to maintain a mutually beneficial U.S.-China relation. One important piece of advice should be that Beijing needs to let the world see it is committed to the rule of law and to political reforms aimed at peaceful and gradual transition to constitutional democracy.

CONDITIONED ENGAGEMENT:
LINKING TRADE WITH RULE OF LAW
Issue Brief no. 23 (May 24, 1996)

The Chinese hardline policy on human rights, trade, arms proliferation, and Taiwan issues has frustrated those who hope that a stable US-China relation will ultimately help China move to a peaceful, prosperous and democratic nation. However, some elements in Beijing would like to benefit from a provoked Washington in order to create a foreign enemy and then use ultra-nationalism to transform China into a powerful state sustained by wild capitalism, military build-up and Fascist political control. If they succeed, the winners will be a small number of empowered official-business elite aligned with powerful multinational financial interest. The biggest losers, of course, will be the Chinese people, but security and trade orders of the region and world will have to be rewritten.

To prevent China from locking itself into this dangerous path, the rule of law is a necessary and perhaps most effective weapon. Linking trade or other bilateral relations with China's progress in the rule of the law should be the basis of the Administration's engagement policy with China. Promoting China's rule of law can effectively synthesize the U.S. concerns on human rights, trade and security issues, and more importantly will be viewed sympathetically by the liberal wing of the Chinese government and people. On the positive side, the U.S. should participate more broadly in China's effort to build the rule of law, and thereby engaging the Chinese society more substantively. On the negative side, the U.S. should stand firm on all the international agreements and regulations reached with the Chinese government. Trade sanctions should be brought in to fight lawlessness of the corrupt Chinese officials or businessmen. Often times, these corrupt elements are also acting against the existing Chinese laws. The fact that certain military and political elements are allowed to stay above the laws of the land has created such bilateral crisis as nuclear technology transfer to Pakistan and illegal weapon smuggling to the American streets. Without the rule of law, their venturous enterprise is sure to continue, though one has to guess their next target.

Indeed, China has a weak tradition in upholding the rule of law, and the dynastic as well as the recent communist politics were rooted in a tradition of rule *by* law, which catered to the impulsive and corrupt behavior of the officialdom. However, some progress was made towards the rule of law since China opened to the outside world, primarily in the area where China has direct contacts with the rest of the world.

The National People's Congress should be credited with drafting a wide range of laws, paving the way for an accountable governance system. But recent political development threatened to derail China's infant legal reforms. First, the good laws are of no use if they are not seriously implemented. The biggest challenge to China's rule of law is that there are no political forces that have enough incentives to successfully push for the implementation of those laws. The corrupt business-official elite find it more profitable in a wild capitalist environment than in one based on the rule of law. In China, laws can therefore be blatantly ignored as long as one has the right connection in the government.

Thus the threat of trade sanctions on lawless behavior can be a powerful leverage to lend support for those in China who favor the rule of law. Without the existence of a constant pressure from the international community, the Chinese ruling elite will always sacrifice the rule of law to its short-term political and economic interest.

Second, the western businessmen are increasingly adapted to wild capitalist practices in China, thus making them the dominant rule of the game in doing business there. This is feeding into a vicious circle, the continuation of which will threaten not only intellectual property rights, but also a wide range of rules and institutions taken for granted in developed countries. As China participates in the world economy with increased intensity and scale, its lawlessness will spread beyond its borders, exacerbating problems in illegal immigration, drug trafficking, weapons proliferation, Mafia and terrorism, environmental protection, not to say increased irregularity and corruption of business practices across the board.

Many have eyed the Chinese market as offering biggest business opportunities in the next century, and they may be right; but without the rule of law firmly established in the land, that market will prove to be a mirage in the sky, luring but forever inaccessible.

Should there be a consistent and long-term China policy, promoting (with both positive and negative incentives) the rule of law ought to be a cornerstone. Democracy and human rights will be nurtured under the transparency, due process and independence of Chinese judiciary system, in the process of which the Chinese political and military Mafia should be defeated.

THE ANNUAL DEBATE ON CHINA'S MFN STATUS

Issue Brief no. 24 (May 27, 1997)

Each year at this time, the American public and the US Congress are torn on the issue of extending MFN (Most Favored Nation) status to China. The debate itself becomes so annoying to the Administration's China policy that Secretary of State Madeleine Albright says she favors permanent MFN status for China. To grant or not to grant MFN status is indeed debatable, but to debate or not to debate is an entirely different matter. The intention to end this debate once and for all is simply wrong and not in the American national interest.

It is the Chinese government which feels most frustrated by the annual debate over MFN status, and it is understandable that it would do everything to make sure that such frustration is felt at the White House. Indeed most people support the president's policy of continuing and expanding trade with China, but this should not be interpreted as this country's putting US dollars in front of US principles. Proving this point is the annual debate on the MFN issue.

Across the Pacific Ocean, behind the few rulers in Beijing, 1.2 billion people are observing this debate closely through foreign broadcasted transmissions. China is a nation disillusioned by communist ideologies and official corruption. The moral vacuum there is made more serious by the regime's crackdown on religious institutions that could serve to fill the vacuum, as they did in other formerly communist countries. The Chinese people are actively searching for a moral order based on principles that the rulers in Beijing cannot offer. That is why there are Chinese people who risk their lives to promote the principles laid down in this country's Declaration of Independence.

The Annual debate on MFN status sends a message to the Chinese people that at least their rights and social justice in general are taken seriously by some people in this country. On the other hand, ending the debate would convey cynicism to these people in China and would tarnish the image of this nation among them.

Entering the post-Deng era, China is uncertain where to turn for its political future. The communist political system is being outgrown by market reform. Its leaders lack the vision to renew China's rich history and tradition in a democratic framework. But most Chinese intellectuals and the Chinese public believe that China's social order and justice can be ensured only in a system of constitutional democracy.

Indeed, without democracy and human rights in China, US-China relations will never be able to reach their full potential in the long run, no matter how cozy they may appear in short terms. Therefore, while recognizing the importance of continuing trade with China, I oppose giving up the MFN debate because it is a symbol of the true heart and soul of this nation.

JIANG ZEMIN'S LACK OF VISION IN US-CHINA RELATIONS

Issue Brief no. 28 (July 11, 1997)

For those in this country who worry about the drifting of current US-China relations, there is an often neglected source of the bilateral problems – a lack of vision and consensus on the part of the Chinese leadership as to what they exactly want from such a relationship. President Jiang Zemin reportedly often comments on the importance of US-China relations, but is never able to articulate why this is so. His predecessors Mao Zedong and Deng Xiaoping were notorious for their tyranny and their dictatorial hold on power, but both had a clear vision of the US-China relationship, and thereby were able to move the relationship to a new plane.

Clearly, Jiang is no dynamic leader. Thus, those who wager too much on him will be inevitably disappointed. Contrary to many western expectations, Jiang is more of a survivor than a leader, and his dominant concern is political survival at home. He repeatedly talks about the three Shanghai Communiqués (which recognize only one China) as the foundation of US-China relations, as if it never occurred to him that Taiwan could be only part of the bigger picture of the US-China relationship. A visionary leader in China would make the Taiwan issue part of a long term, strategic Sino-American relationship rather than base ties solely on cross-strait relations.

Jiang has consolidated his position and holds relatively unchallenged power in China, which does not, however, imply any outstanding qualifications for real leadership. Indeed it is not the first time the world has seen an inept leader take charge of a country at the death of a strongman. Jiang has caved in to the agenda of the People's Liberation Army on the Taiwan issue, though most generals were his appointees. Of course, the situation of Chinese international relations could be worse under the guidance of another Mao-figure, but the current situation is just as threatening. Judging from the PLA's record, it also has no qualms about abusing its power and crushing popular movements. The prospect of their control of China is no good news to the world.

It is a sad fact that the world's most populous nation is headed by a man without a world vision. Deng's death leaves China at crossroads in diplomacy, but it is difficult to rejoice at the thought of crossing into the next millennium with an opportunist like Jiang. In one sense, there is no longer an immediate threat of abuses by an egoistic dictator like Mao Zedong, but the bad news is, the current leader appears to be thoroughly mediocre and in no position to improve China's international situation.

In the short run, Jiang's apparent mediocrity may well undermine the chances of success at the upcoming summit between him and Bill Clinton, but its long term damage would be the loss of a guided sense of direction as China seeks to integrate itself with the world. As China strives to modernize itself, it is perhaps the most unhappy combination: the inept and lagging leadership and a racing economy and society running rapidly toward an uncharted future.

THE NATURE OF THE SCORPION
Issue Brief no. 36 (September 5, 1997)

Here's a story familiar to many. A scorpion asks a frog to carry him across a river. The frog says, "Well, if I do, will you sting me?" "Nonsense!" replies the scorpion. "Why would I be so stupid? Don't you think I know that if you sank I would drown, too?" Makes sense. However, the scorpion stings the frog midstream anyway. The frog cries out before sinking under, "Why have you done this? Now we both will die!" The drowning scorpion answered, "I couldn't help it because it's my nature to sting."

The nature of the Chinese regime is more complicated, but its dark side is not unlike the scorpion's. Because of its nature, the regime sometimes does things that may appear stupid, irrational, or even against its own interests. To much of the world, including many Chinese, the imprisonment of Wei Jingsheng and Wang Dan is unnecessary and counter-productive. The point is that the communist leadership cannot help it.

Indeed, Chinese leaders are often portrayed as "valuing face" (*yao mian zi*), and their feelings are fragile and vulnerable to straight-forward criticism, especially of their poor human rights record. To accommodate the sensitivity of the Chinese leadership, the Clinton Administration has done its best to avoid publicly criticizing Chinese leaders. Instead, the Administration has sought to "resolve differences through private meetings," a tactic said to be more effective when working with Chinese officials.

This could be correct, as the Chinese leaders do seem to resent losing face. But if the Chinese leaders were true face savers, why would they constantly provoke international indignation by persecuting Chinese dissidents? And if President Jiang Zemin valued his image, why did he let the world see his shamelessness and cowardice by personally ordering long prison sentences for Wei and Wang when they already lived under house arrest? Perhaps Mr. Jiang cannot help it.

Now Mr. Jiang must cross the Pacific for his state visit to Washington, and he has asked President Clinton to spend more political capital to cover for him. But will Mr. Jiang act like the scorpion, even though he is serious about improving US-China relations? Temporary tolerance (likely to be shown before Jiang Zemin's visit to the United States) may be due to circumstantial calculation, but suppressing dissent is part of the regime's nature. The Administration should therefore seek substantive concessions on human rights before welcoming Jiang Zemin and attempt to make the regime's poisonous sting and dangerous instincts ineffective.

A LEADER WITHOUT A PEOPLE

Issue Brief no. 36 (September 5, 1997)

In less than a month, President Jiang Zemin will come to the United States, presumably as China's number one guy representing one fifth of the human race. With his position further consolidated in the 15th Congress of the Chinese Communist Party (CCP), Jiang is widely viewed as the man with whom the western governments have to do business. Indeed, Jiang appears to be in charge in China, but that does not qualify him to be a leader. A leader must be able to lead the majority of his people. Like Louis XIV, Mr. Jiang may outshine all the smaller stars of his court in the Zhongnanhai compound, but he is no leader of China.

On June 25th, the Chinese Public Security Ministry reportedly issued an internal report stating that the number of Chinese Christians has reached thirty million in urban areas. The report says that the Chinese Christian population has grown by about fifteen percent each year since 1990. Moreover, there are two million Chinese Communist Party members who have been converted to Christianity, and the number is growing. This shows that more and more people are turning their backs on the CCP, though Jiang still believes that the CCP is the only qualified leading force in China.

At approximately the same time, the Chinese Academy of Social Science (the primary government research institute) conducted a survey of 2,500 people in Beijing, Tianjin, Shenyang, Dalian, and Shijiazhuang. One of the questions asked was: Do you consider that the reports in the state/party newspapers are trustworthy? Only twelve percent of those polled gave affirmative answers. People do not trust what the leaders have to say, even though Jiang believes he is the trusted leader of the Chinese nation.

A leader who does not have his people's love and trust is no more than a miserable little puppet of a few. Indeed, Jiang belongs to a small clique of the communist elite, whose power is not based on the consent of the people but on coercion and brute force. To keep his position and to serve the interest of the communist elite, Jiang Zemin jailed dissidents like Wei Jingsheng and Wang Dan. He therefore lacks the basic decency required for a figure to be treated as a respected national leader. If Mr. Jiang is disappointed with his treatment in this land, I think someone in this country should say to his face: "If you want respect here, please get it first in your own country from your own people."

CHINA'S POLITICAL REFORM
AND US-CHINA RELATIONS

Issue Brief no. 42 (October 17, 1997)

On October 17, the *People's Daily*, the mouthpiece of the Chinese Communist Party, carried an editorial which calls for the acceleration of political reform in China. This may be the first official indication after the CCP's 15th Congress of the direction of political reform during Jiang Zemin's reign. This is not much of a noticeable change compared with the rhetoric of previous eras. However, the stressing of the need for the rule of law and for some division of government is a welcome sign, especially in regard to the upcoming Clinton-Jiang summit.

The leaders in both Washington and Beijing have recently alluded to a "strategic partnership" as the future they envision for the relationship between the US and China. But what elements does this partnership include? To President Jiang Zemin, it may entail Sino-US cooperation in trade and security issues. The question of admittance into the WTO, the Taiwan issue, and Korea may be high on the agenda. But are these enough for a true partnership? The answer is no.

A strategic partnership must above all be built on compatible socio-political institutions in the two nations, not on the leadership's good intentions towards each other. China's democratization is therefore a necessary link in forming such a partnership.

First, close ties between the two countries need broad-based public support. If the Chinese government continues to imprison those who aspire to democracy, the development of such close ties is simply politically unsustainable. Moreover, if China is not democratized, ultra-nationalism will be the only candidate to replace official communist ideology. In such a case, support within China for a true partnership could be very shaky.

Even on the economic side, China's political system has caused a bottleneck in the flow of cooperation. Many of the current trade conflicts can be traced back to China's weaknesses when it comes to the rule of law and the control of official corruption, which can never be resolved without political reform in the direction of a constitutional democracy.

What about the Taiwan issue? If both sides of the Taiwan strait were true democracies, then there would be no insurmountable problem in reunification. Now both the mainland and Taiwan have nominal interests in improving their relations, but how those interests become substantiated depends on how compatibly the two social systems can respond to each other. At this moment, they don't respond compatibly at all. If China became a democracy, the Taiwan issue would largely be removed from the negotiation table between China and the United States, because the Chinese could handle the reunification by themselves.

In short, China's political reform insures stable long-term US-China relations and perhaps may be the cornerstone of the partnership. The trend towards globalization is not just in terms of trade, but more so in the area of the compatibility of socio-political institutions. The *People's Daily* editorial speaks about China's political reform towards a parliamentary-like system with the rule of law, which, though not enough, needs to be encouraged. The crucial step in China's democratization process is abandonment of the one party monopoly on political power through the embracing of pluralism based on a free press and the freedom of association. Until this happens, the strategic partnership between the two nations can be nothing more than a muddling-through process.

THE GOOD, THE BAD, AND THE UGLY OF JIANG
Issue Brief no. 43 (October 31, 1997)

The week-long state visit by Chinese president Jiang Zemin offers a good opportunity for the American public to see him at close range and understand the mentality of a communist leader who claims to control almost one-fifth of the human race. At close range, one can see the good, the bad, and the ugly sides of this man.

The good side. Mr. Jiang is good at appealing to familiar American themes for a public show. He can go on dancing hula with the Hawaiian locals to show that he is in tune with American ways. He can twist the American historical experience to justify China's hard line on Taiwan and Tibet. He managed a smiling face in spite of the odds against him because of China's human rights abuses.

The bad side is that Mr. Jiang remains part of the evil called communism that has cost about 60 million in human casualties in China. He did not repent, not even in terms of a "necessary evil." He still thinks turning the streets leading to Tiananmen Square into a killing field eight years ago was a "correct decision," and he showed not the slightest moral regret. In terms of brutality and cruelty, he is not very different from any other tyrant in history. For the sake of preserving his power, he has no moral bottom line.

The ugliness of this man shows when you add the good and bad together. He is a hypocrite. He enslaves his people, but pretends to be comfortable with the ideals of Abraham Lincoln. His human rights vision is no more than the degrading "fed and happy" condition where the Chinese people can eat and be clothed, but not talk. He insults the Chinese nation in front of the world by believing in this "pig-raising style" of human rights.

Indeed, Mr. Jiang appears not at all afraid of President Clinton's criticism of his regime's human rights abuses, as long as such criticism remains lip-service from the American leadership. But he is afraid of the pro-democracy demonstrators outside the White House and the ones following his trail. He did not go to see the Liberty Bell as planned because there were several hundred people protesting China's human rights policy at a public place nearby.

Mr. Jiang feels most comfortable in the company of businessmen, and perhaps he has more of a trader than a statesman in him. He does not seem to have a soul, though he does show a lot of shrewdness in using his power to trade. I put this trait also in the category of the ugly.

THE WRONG SIDE OF HISTORY
Issue Brief no. 44 (November 7, 1997)

President Clinton made the right comment that the Chinese leadership is on the wrong side of history regarding the June 4th massacre in 1989. But Mr. Jiang Zemin tried to convey to the American public that the massacre was necessary and "correct." His think tanks cooked up a few arguments which Jiang used here and in China to excuse the bloodshed. Let us look at them briefly.

Excuse No. 1. *China had to maintain stability, which required a crack down on the students in 1989, in order to develop its economy.* This insults both the memory and intelligence of the American and the Chinese people. First of all, the students were peaceful and orderly. The only disorder in Beijing was when the government turned violent, using machine guns and tanks to disturb the peace. Second, can Mr. Jiang explain why he thinks the democratic reform demanded by those students will lead to chaos, while tyranny will ensure order?

Excuse No. 2. *Chinese communists serve the interests of the majority of the Chinese people, and to sacrifice a few hundred (or a few thousand) was for the common good.* It is perhaps not even worth commenting on the fact that corrupt officials are stealing from and abusing the Chinese people. But suppose the deaths of a few hundred terminally ill patients would serve the "common good" of saving medical care and improving the economy. Would you kill them for the sake of the economy? Mr. Jiang does not seem to understand the value of human life, not to mention that he does not respect human rights.

Excuse No. 3. *The June 4th Incident happened eight years ago, and we should all look forward into the future. See that the Chinese people are better off now than they were eight years ago.* Would you say, Mr. Jiang, that a crime should not be condemned if it occurred in the past, because the criminal says that we should look into the future? Why does not Mr. Jiang dare to tell the Japanese, "Forget the history of fifty years ago, and let us look forward?"

Excuse No. 4. *Because the US and China have more common interests to develop, we should not allow different views on the June 4th Incident to hamper our business deals. We should not interfere in each other's internal matters.* If someone abuses his children or even kills them, would you expect his neighbors to say, "We can still work together on a common driveway?"

There may be a few more such excuses used by Jiang Zemin and his colleagues. They all show that Mr. Jiang lacks the basic understanding of the value of human life and the meaning of human rights. He does not repent for the killing of those innocent victims. He remains a self-righteous communist, on the wrong side of history.

"GOOD FEELINGS" IN US-CHINA RELATIONS
Issue Brief no. 45 (November 14, 1997)

In the wake of Clinton-Jiang summit, many have become optimistic about US-China relations, believing the current atmosphere will continue at least for the rest of Clinton's presidency. US ambassador to China James Sasser reportedly described such warm relations as "the era of ... good feelings between China and the United States" (Reuters 11/13/97).

I read this news with great sadness. The US may continue to do business with China and may work with Chinese leaders on security and other issues. No Problem. But the leaders in Beijing still refuse to repent for the massacre in 1989 and still insist on political dictatorship, so I have a reason to expect the Administration officials not to be carried away, but reserve the sense of moral indignation. "Good feelings" is certainly the wrong phrase because it sends the wrong message. These words cover up the real source of potential conflict: America is a democracy, and China is a communist regime. This is something the Administration should pay more attention to.

As long as such fundamental differences in government remain, the US and China will remain distrustful of one another, and any good feelings are bound to be superficial. Therefore, an inalienable part of the Administration's China policy should be the active promotion, both in words and deeds, of China's democratization. A prosperous and strong China may or may not be in the American national interest, but a China that is prosperous, strong, *and democratic* is undoubtedly in the US interest.

Thus, there is nothing wrong with engaging China or having a dialogue with the Chinese leadership, provided these two measures serve to convert China to democracy. President Clinton has long worked to place engagement and dialogue at the center of his China policy. Now it seems he has achieved this goal. But he must show that these measures are actually the means, not the end. Clinton says the best way to change China is to engage it, so he now is supposedly in a better position to push the Chinese leadership to change its political system to a democratic one. Therefore it is time for President Clinton to put more, not less pressure on Beijing on issues related to human rights and political reform.

I hope that the president will write to Jiang Zemin, saying that the release of political prisoners certainly will reduce some bad feelings from the American people towards the Chinese government, but if China becomes a democracy, American good feelings towards China will be abundant.

CHINA'S STAND ON THE IRAQ CRISIS
Issue Brief no. 56 (February 12, 1998)

Recently, the Chinese media has devoted much of its attention to the current Persian Gulf crisis. Chinese foreign diplomats have repeatedly appeared in the Chinese press urging the United States to seek diplomatic and peaceful ways to end this crisis. China objects to any use of force by the US on Iraq and urges Saddam Hussein to cooperate with the United Nations weapons inspection team. The Chinese position is based on the fact that Iraq is a member of the UN and that as such its sovereign rights should be respected. Indeed, compared to its role during the 1991 Persian Gulf War, China appears much more confident and aggressive in pushing its own agenda in this international and geopolitical arena.

The Chinese position can be interpreted in several ways from its internal politics. First, the Chinese leadership still worries about the intervention of Western powers in its internal politics, especially considering that China's political system is highly disfavored by the latter. Thus, the sovereignty of Iraq is seen as somewhat compatible with the Chinese "sovereign right" to handle its own internal affairs, i.e., to suppress political dissent.

Second, there is the shadow of the Taiwan issue. Any regional instability caused by conflicts in the Taiwan Strait may lead to American (and possibly Japanese) intervention in the area. The Chinese would like to emphasize the supremacy of sovereignty in the issue of Iraq because of a fear that the crisis there may set a precedent for US intervention in the Taiwan Strait.

Third, China needs to court the Islamic world to quiet its western frontier, which is largely populated by Muslims. The independence movement in Xinjiang Province put pressure on China to maintain a good relationship with the Islamic world so that China might contain such independence movements.

Fourth, China sees this as a golden opportunity to project itself into the international arena without much effort. Afterall, the Russians and some other Islamic countries like Egypt and Turkey are in the forefront, and the Chinese will remain in the backseat only to pay lipservice. Moreover, the Chinese stand increases its leverage against the United States, considering China is a permanent member of the UN Security Council.

In short, China is beginning to flex its diplomatic muscle against the US, even though it is not ready to flex its military muscle. President Jiang Zemin wants to work with the US to gain needed capital and technology, but he also wants to undermine the dominance of American influence in regional and international affairs, because he believes that such influence may jeopardize the Chinese political system and dictatorship at home.

BEYOND TIANANMEN?

Issue Brief no. 66 (May 1, 1998)

During her visit to China, Secretary Albright stated, according to Reuters, that the Clinton administration wants to "get beyond the Tiananmen Square Massacre". I wonder what she actually meant by: "We are looking towards the 21st century in terms of our relationship with China and that is the focus of the summit—to try to look forward." If she meant to say that this summit would provide a turning point where the United States would no longer consider the Tiananmen Square Massacre as a factor in US-China relations, it was a big mistake. Or, if she meant to say that the United States could pretend that what happened nine years ago at Tiananmen could be brushed aside as something insignificant in US-China relations, she was wrong.

The fact is, among the millions of people who participated in the 1989 democracy movement, no one has forgotten what happened, in spite of the Chinese government's efforts to make people forget. The victims of the massacre will not forget, the relatives and friends of the thousands who lost their lives will not forget, and all those who watched the bloodshed on the television screen will not forget. Nor can the Chinese government forget that incident which still wakes up Li Peng and Jiang Zemin in the middle of the night. The dead still haunt them.

Indeed, the Chinese government has tried hard to get beyond Tiananmen Square in the past nine years, wishing to erase this movement from the memory of the Chinese people. Perhaps the leadership in Beijing will come to realize the greatest threat to its regime is that people cannot forget. And there virtually has been an ongoing battle during the last nine years between the government which wants to make people forget and the people who try to keep the memory alive. To friends and relatives, the deaths of thousands of martyrs in that movement do have meaning. These heroes live in the hearts of the people and remind them of a dream shared by all Chinese citizens— a dream of a free and democratic China.

The end of communist regimes in Eastern Europe started from Tiananmen Square. It was also the starting point for a new and democratic China. Any allusion to getting beyond Tiananmen is clearly disregarding history. Moreover, the best way to prevent similar human tragedies in the future is to remember the tragedies of the past. This is not only true for the people, but also true for the officials in the Chinese government. As long as Jiang Zemin refuses to repent for the bloodshed, President Clinton should continue to remind him that he is "on the wrong side of history."

THE PAKISTAN FACTOR

Issue Brief no. 69 (May 29, 1998)

The Pakistan nuclear explosions are a watershed event for US-China relations. In US policy circles, this may have been the darkest day for the democratic peace contenders who look to "enlargement of the free market and democracy" as the major goals of US diplomacy in the post cold war era. It seems that the realist view of global balance of power and geopolitical competition is a better tool to work out foreign policies. This indeed may give the Clinton Administration further incentive to de-emphasize human rights and pro-democracy issues in the US-China relations.

On May 28, President Clinton reportedly called Jiang Zemin for the first time using the hotline which was set up during Secretary Albright's visit in Beijing. As if symbolically underscoring a growing US-China partnership, Clinton conveyed two messages to Jiang: i) he would come to Beijing in spite of the recent Congressional call to postpone the visit, and ii) in return, Jiang was urged to pressure Pakistan not to explode its nuclear devices. (Jiang wrote a letter to such effect to Prime Minister Sharif as an act of good faith to Clinton.)

Now in the aftermath of the five nuclear blasts by Pakistan, security concerns become the driving force likely to shape the Clinton-Jiang summit scheduled for late June. Meanwhile, China is getting extremely suspicious of the US's intention in playing India (and Japan) to check China, in using Taiwan to contain China, and in supporting the ASEAN nations to resist China in the South China Sea. So on and so forth as the geopolitical talk already goes around the policy circles in Beijing.

Besides the empty rhetoric of "strategic partnership", the question is: to what extent is the US willing to accommodate China as a rising superpower? Will the US gradually give up Taiwan and neutralize Japan to recognize the Chinese sphere of influence as a regional power? What about the South China Sea? In the language of big power politics, the US-China relationship is primarily one of contention rather than of cooperation or "partnership". For the Kissinger-type believing in the miracle of the balance of power, perhaps the biggest danger is underestimating both the skill and ambition of Beijing in playing the same game.

Therefore, in spite of some failures of the democratic peace arrangement in the Asian subcontinent, a real and long term "US-China partnership and peace" must be based on the assumption that China is a benign power. And looking at the history of mankind, a large benign power can only be achieved through developing firm roots in internal democratic institutions. Thus, while the Pakistan factor focuses the attention to the external or geopolitical aspects of the Chinese regime, in the long run policy thinking regarding China cannot afford to lose sight of supporting its internal democratic changes.

ENGAGING CHINA'S THIRD DIMENSION
Issue Brief no. 70 (June 5, 1998)

As the date of President Clinton's visit to China draws closer, the debate on China policy also intensifies. Much of usefulness of this debate or propositions would, I think, depend on an objective perception of China, or on whether the policy-making community can transcend a simple, holistic view of China.

China is not a friend-or-foe-type personality. Nor is it an evil empire or emerging capitalist. Instead it is a country characterized by a rapidly evolving system of governance which is gradually reaching the threshold of fundamental and unprecedented social transformation. This development is indeed unparalleled in the last 2000 years of Chinese history. To be sure, the interaction of three organizational complexes--- government sector, business interests, and civic organizations- -promise to shape China's identity in the next century. At the moment, the last one is the weakest but potentially the most crucial dimension that will determine whether China is a strategic threat or partner to the United States in the next century.

Without this third dimension as a linchpin, political power combined with monopoly business interests will create a corrupt, unstable China. Under such conditions, internal chaos and external aggressiveness are the two more likely consequences that will undermine both regional and global stability. And democratization will be a tenuous prospect, and will easily fall to the prey of the combined interest of politicians and capitalists. The rule of law will not work, either.

But China does have some potential aided by its tradition to develop the third dimension to prevent such disastrous consequences. It has a long history of civic self governance in which no government offices existed below the county level. Moreover, the experience of other nations shows that the third dimension may be established and integrated through modern independent media and educational institutions. In 1997, American non-profit organizations employed about 10 percent of the US population and consumed 143 billion dollars. The challenge confronting American NGOs is how to most effectively minimize the impact of business interests and the reach of the state in their sector.

For the Chinese, however, they face the momentous task of legally and institutionally nurturing true non-profit or non-governmental organizations to take over the space currently being both abused and unattended by the political and economic power houses. They then need to keep the paws of the business and government out of their domain.

Thus, while President Clinton has geared his China policy toward engaging government and business interests, he should find ways to advance the efficacy of the emerging third dimension in Chinese society. He should support the expansion of the Chinese civic organizations (not fake, government-controlled NGOs), and help American NGOs to engage their counterparts in China.

THE LEAST CLINTON CAN DO
FOR THE CHINESE DEMOCRATS
Issue Brief no. 71 (June 19, 1998)

Next week, President Clinton will step into Beijing's Tiananmen Square, making him the first US president to do so since the bloody massacre nine years ago. For the small but persistent pro-democracy movement in China, the question is: What can President Clinton do to promote their cause? There are both high and low expectations expressed by some dissidents in China. Let us look at the four basic ones that are reported in the press.

First, they want to hear the president publicly commend the democratic movement while at the same time condemn the massacre in 1989. They do not want to see the president help the unrepentant regime to cast off the shadow for the killing of peaceful demonstrators nine years ago.

Secondly, they want the president to meet with them. If the president is too busy with his talks with the Chinese leaders, fine. But would one of his several hundred officials going with him care to meet with some of the dissidents? No one among the dissident community is against the Administration's engagement policy as long as it is a balanced and principled one.

Third, they hope President Clinton is instrumental in pressuring China to sign the U.N. Covenant of Civil and Political Rights, and then ensure its implementation. They want Clinton to get right into specifics with Jiang in chartering a clear course for full implementation of the U.N rights covenants. This is the area in which they hope Clinton can act more aggressively.

Fourth, they want President Clinton's effort to build a strategic partnership with China to be sensitized to China's democratization. President Clinton needs to remind Jiang Zemin that political reform and democratization are inevitable for the development of such a "strategic partnership". To accomplish this, Clinton should push the regime to release several thousand political prisoners still held in custody.

Indeed the list can go on. But I hope President Clinton and his advisors will think what they can specifically do for those who risk their freedom and life for the very principles written in the Declaration of Independence. If he can indeed do something specific for them, they will be grateful. If he can't, they don't want to hear any empty rhetoric and apologies.

CLINTON'S CLOSE ENCOUNTER OF THE THIRD KIND
Issue Brief no. 72 (June 26, 1998)

In the eyes of Chinese public, President Clinton has come to China, representing not only America but also the Western powers collectively. The historical experience of Chinese encountering foreign powers lies deep in the nation's memory, which in turn shapes their perception of the American president. Based on their historical experience, the Chinese people expect three kinds of encounters.

The first kind of encounter invokes the memory of "alien" guests who paid tribute to the Middle Kingdom. This used to be a century old ritual in which the alien leaders were made to recognize the glory and power of the central kingdom. And in return to their display of respect, or kowtowing, the Chinese ruler would reward the guests with generous benefits and gifts. Indeed, if the Chinese media is able to depict an overly deferential Clinton merely advancing trade benefits for corporate America, many Chinese citizens would see him through the lens of the century-old game of "managing the barbarians".

The second kind of encounter, based on gunboat diplomacy, consisted of the Western colonialists path-blazing into the middle kingdom spreading fear and destruction on their way. Defeated and weakened, the Chinese rulers kowtowed to the arrogant foreigners who had no regard for Chinese culture, law or tradition, not to mention the Chinese people. Recently, when the mayors of Xian and Shanghai got rid of the street vendors to make way for President Clinton, many ordinary Chinese may get offended. For it was too much like a historical replay of one particular scenario: the rulers went out of their way to please foreigners by cracking down on the common people or interrupting their daily routines.

Of course, what I hope for is none of the above, but an encounter of a third kind, namely, an equal-footed and principled encounter. The equal-footedness lies in President Clinton's show of understanding of the Chinese (not the communist) culture and tradition. He needs to be more aggressive in reaching out to the ordinary Chinese citizens (not officials), candidly expressing his views on those issues that are important to the Chinese public. The principledness depends on whether Clinton stands firm on promoting the values of freedom, human rights and democracy. These values are blunt and need to be expressed bluntly. Standing firm means no tampering or soft peddling. Otherwise, Clinton risks being perceived by Chinese people as either an arrogant Western imperialist or a kowtowing tribute bearer.

AFTER THE FIREWORKS
Issue Brief no. 73 (July 2, 1998)

In the Western, and to a lesser extent, the Chinese media, the Clinton-Jiang summit appeared like a short burst of bright fireworks, a show with brilliance, surprises and some cheering to the credit of both leaders. Then things will go back to normal. Or will they? In the upcoming days and weeks, perhaps the smoke after the fireworks will dominate the sky, obscuring the long term significance or lack of significance of the summit for peoples both here and in China.

First, the summit will not likely have any immediate impact on Chinese political liberalization. A relatively smaller number of people actually watched the live coverage of the Clinton-Jiang debate, either because they were at work (near noon time) or because the decision to carry it live was made at the last minute without pre-informing the public about such an event. Nor were the transcripts published in the Chinese newspapers. Even if they were, to most Chinese, Clinton's messages remained at an abstract and philosophical level, bearing little, if at all, relevance to their daily lives, because the president glossed over those touchy issues most relevant to the Chinese public, i.e., the labor plight, unemployment, rampant corruption, moral decline, crime rate, etc. These issues loom large in Chinese citizens' minds and Clinton failed to tap into that part of the public's mentality.

Second, in the eyes of the Chinese public, Jiang's humiliating performance in debating Clinton has caused the nation to lose face. Jiang will face heated criticism from the Party and military hard-liners who will attack him (which is very likely) for giving up too much (arms proliferation and human rights) while gaining little on Taiwan from the United States. The summit is over but Jiang's troubles at home have only just begun.

Third, back home, President Clinton's skill in debating Jiang may have saved him some criticisms over his soft human rights stand, but he will have to face the congressional grilling on the lack of progress made in trade deficit and security concerns. Meanwhile, he will also come under mounting criticisms for speaking about the three NOs concerning Taiwan in Shanghai. The ripples created in

Taiwan, Japan, and India will come back to make some waves both at home and abroad.

Indeed, the Clinton visit went as smoothly as both Clinton and Jiang could have hoped - a glamorous, as well as symbolically meaningful tour. But the hard differences between the two sides remain as wide and deep as before the summit. The good atmosphere may count as good fireworks to watch, but such a display will quickly dissipate into thin air. Besides seeing an equal exchange of face-saving gestures, the world is now more interested in understanding how much actual progress has been made as a result of the summit.

JIANG ZEMIN'S POST-SUMMIT MANEUVERING
Issue Brief no. 75 (July 24, 1998)

The real significance of the recent Clinton-Jiang summit is something to be assessed through time by future historians, but one can be sure that it has had a bigger impact on China than on America. Weeks after the summit, Jiang is still busy reacting to its fall-out.

Since the summit ended, the tide has begun to turn across the Taiwan Strait. After publicly stating the three NOs, President Clinton left Taipei with no choice but to talk with Beijing. Unable to play an American card, Taipei subtly changed its strategy towards the mainland. President Lee Teng-hui said a few days ago that China's democratization is the only chance for cross-strait unification. Even Hsu Hsin-liang, former party boss of the pro-independent DPP, made a surprise call for China-Taiwan unification under one country, one (democratic) system.

After all, this was what Jiang had wanted from the summit via Washington: political dialogue and expanded relations across the Taiwan Straits. Now the question is whether he can swallow the fruit without choking himself. Can Jiang Zemin manage a good atmosphere for a Sino-American and China-Taiwan honeymoon while stemming the domestic forces for democratizing Chinese political system?

Jiang Zemin's desire is to have the best of both worlds: taking back Taiwan while keeping the communists' monopoly on power. Thus, the first thing Jiang did after the summit was to have 5 million Chinese officials focus on "unifying thinking" (*tong yi si xiang*) by studying Deng Xiaoping's theory of socialist construction. The public campaign of the Chinese propaganda machines resemble the former campaigns against "bourgeois spiritual pollution", though the difference is that this time part of the pollution was left behind by a US president. But this can only add confusion to an already confused public, which is increasingly exposed to the uncontrollable dissemination of information from outside China.

Second, Jiang tried to *contain* Chinese dissidents through whatever means because eliminating them would ruin the atmosphere he tried to nurture around the summit. Jiang needs an open and tolerant image to have the US on his side, while inducing Taiwan to the fold. Containment is better than elimination, but it does not constitute engagement with the democrats.

Lastly, Jiang tried to streamline the regime's security and military apparatus, starting with a crackdown on illegal smuggling. Corruption has eaten into the heart of these forces, making them a problem, not a solution to China's growing social chaos, especially in those regions of which Beijing has less direct control. But Jiang's dream world will quickly dissolve if Zhu Rongji fails to reform Chinese ailing economy, a task made more difficult by drastic economic slowdown and mass unemployment in China confounded by the Asian economic crisis.

PART SIX

THE MAKING OF JIANG ZEMIN ERA

THE RISE OF NEO-CONSERVATISM IN CHINA

China Focus, Vol. III, no. 1 (January 1, 1995)

As different factions are posturing for the post-Deng power struggle, a showdown seems inevitable the moment when Deng Xiaoping goes to meet Karl Marx. At this point, no one can tell who will be up or down or survive in reshuffling period. The democrats are actively working for a peaceful transition to constitutional democracy, but whatever road China embarks on, neo-conservatism will be a factor to be reckoned with for a long time.

Neo-conservatism surfaced a few years ago as cultural and ideological hearsay in Beijing and Shanghai intellectual circles, but no one took it seriously until late 1994, when it became a strong political force. It is now a major movement with a chance to dominate China in the post-Deng era.

There are three immediate causes for the rise of neo-conservatism in China: the downfall of the former Soviet Union, the new class of entrepreneurial government officials, and the growing spirit of nationalism. To round out the picture, add to these the influence of former hard-line communists, the newly rich, some military commanders, a small number of top technocrats, some relatives of high cadres, and a few ultra-conservative intellectuals. Jiang Zemin would like to head this new movement, but his ideological fitness has not inspired confidence among inner circles.

The political causes: The disintegration of the USSR impacted mightily on the Chinese ruling elite. With the 1989 democratic movement still fresh in their memory, they took every measure to prevent China from falling into Gorbachev-style political liberalization. Any show of dissent was severely dealt with. At the same time, market reforms were pushed ahead in hopes of improving people's living standards, thereby alleviating pressure from the Party's lower-echelons. This led to a lopsided structure that exhibited blatant political and police control but considerable economic and social freedom. This structure won the hearts of almost all former hard-liners and a number of top-echelon bureaucrats and technocrats. They felt it the only way for them to survive the inexorable down-fall of communism with their power intact. In fact, so successful have they been at frightening the upper classes with the specter of social unrest that their power has actually expanded.

The economic causes: Early on, the economic reform produced a new social stratum, peopled mainly by government-based entrepreneurs who thrived amid both market opportunities and official red tape. Dwelling in the interstitial areas between polity and economy, they were well-placed to use power to make money. They became immensely rich by plundering public property or making it their own through legal or illegal means. Whether in the stock exchange, the under-regulated financial market, land speculation, or foreign investment, they were the ones who cashed in on insider trading and other forms of corruption. These former (or current) officials of the bureaucracy constitute a considerable segment of the newly rich. They have a high stake in the current anti-democratic regime and are fearful of any social changes that might undermine their power. Their interest is in keeping down the wages, as well as the rights, of the working people. They hope to see a China ruled by a strongman sympathetic to their interests and capable of maintaining strict order throughout the nation. Some of the transitional corporations are perceived as aligned with this new class in China.

The cultural causes: Of course the events described above would not be so serious without the rise of ultra-nationalism. Ever since the first opium war, China has suffered repeated defeat and humiliation by Japan and the West. Historical memory runs deep in the nation, and the perception of external danger, military or non-military, is pronounced in the public mentality. Some intellectuals have trumpeted the supremacy of national interests and international rivalry, creating a political ideology to replace Communism. They also champion traditional Chinese culture, especially those parts that favor elitism, mass obedience, stratified order, and loyalty to rulers. They openly claim that democracy is not suitable to the Chinese condition, now or anytime soon. They use the decline in public morality as an excuse to impose a state culture or ideology on the populace. Indeed, the patriotic education endorsed by the state propaganda machine, with its historical revisionism, seems to have already become the cultural mainstream of China.

If, by chance, the neo-conservatives are triumphant in post-Deng China, the country's political landscape will be transformed. Communism will end and the era of neo-fascism, albeit with Chinese characteristics, will begin. Politically, any challenge to one-party rule will be suppressed brutally. Human rights will deteriorate further. The media, as well as public opinion, will come under ever-stricter control. Maintaining social order will be the main priority of public policy. A series of anti-crime and anti-corruption campaigns aimed at local officials and independent small entrepreneurs will be launched to restore public confidence and win public support. Nationalism will be the rallying cry from Urumqi to Guangdong, and the military will receive a big boost, becoming less involved in civilian fighting but a stronger for unified leadership and central control.

China will adopt a stronger stand toward the issues of Taiwan and Hong Kong. Its military power will be extended over a larger area, and its foreign policymakers will speak from a position of military and economic strength. Spokesmen will demand that the international community play by rules acceptable to China.

Economically, there will be further integration of government officials with the new entrepreneur elite. State-owned enterprises will be largely transferred to their control. There will be no room for the rise of the middle class, which will have to choose between being coopted by the new bureaucrat-entrepreneurs and joining the working class. China's economy will be controlled by the state in macro aspects, favoring the oligopoly structures dominated by the new elite. The economic reform will continue. The rules of the market and private property rights will be substantiated as soon as the new elite has completed redistributing public property into their own hands.

STATE POLICY AND CHRISTIANITY IN CHINA
China Strategic Review, Vol. I, no. 1 (February 29, 1996)

After the "Third Plenary Meeting of the Eleventh Central Committee (1978)," the Chinese Communist Party (CCP) softened its policy on religion. They no longer banned religious activities for the purpose of "wiping them out", but rather sought to contain, in a much subtler manner, religious practice in order to boost its international image. After formally ending of the Cultural Revolution, Deng Xiaoping sought to strengthen his legitimacy as a ruler, and felt that thawing religious repression would serve that end. He also hoped that moderate policies on religion would strengthen rather than weaken the public support for the Party's leadership. This policy shift gave a big boost to the legitimacy of the state-controlled religious agency, the Three Self Patriotic Movement Committee (TSPMC), and its affiliated religious organizations, though they are strictly monitored. Thus, through TSPMC, Christianity was made part of the Communist governance system. At the time, most Chinese Christians were senior citizens, and government leaders felt Christianity would remain confined within this small community.

However, the leaders had misjudged the ramifications of their thawing policies, because an increasing number of young people embraced Christianity. The rapid ascendance of Christian influence in China during the 1980's and early 1990's presented a grave challenge to the Communist party system and caused the regime to review its relatively tolerant religious policies. On January 14, 1996, local officials were summoned to Beijing to discuss the issue. There are indications that the leaders of the post-Deng era are shifting toward harsher and more repressive policies to contain the spread of Christianity.

Early Persecution of Christians
After taking power in 1949, even though Marxism was contradictory to the doctrines of Christianity, the Communist

Party adopted a tolerant policy toward Christianity in order to win support and cooperation in establishing a new social order that had been undermined by decades of war. Weary of the atrocities of the civil war, Chinese Christians generally welcomed the order that the new republic victory brought about. The brief tolerance of religious activities won many Christians' support of the regime, and when the Party called on them to form a patriotic organization to handle church affairs, independent of foreign Christian communities, little opposition was voiced. Those who did not go along were labeled as tools of imperialism's invasion against China. In 1951, the Three Self Patriotic Movement Committee (TSPMC) was formally established, and all different denominations were called together to worship, as if they already attained unity in Christ through the atheist government. Most Chinese Christians did not know that the cut-off of the Chinese churches from the ecumenical churches was just the first of a series of steps aimed at eliminating Chinese Christianity. The resultant persecution and state-controlled. movements made the TSPMC into a half-religious, half-political monster. It was administrated by the CCP's united front department. As soon as the isolation of Chinese churches from the outside world was achieved, the regime quickly moved to harsher policies with outright persecutions of Christians in a sequence of political movements aimed at "rooting out" bourgeois influence. Such persecutions culminated in the 1960s when all religious services were banned, Bibles were burnt and numerous Christians were arrested and killed for their faith during "the Culture Revolution". But to the surprise of many state officials, the Chinese Christian communities earnestly persevered. Despite thirty years of state-created terror and persecution, the churches remained alive and active through unofficial meetings and communions. The Christians simply refused to worship Mao as a god figure though his personal cult had swept through China under the state auspices.

According to Marxism, religion will diminish and die out with the diminishment of private ownership and exploiting classes. Rigid followers of Karl Marx successfully replaced private ownership with public ownership, and wiped out their class enemies through execution and persecution. But religion did not fade away as theorized.

Meanwhile, the economic and social policies were in a total disarray. The ten year Cultural Revolution opened the eyes of the people to the plight of the economic and legal system pronounced to be the most advanced in the world. New inequalities in wealth distribution, poverty of ordinary citizens, and grave social injustice seriously undermined the Party's legitimacy to rule. Disillusioned with communism, people returned to religion to find balance in their mind, comfort in their heart, and above all, to heal their sufferings. If the communists earlier believed ignorance was the root cause of religion earlier, they now realized that hard political and economic realities had played a role in people's religious inclinations.

Reform was in the air in the late 1970s, at first as desperate measures to prevent the collapse of the party state. China had suffered great losses due to a closed-door policy, and to revitalize the economy the leaders now had to open to the outside world in order to reform their stagnant economic system. But such new policies would increasingly expose China to the outside world's religious influence, especially with ever increasing international economic and cultural exchanges.

The leaders in Beijing also recognized that religion, unlike an ideology, is fairly independent of economic and political systems. It is relatively stable and slow to change in essence and form, and even rapid social and economic changes cannot wipe out a religion. This judgment led Party leaders to adopt a policy establishing a much longer time line for religious forces to die out in China's socialist system.

All these factors and perceptions required new strategies in dealing with religion. In the late 1970s, the Communist Party abandoned their earlier harsh policies of persecuting Christians, and a new religious policy began to take shape.

The New Religious Policy in the Reform Era

The groundwork for the new policy was first documented in "Fundamental Viewpoints and Policy on Religious Issues in Our Socialist Period", a formal Party directive by the Central Committee of CCP released in 1982. This document was meant to be a guideline for religious work in the new reform era, and a basis for resolving all religious problems. It contained three important policy points. First, that freedom of belief should be respected and protected. This claimed to ensure individual freedom to choose what to believe and what not to believe, but also provided that the Party members had the right to aggressively propagate atheism. Separation of religion from politics would be encouraged, and administrative measures would not be used to force individuals to accept or refuse a certain religious belief. Second, state control and management of religious affairs would be brought into a legal framework. With the permission of the Ministry of the United Front, all religions would enjoy the right to open schools and print and distribute religious books and scriptures as long as these activities did not interference with governmental and public affairs. Religious activities perceived as against state security were strictly forbidden. The three self principles (self-preaching, self-sustaining and self-governance) in dealing with Christianity is reiterated in this document. No foreign church organizations were allowed to interfere with Chinese church affairs, and all funds from foreign religious institutions must be declined. Third, religion is expected to serve government policies in promoting economic development and relations with the outside world. Such activities by religious communities would be under the leadership of the Ministry of the United Front, and religious leaders would serve as the bridge between the Party and their respective communities. Clearly the new policy underlined the need of the Party to use religious organizations to serve the purpose of the regime. The interest and mission of religious communities were secondary to Party interest. It was unclear, however, whether the leaders anticipated whether this new policy was a double-edged sword. While religious groups could be used to advance the Party's interest, there was a risk that their influence could expand to the point of challenging the Party's monopoly of power. Indeed with the genie out of the bottle, there was a rapid growth of believers that astonished the leaders in Beijing. The next decade saw a deepening of the policy paradox between using and controlling Christianity. Some elements within the Party became eager to reverse the somewhat tolerant policies in order to stop the spread of Christianity, but they have not found ways of doing that without serious cost to China's international image and its policy of opening to the outside world.

The wakening of Christianity in China before 1989

The response of the Chinese Christian community to the new policy was quick. In many cities long lost church properties were taken back, and regular worship services were conducted in almost all the major cities in China. These services quickly attracted young and old to the churches. Fourteen theological colleges and universities were reopened to educate a younger generation of Christians to be preachers and church leaders. Now thousands of these graduates have become pillars of the churches, actively preaching gospel in cities and the countryside.

The once severed relationships with outside world churches were in time reestablished. The Nanjing Faith Funds Foundation was set up shortly after the implementation of the new policy. Under close state monitoring and supervision, the foundation is allowed to accept overseas funds to print Bibles and other church materials. More than nine million copies of the Bible were printed in Chinese and several minority languages since the foundation was founded. In 1994, annual publication of Bibles reached one million and six hundred thousand copies. But this number was still unable to meet the demand of the rapidly expanding Christian community. Once secret meetings in private homes experienced new found growth and became more open. More and more young people joined the old congregation.

Christian influence also spread into the academic community, especially among young and middle-aged intellectuals. Disillusioned with communist doctrines, they turned to Christianity with great interest. Many books on Christianity were translated into Chinese, and religious studies became popular in academic circles. In turn, their studies and papers on religious issues popularized Christianity among the Chinese public. The false ideas about Christianity as one form of superstition, which had been churned out by Party propaganda machines, were soon defeated. Christianity won the respect of many Chinese.

In short, with the new policy of permitting limited freedom of religion, Christianity was able to quickly take root among China's new generation as an alternative to communist ideology. This prepared the ground for Christianity in China to take off, some predict it will soon outnumber Buddhists. But will China become a Christian nation in the next century?

The Revival after 1989

The crackdown on the pro-democracy movement in 1989 marked a turning point in both government policy and the people's attitudes toward Christianity. The Christian community was supportive of the student movement, and the Chinese government realized that the growth of Christianity was becoming an opposition political force. This view was reinforced by the collapse of the former Soviet Union and East European countries, where Christianity was instrumental to the formation of democratic coalitions that hastened the collapse of government dictatorships and midwifed the arrival of a free society .

As democracy became taboo after the 1989 "June 4th" massacre, a great number of democratic aspirants turned to Christianity for consolation and realignment. According to a survey conducted by the Central Institute of Educational Research soon after the massacre, only 2.96% of the 500 students in Shanghai claimed to believe in communism, while 41.8% said they believed in God. This was in sharp contrast to the same survey done in 1982 when 60% said they believed in communism and only 8% believed in God. In 1993, Beijing University offered a series of lectures on religion which attracted thousands of students. One lecture, "The Holy Bible and Christianity's Impact on Western Culture," drew a full house with people standing in the hallway. In Nanchang, capital city of Jiangxi province, more than 2,000 young people reportedly attended weekly Bible Study gatherings. A report from Zhejiang province said that of six thousand university students surveyed, fifteen percent of them claimed to be Christians, and 627 out of surveyed 871 high school students said that they went to churches regularly.

The statistics of Christians in Gongzhuling, a city of 1.8 million in Northeast China further indicates changes in the Christian population after 1989. The city's total number of Christians in 1988 was under 200, but in 1989, more 2,000 people were baptized as Seventh-Day Adventists, the smallest denomination of the "Three Self Church." Four years later, the Adventists in this area increased to more than 20,000, making up 2% of the total population.

It is difficult to determine how many Christians are in China now. Yet it is interesting to note the difference between government and non-government statistics on the total number of Chinese Christians. Governmental statistics in 1991 reported 4,5000,000 Protestants and 3,500,000 Catholics in China. However, according to research done by a non-official institute in 1992, as reported by *MINBAO* in Hong Kong, there were 63,000,000 Protestants and 12,000,000 Catholics. The difference between the official and non-official reports is that the government figure does not include the fast growing underground churches. Which estimate is closer to fact? Based on distribution of Bibles printed in China, i.e., ten million copies after 1982, and probably the same number smuggled into China during the same period, the internal investigation by the Chinese state security might have revealed the true picture.

In November 1995, the State Council, China's highest administrative organ, released a document issued by the Ministry of Public Security entitled "On Further Reinforcement of the Leadership and Supervision Towards Religious Groups." Attached to it is an investigative report ("Regarding the Situation of Religious Groups and Their Activities in City and countryside"), which was drafted jointly by the Ministry of Public Security and the Ministry of Civil Affairs. This report claims that there are 25,000,000 Protestants and Catholics in China now.

Despite the different projections, the figures evidence a revival of Christianity in China today. This reality has also led to changes for the TSPMC. Formed in 1951, TSPMC officials have been strictly controlled by the Chinese government, and were used to administer and limit the growth of the Chinese Christian community. They are nothing more than a tool of the government. To some extent, they took part in the long persecution of Christians. But the TSPMC's position has been changing recently, as they attempt to draw away from Beijing policies. Ding Guangshun, President of TSPMC, had the courage to speak out against the interference of local government in religious affairs at the Eighth National Political Consultative Conference in 1993, an act unheard of throughout communist rule. In 1992, the TSPMC appealed to the Central Government to acknowledge those in unregistered family churches or other underground churches as legal Christians. It is not difficult to predict that TSPMC will play a new role in the revival of Christianity in China.

The Present Situation

When compared with China's huge population of Considering the 1.4 billion, Christians are still a "little flock" and a minority, but their influence has been steadily increasing. In 1991, the State Council issued an administrative directive ("Notice of Problems on further and better

Administrating Religious Works"), which shows signs of reversing the 1982 policy. In the 1982 document, it is claimed that "Marxist and all patriot religious individuals could and must be united into a front for the modernization of socialist construction". However, the 1991 document views religious work as the struggle between infiltration and anti-infiltration, subversion and anti-subversion, peaceful evolution and anti-evolution. In 1994, two additional regulations, i.e. "Regulations Regarding the Religious Activities Within the Border of the People's Republic of China" and "Regulations Regarding the Religious Activity Places", were released. Authority was given to county-level governments to control religious activities instead of letting religious communities to arrange and control their own activities. Clearly this is a further reversal of the policy designed in 1982. All these documents indicate that the Central Government is adopting a more conservative policy to control and limit religious activities. In the national meeting of religious officials in Beijing on January 14 1996, a timetable was set for a regulative and control system on religious groups to be in place by the turn of the century. In November 1995, another document "On Further Reinforcement of the Leadership and Supervision Towards Religious Groups," issued by the Ministry of Public Security, reportedly contained passages of a speech by the Party General Secretary and President Jiang Zemin. Jiang reportedly described new policies over Christianity as "a war to be conducted quietly," and warned that the graveness of the situation cannot · be underestimated. Given these developments, one can expect more restrictive laws and measures against Chinese Christians to be implemented in the near future. There will be more arrests and other forms of persecution in order to limit the development of Christianity. But all these efforts probably will not achieve their desired goals. China's Christianity has reached a critical threshold in both number and organizational strength. More persecution can only help spread the gospel among the ordinary people, who are disillusioned with corruption and Chinese politics.

Moreover, forty years of struggle with Communism has made Chinese Christians capable of dealing with different forms of the government persecution. Perhaps it is safe to say that in the post-Deng era, Chinese Christianity will be one of the major political forces that will help promote China's peaceful transition to constitutional democracy. Only in a true democracy where freedom of religion is guaranteed, can Chinese Christians rid themselves of persecution.

CHINA WITHOUT DENG
Political Trends In 1997 and Beyond

China Strategic Review, Vol. II, no. 1

(January/February 1997)

With the passing of China's paramount leader Deng Xiaoping, state control has officially passed to a collective group of Communist elites who enjoy neither the stature nor the prestige of their predecessor. While President Jiang Zemin has managed to successfully balance his political rivals against one another in the short run, an intense if not covert struggle for power is sure to occur during the months leading up to the 15th Congress of the Chinese Communist Party (CCP) set for October. While the upcoming congress appears to be solidly under Jiang's control, several factors could emerge to loosen that control and color the general outcome of the congress.

Chairman Jiang?

First, there will be serious disputes over the limitations placed on Jiang Zemin's power. Central to those disputes will be Jiang's desire to become Chairman rather than General Secretary of the Chinese Communist Party, a post he currently holds in addition to being the Chairman of the Central Military Commission and the President of China. The distinction between Chairman and General Secretary is a crucial one in the world of Chinese politics. The General Secretary has one equal vote and is largely responsible for coordinating the activities of the seven member Standing Committee of the CCP. It is an unwritten rule in the CCP that the title of Chairman historically has been reserved for Mao and implies much greater political weight than does General Secretary. As Chairman, Mao had the power to dictate party issues and overturn decisions enacted by a majority vote. Thus for Jiang to become Chairman would be a symbolic as well as tactical victory, conferring the power to rule virtually by decree while simultaneously acknowledging his place as a paramount figure in Chinese history.

Jiang has other more pressing political motives for becoming Chairman. Currently there are a number of factions at the center of the CCP power system which publicly support the "Jiang core" but privately question the President's ability to lead. These factions prefer instead to govern through "collective leadership." The collective consists of the seven members on the Standing Committee of the CCP Politburo. Each member has his own power base which is supported by a certain number of party elders. While none of these members had the ability or desire to challenge Jiang Zemin while Deng Xiaoping was alive, Deng's death has opened the door for potential coups.

Mindful that he does not have sufficient political support to become the paramount leader, Jiang is seeking to form an alliance with the powerful Premier Li Peng, Jiang's political ally and principal behind-the-scenes rival. Li's stature is at least equal to Jiang's and his two tenures as Premier is set to expire this year as mandated by China's constitution. Jiang would prefer that Li remain Premier past the two terms in order to keep him from launching an open political challenge for the Presidency. But extending Li's tenure requires a constitutional amendment be passed by the National People's Congress, a highly improbable option given that the NPC is currently controlled by Qiao Shi, a political opponent of the Jiang-Li coalition. If this issues remains unsettled and Li is forced to vacate the Premiership, he is sure to challenge Jiang for the Presidency. The only alternative would be for Jiang to obtain the title of Chairman of the Party and appoint Li as Vice-Chairman, effectively creating an Jiang-Li alliance.

But there is significant opposition to Jiang's designs by Party elders who consider his plan to be a flagrant dismissal of the party's prior consensus. If Jiang fails to acquire the Chairmanship, his opponents may force him to relinquish the presidency to Li, a move that would delay his ultimate goal of acquiring the status of Mao or Deng. Jiang may move to silence his opponents, but overly aggressive maneuvering could heighten party factionalism thus ensuring that intra-party power plays will continue well beyond the fall congress.

It is likely that some sort of Jiang-Li alliance will emerge whether or not Jiang is able to push his plan through, thus ensuring that a conservative shadow will hang over the next term of the CCP leadership.

High Level Worries

Surpassing the CCP's introspective concerns over internal political struggles is an overarching concern about the party's predominate role in Chinese society. In the months following Deng's death, the CCP's most pressing task is to maintain an orderly political setting by insuring that challenges to one party rule are suppressed. To achieve these ends, the government will focus primarily on two potential distractions: opposition forces and potential social turmoil resulting from the current economic conditions.

Dissent and the Media. The CCP intensified political repression in 1995 and 1996, making the latter the most politically repressive year since 1989. The arrest of Wei Jingsheng in 1995 was staged to send a warning to China's opposition forces. But this warning went unheeded as opposition forces rallied in 1996. Some activists boldly appealed for the impeachment of Jiang Zemin, claiming he violated the Chinese constitution by forcing the Chinese military to accept the absolute command of the CCP. At the same time, international support for the opposition movement grew, causing the CCP to respond by arresting and sentencing vocal activists such as Wang Dan and Liu Xiaobo.

Individual activists were not the only victims of repression. Although China has some of the world's strictest regulations governing the media, the nervous leadership does not think they are strict enough.

It is true that control over the press relaxed to a degree under Deng and the thaw in state control allowed a number of popular newspapers and magazines to emerge. While most of these publications carry only gossip-like reports, some report on meaningful party events, printing stories about official corruption, internal power struggles and secret deals forged in the top decision making organs.

In addition to these newspapers and magazines, a number of popular books have been published that offer commentary on timely social issues. While these books claim only to address specific problems without any intention of challenging communist ideology, they do expose embarrassing facts about the party.

The number of television and radio networks has also grown during the reform years to some 4000 stations nationwide. Because many of the localized TV stations lack the funding to produce their own programs, they have to air programs produced in Hong Kong and Taiwan. Beijing officials consider these popular programs to be major sources of "spiritual pollution" because they sometimes contain violence and pornography. But underlying the CCP's concerns over the prurient nature of foreign broadcasts is a more fundamental worry that these programs distract viewers from official CCP propaganda and add to their cynicism about the political system. In order to contain these problems the CCP is reportedly considering legislation that would close a quarter of Chinese media outlets, including publications for internal references (*nei bu can kao*) which are only distributed in the lower echelon of the state apparatus.

Labor's Discontent. The CCP leadership is especially sensitive to the possible integration of political dissent, which exists mainly among intellectuals, with politically disconnected and economically marginalized workers and peasants. Since early 1996 thousands of workers and peasants have organized strikes, demonstrations and even violent protests. Although the official media in China are barred from reporting these incidents, the protests have made the CCP leadership extremely anxious.

To prevent any further escalation of large-scale unrest, the ruling elite is using monetary handouts to mitigate the collective discontent of unpaid workers. State banks are instructed to give "unity and stability" loans to failing enterprises so that they may pay long overdue salaries to their employees. CCP leaders have declared that no IOUs should be issued in place of actual payments while state leaders have begun to visit economically underdeveloped regions. Meanwhile, China's security forces maintain a close watch on workers to prevent any efforts to organize.

All these issues exacerbate the CCP's concerns over the decline in public support and acceptance of one-party rule. The upsurge in dissident activity, an increasingly vibrant media and the looming potential for broad-scale social unrest from workers are concerns which are sure to hang large over congressional proceedings and the battles for power among nervous CCP elites. It is logical to expect that the CCP will continue to enact repressive measures on all fronts throughout 1997.

Escalating Nationalism

The book *China Can Say No* symbolized the importance and escalation of nationalism as an ideological substitute for communism. However complicated the reasons for this escalation, the fact is that it is welcomed, endorsed, and fueled by the current regime.

China's post-Tiananmen crisis of ideology has caused communist leaders to seek ways to rally and mobilize the people. Some CCP strategists suggested that nationalism could be used to fill the ideological vacuum. Thus with official endorsement, nationalism gradually emerged as the intellectual and spiritual parent of China's surging neo-conservatism.

China Can Say No immediately caught the attention of the international community and is evidently backfiring in China's international relations. As a result Beijing has been trying to distance itself from this extreme nationalism. However, it is an open secret that nationalism is supported by high ranking CCP officials. It has been promoted to such a scale that it will be very difficult to curb. More importantly, without this brand of nationalism the CCP has little ideological influence over the people, a fact which threatens the CCP's legitimacy. Therefore, we can only expect increased nationalism in China, especially in the context of Hong Kong's reversion.

Hong Kong's reversion signifies to many a glorious rebirth for China. Besides being a monumental political test of Jiang's leadership abilities, it is an event which symbolizes China's return to world power. While this is indeed an event worth celebrating for the Chinese people, it is also an opportunity for the CCP to glorify itself through nationalist propaganda. A China driven by nationalism will definitely alarm other countries and hinder the development of democracy.

Hopeful Democrats?

Chinese democrats should not be overly optimistic about 1997. The CCP will impose tight controls on domestic affairs while Beijing's international policy will continue to be hard-line. In this repressive environment are there still chances for the democrats to affect change? Will there be a political opening?

There are two issues that may strengthen China's democracy movement in 1997. The first is the reversal of the June 4th verdict. Since Deng's death, the Chinese public has become increasingly vocal in their demands that the government recognize the 1989 democratic movement as a patriotic movement. There have been calls for a public denunciation of the government's use of force against the peaceful demonstrators. No faction within the party wants to appear unresponsive to public desires, instead they will attempt to appear liberal-minded on the issue in order to extract political gain by improving their public image. A reversal of the Tiananmen verdict would set the stage for a more liberal faction to take control while energizing democratic elements at the local level.

The second issue is rampant corruption. Public antipathy has grown as corrupt officials abuse their power for personal gain while the conditions for the urban working class continues to deteriorate. The task for China's democrats is to harness public resentment and transform it into substantive demands for political reforms, including greater accountability for government officials, a freer media and other legislative measures which will build an institutional basis for political pluralism.

The Chinese democrats should also capitalize on the power struggles unfolding in the upper ranks of the party. There is no indication that Jiang will be able to eradicate his opponents and their presence represents a de facto check on Jiang's power; a rare window of opportunity to insert some formalized system of checks and balances into the state apparatus. Qiao Shi has transformed the formerly rubber-stamp National People's Congress (NPC) into a separate power base that is reasonably able to launch challenges against Jiang Zemin. Li Ruihuan has used the Chinese People's Political Consultation Committee (CPPCC) to advance his agenda and recent reports suggest that his followers have proposed to transform the CPPCC into a western-styled Upper House while letting the NPC functions as the Lower House. Tian Jiyun, another ranking reformer, is likely to throw his weight against Jiang's attempt to dominate China's political landscape. Zhao Ziyang and Yang Shangkun, both ousted from the ruling clique but still politically viable in the provinces and the military, are also potential challengers.

In the CCP's history, no factions have been allowed to exist legitimately. As a result factional power struggles have always been bloody with the dominate faction brutally suppressing its opponents. In the post-Deng era it is possible to officially or tacitly legitimize the existence of these factions, a move that may pave the way for political pluralism. These de facto political factions, if transformed into de jure political units with substantive power, could serve as an embryonic system of checks and balances that leads China away from the current authoritarian model to a more inclusive and representative one.

If the communist political power comes from the barrel of the gun, democratic political power must come from the conscience and rationality of ordinary Chinese citizens. Thus in 1997 the challenge to the Chinese democrats is not to face down the regime with a display of courage, but to combine bottom-up democratic pressures with opportunities presented by the unsettled power struggle at the top. This year will be a difficult one, but it is still possible to achieve selected institutional break-throughs that may set China on a secure path for a peaceful and orderly transition to constitutional democracy.

METAMORPHOSIS OF CHINESE NEO-CONSERVATISM
Can It Dominate the Post Deng Era?

China Strategic Review, Vol.II, no. 2
(March/April 1997)

Among the many political trends in China today, neo-conservatism has been very influential. It is beginning to be felt in almost all aspects of Chinese political and economic life, although its policy implications have yet to be seen. Indeed a trend still in its formative stages, it defies clear definition. After Deng's death, China's political uncertainty offers an opportunity for further evolution, the consequence of which has important and long-term implications for China's political development into the next century. It is a political phenomenon well worth close attention.

From Neo-Authoritarianism to Neo-Conservatism

The term "neo-conservatism" was quite unknown to most Chinese before 1989 and not widely used in China's political circles until the early 1990s, when its exponents like Xiao Gongqin and He Xin began using the term to denote a less communist-colored but non-democratic alternative to China's political development. In a nutshell, neo-conservatism hopes to smooth out the discrepancies and conflicts between China's market reforms and rigid political controls.

Before proceeding to fully analyze neo-conservatism, it is worth the effort of tracing its evolutionary path from "neo-authoritarianism," an earlier ideology which came into vogue during the late 1980s. Hereditarily linked, the essence of neo-authoritarianism is its carrying out of free market economic reforms under rigid, if not repressive, political control, while postponing democratization to a indefinite future. At the time, neo-authoritarianism was considered an emerging ideology with obvious conservative tendencies mixed with a slight liberating element. It was conservative in the sense that it was elitist and stressed a high concentration of power as a necessary prerequisite for free market economic reform. Some thinkers openly called for a reform-minded authority figure like Mikhail Gorbachev in the former Soviet Union. Remember, this period was before the downfall of the Soviet Union when Gorbachev was at the height of his power and influence. In fact, Zhao Ziyang was considered a candidate for such a figure by many neo-authoritarians at the time. It was slightly liberating because neo-authoritarianism tended to negate orthodox Maoism while supporting China's economic reforms.

According to neo-authoritarian principles, only with the success of economic reform, can a democratic political system be established. The "Four Little Dragons" (Taiwan, Hong Kong, South Korea, and Singapore) of Asia, they argue, are successful examples of such reforms. Though strongly inclined towards political conservatism, neo-authoritarianism in the late 1980s never tried to rule out that democracy is both inevitable and desirable in the end. In post-Mao China, this also reflects a willingness to abandon communism as the dominant ideology.

Since the Tiananmen incident, drastic changes have taken place in China's political atmosphere. In order to stop the influence of liberal democratic ideas from the West, the government began to reinforce official ideological control. As a result, ultra-leftist ideology gained the upper hand in preventing the effective spread of liberal ideologies. No other voice could be heard through the media, apart from the rigid official ideological doctrines. The strengthened official ideological control and the downfall of Zhao Ziyang shattered for many the hope that the slight liberating element in neo-authoritarianism might evolve into Gorbachev-styled open-mindedness for political reform.

The speeches made by Deng Xiaoping during his inspection of southern China in 1992 somewhat undermined the extreme rigidity of the ultra-leftist rhetoric in the media, setting the stage for some non-orthodox ideas to emerge in the public sphere. Under pressure from Deng and his reform-minded followers, the ultra-leftist media began to allow some views other than the usual orthodox communist views to be expressed, though Western liberalism, which came into currency before the 1989 democratic movement, was still kept at bay. This provided the necessary political opportunity and right climate for neo-conservatism to rise.

Moreover, the reforms and the open door policy have created their own share of serious social and economic problems such as inflation, corruption, moral decay, and deterioration of social order. These problems and a fear of chaos created political platforms for the neo-conservatives to revive some of the earlier neo-authoritarian arguments in new political circumstances. Their proposal emphasizes political and economic stability and control while intending to restore moral values based on the conservative elements of Confucianism.

Political Traits of Neo-conservatism

Similar to neo-authoritarianism, neo-conservatives advocate an authoritarian approach to politics. In other words, it prefers strengthened political control and concentration of power so that the spread of Western liberal institutions and influence can be kept in check. While neo-authoritarians talk about gradually establishing freedom and civil liberties under the leadership of a political authority after the success of the economic reform, they remain vague about whether China would adopt a democratic political system at the end of the process. They insist only that it carry the label "China styled." In the eyes of some neo-conservatives, even if democracy is desirable, it would have to be quite different from the Western models, not to mention that it would take an indefinite period of time to establish because of issues such as different regional conditions, the low education level of the masses, the backwardness of the economy, and so on. For a while, much of the neo-conservative writings focused on the analysis of different national conditions, but arriving at a more or less similar conclusion that a concentration of power, not democracy, would work for China's conditions. In the neo-conservative perspective, the success of the "Four Little Dragons" is based on restraining the demand for democracy while developing the economy. However, they do not explain why there is invariably a democratization movement after the success in economic development. Such neo-conservative views are fully expressed in journals like *Zhanlue yu Guanli* (Strategy and Management).

Turning Back on Market Reform

In terms of China's future economic system, some neo-conservatives advocate strengthening development in publicly-owned sectors of the economy while restraining growth in privately-owned sectors. They insist that government economic policy should support the public sector and facilitate its development in spite of the extreme difficulties it faces. Although failing to offer viable policies to resolve the grave economic problems facing these public sectors, they nevertheless consider any further softening of government intervention in state enterprises to be dangerous and something that should be prevented.

In fact, such neo-conservative attitudes towards private and public sectors of the economy have become government policies, at least for now. Privately-owned enterprises do not enjoy the luxury of similar government support. It is difficult, if not impossible, for these enterprises to secure loans from banks. According to statistics, only thirty percent of the financial resources used by privately owned enterprises is from Chinese commercial bank loans.

Favoring Centralization

Hu Angang and Wang Shaoguang, though both trained in Western institutions, gave voice to China's neo-conservative thinking regarding economic policy. They claim that the financial difficulty faced by the central government is caused by the excessive decentralization of power, which leads to conflict between the central and local governments and in turn will lead to the break-up of the country. However, the reality is that there is still not enough decentralization of power in China today, especially in the western and central areas where the central government's control is so excessive that it has stifled local creativity and initiative and hampered the economic development of this area. The key to development in this area still lies in the strengthening of reforms and further opening-up to the outside. Only through continued decentralization will it be possible to provide the area with the opportunity for economic development.

The coastal areas in eastern China also face similar issues of further decentralization of power, which surely will encourage local economic development. Judging from the current overall situation in China, a threatening break-up of the country because of the decentralization of power simply does not exist. Only by developing a market economy with continued economic growth can a unified Chinese market be created, which will result in the cooperation among and union of all the regions. This makes a potential division of the country virtually impossible. The claim that China will break up due to too much decentralization may help to hinder any further development in China's economic reforms. Neo-conservative views have been praised by some government agencies, but have yet to become government policies.

By their logic, the neo-conservatives even propose abolishing special economic zones, opposing any radical economic reforms, such as letting some people in certain areas get rich first. They argue that such policies have already caused serious polarization problems and, if not corrected, will endanger national security.

Nationalist Attitudes Toward Culture and Ideology

Neo-conservatives oppose the invasion and ever-increasing influence of Western culture. They are against "total westernization". However, they also disapprove of the official indoctrination of the masses by the hard-line leftists. Aware of the incompatibility of the orthodox official doctrines with the

needs of modernization, neo-conservatives continue to argue
that neither Chinese intellectuals nor ordinary people would
be convinced by old-style communist indoctrination. The
political game played by the old leftists will not be effective
because it lacks creativity. Therefore, according to neo-
conservatives, a new way of thinking in terms of ideology and
culture must be found in China to replace the old ideological
doctrines. This new way of thinking is to advocate traditional
Chinese culture while negating Western culture. Since the
early 1990s, this neo-conservative view has found expression
in articles evaluating the clash of civilizations as proposed by
Samuel Huntington.   One controversial article regarding
Western civilization was written by Sheng Hong in a 1994
issue of *Strategy and Management*.   Although Sheng himself is
not an ultra-leftist, his view advocates the total negation of
Western culture.

Under such circumstances, nationalist sentiment has risen
in recent years, used by the ultra-leftists to wage an anti-
Western nationalist campaign. The book *China Can Say No* is a
typical work representing the ongoing nationalist trends. Neo-
conservatives have gained some inspiration from the revival
of traditional Chinese culture, which not only counteracts the
invasion of Western culture, but also replaces the unwelcome
official ideological doctrines. In this sense, their version of
"fostering tradition" (*fayang chuantong*) is more complex
theoretically and may differ with the narrow-minded
nationalism advocated by government propaganda. However,
the result of their work, at least in light of the current
situation, is contributing to the rise of nationalism in China.

Abandoning Communism?

The characteristics of the neo-conservatism described
above differentiate it from ultra-leftism in China. In their
articles, neo-conservatives seldom mention Marxist ideology
or even quote its sayings. However, they are known for their
approval of the centralization of state power and their support
of Communist Party leadership. While they like the idea of

free market competition to a certain extent, they are, however, against both private property rights and the decentralization of power among the regions. They would like to place the reforms under strict state control. They favor the development and strengthening of government enterprises while restraining the private sectors. In fact, they do not like either Western culture or the official Marxist-Leninist ideology; what they do like is maintenance of traditional Chinese culture. In conclusion, they are not dogmatic ultra-leftists, but conservatives with a sense of modernity, if not liberal ideas.

The Role of Neo-conservatives in Post-Deng China

In today's China, neo-conservatism is a very influential political trend whose function in Chinese politics and economics cannot be ignored. Many current political and economic policies are linked to it. Generally speaking, neo-conservatism is conservative by nature, in that it emphasizes political stability based on elite, if not communist, control. It must be pointed out with due fairness that neo-conservatism has a wider world view than Chinese communism, which is the reason why it gained some influence among the new generation of intellectuals.

The major difference between neo-conservatism and ultra-leftism lies in the fact that the former does not oppose adopting a free market economy while the latter does. Fully aware of the deep crisis in Marxism and Leninism, neo-conservatives are trying to find an alternative to the ultra-leftist strategy of turning back the clock. Under such circumstances, neo-conservatism is called "communist liberalism" by many in China, that is, "liberalism" within the framework of communist rule. They try to preserve the elitism of the communist power structure while abandoning its ideology.

In fact, it is the balance struck between neo-conservatism and liberalism that has been keeping China on a road of reform and development. As neo-conservatism gains influence among many Chinese intellectuals, including young intellectuals and government officials, many of its ideas are being adopted and implemented as concrete policies. In the post-Deng period, neo-conservatism may become one of the major political trends in China. It will help keep social stability high on the agenda of government policies, even to the extent of slowing down, if not reversing, the reforms inherited from Deng's era.

The major problem of neo-conservatism is its elitism and overemphasis on political and economic order and stability. Its obvious flirtation with fascism will bring strong opposition from the public and liberal intellectuals. Because it denies the constructive function of democracy and creativity in the development of the market economy, it is unlikely to provide genuine solutions to China's ailing political system. In the long run, although neo-conservatism can temporarily alleviate some of the symptoms of China's ills, it cannot cure them. As a result, the creative role in Chinese political and economic reform has to be shouldered by Chinese democrats.

THE EMERGENCE OF THE ULTRA-LEFT
IN POST-DENG CHINA
China Strategic Review, Vol.II, no.2 (March/April 1997)

The direction China's political development will take after Deng's death now becomes a contending issue in which different political forces are trying to play a larger role. This essay will analyze how the Chinese ultra-leftists or orthodox communists fit into this bigger picture, and predict their impact on China's political evolution.

Specifically, I will analyze the socio-political resources of China's ultra-leftist political force by tracing its reformation after the Cultural Revolution; and by investigating its latest activities in the political arena, I hope to explore the political role and orientation that China's ultra-leftist force would assume in post-Deng China.

An Often Over-looked Political Group?

Most people believe that it is impossible for China to return to closed-door isolation as in Mao's era, however, how exactly China is going to further its open-door policies in its reform process is still a topic on which no consensus exist.

The uncertainty is partly due to the fact that the communist regime does not have any viable solutions to tackle the problems and conflicts that China now faces. Due to the lack of internal uniformity in the politics of post-Deng China, a no-further-reform status will likely encourage a political leaning to the left in the near future. This is because China's political system has changed little in spite of a rapid process of economic liberalization in the last two decades, and the political default is very favorable to the ultra-leftist agenda. Thus, like a ship sailing against the opposing current, no advancing forward means a backward shift, which will result in the usage of Maoist controlling mechanisms.

Of course, China's present political uncertainty will also provide opportunities for China's political reform and democratic movement, which will certainly put the ultra-leftists on the edge. The over-seas Chinese intellectuals tend to have over-optimistic expectations for the chances for China's democratization while underestimating the danger and potential strengths of the ultra-leftist faction. Actually, the ultra-leftist political force in Chinese politics has always existed, but it has often been overlooked.

The Daring "Ten-Thousand Word Letters"

At the beginning of last year, the Hong Kong press published the first leftist article entitled "Wan Yan Shu" (The Ten Thousand Word Letter), which received immediate attention both within China and abroad. This article was treated like a scandal in the overseas Chinese communities, yet received commendations and praises from elite government circles in China. The political impact of the event also was reported by the Western media.[1] In view of this article's being able to create such a political incident, one has no difficulty in perceiving the political force and influence of China's ultra-leftists, who actually did not vanish with China's reform and development.

The ultra-leftists' third "Ten Thousand Word Letter" came out in China immediately after Deng's death and began to be known overseas.[2] This article should have been written before Deng's death, but, the fact that they published it immediately following his death still demonstrates their hard-line determination and audacity in challenging Deng's reforms and open-door policy. Obviously, the comeback of the ultra-leftists toward the center of China's political arena is only a question of time. But the issues of concern here are how much force they can gather and what kinds of social resources they can take advantage of under the current circumstances and to what degree they can impact China's political evolution.

---

[1] See *The Washington Post*, Oct. 17, 1996.
[2] See *Kaifang Monthly*, March 1997.

The Ultra-leftist Regrouping After Tiananmen

Looking at the tip of the iceberg, one sees that the ultra-leftists are dominant only in the field of political theory. Indeed, after the student demonstrations on June 4, 1989, the Chinese communists imposed strict ideological control over ideology, striving to wipe out the influence of liberal intellectuals. In this regard, the ultra-leftists and the communist leaders in power have very much in common, which is why there was a swing to the left in China's ideology before Deng's trip to southern China.

During this period, when the liberals were suppressed, the ultra-leftists conducted the first efficient regrouping since the Cultural Revolution (1966-76). They openly blamed the crisis of 1989 on the reform policies, which have allowed the west to adopt a policy of "peaceful evolution" (he ping yan bian), a term in communist often denotes a sense of insidious attempt by the west to wipe out communism through internal differentiation. They argued that the downfall of the former USSR and Eastern European communists was the result of a successful western strategy of "peaceful evolution".

It was also during this period that they started to control ideology and some sectors of political theory. This control is not confined to ideology and theory, however, but actually extends to all organizations and institutions related to ideology, including all newspapers and magazines. Furthermore, they took advantage of their acquired power to start new magazines and papers. During this time, the only unified voice all over the country was that of the ultra-leftists in the press. In fact, this can be seen as more or less a counter-attack on Deng's reforms and open-door policy from the ultra-leftist faction.

Relentless Press Control

Since then, the status of China's press under the control of the ultra-leftists has not changed. The communist leaders in power had to continue the reforms under Deng's pressure, especially after Deng's campaign in Southern China in early 1992, but they also supported the orthodox ideology and political theories. The change of tone in the press favoring reform after 1992 seems to have been involuntary and reluctant. Although there was a great number of articles and press releases which came out in support of the reforms, numerous articles by the ultra-leftists were published at the same time to express their views and opinions in various forms, distancing themselves from Deng's reform policies.

Ironically, these views prove compatible with the need of the communist leadership to consolidate ideological control. The communist leaders in power, therefore, without being really serious in dealing with the ultra-leftists' ideological challenges to reform policies, maintained a policy of tolerance. Only in a few extreme cases did the top leadership in the CCP deal with the ultra-leftists ideological assault on reforms. One such case was Sha Jiansun, the vice-chair of the Party History Research Office of the CCP Central Committee, who attacked Deng's reforms and open-door policy and thus, was forced to resign from his position. Nothing was done to those ultra-leftists who were less blunt or who were moderate in attacking the reform policies; they were sometimes even encouraged.

The first and second "Ten Thousand Word Letter," as far as is known, were handed over to the top officials of the CCP, including Jiang Zemin himself, but received no negative responses. It is apparent that the current top leaders of the party took no stand against the ultra-leftists. This neutrality actually has encouraged the ultra-leftists. It is expected that the recent third "Ten Thousand Word Letter" will not be the last one. This kind of ultra-leftist criticism will no doubt become more frequent and more strategic. The ultra-leftists hope to use this format to propagate their thoughts and even to attempt to spread their propaganda overseas, so that their influence will reach back from abroad to people in China with greater and better results. In fact, this has already become an efficient means for ultra-leftists to overcome their disadvantageous position as a small political faction and to enlarge their influence.

It seems that the ultra-leftists have control over only a handful of newspapers and magazines, such as the Department of Theories of *The People's Daily*, *The Guangming Daily*, *Qiu Shi* (Seeking Truth), *Sixiang Zhanxian* (Thought Frontiers), *Zhong Liu* (Mainstream), and *Front Line*. Also under their control are some university journals, one of which is the academic journal of the People's University in Beijing. These papers and magazines are nothing significant in terms of popular support, but, due to the fact that they are the most important and influential press media in China, these papers and magazines do have very powerful political impact.

In addition, Deng Liqun, spiritual leader of the ultra-leftist faction, by taking advantage of the Tiananmen incident, established the Research Academy of Contemporary China, a ministry-level entity in China's administrative hierarchy. Many left-wing party demagogues and ultra-left theorists have gathered there to write and do research on post-1949 China history. They are in fact taking an ultra-leftist standpoint to assess post-1949 history, preparing for a future theoretic negation of the reform and open-door policies. To date, the academy has already published numerous volumes of the *Guoshi Nianjian* (Almanac of the State Affairs), in which the history of communist China after 1949 is systematically expounded upon from an ultra-left viewpoint.

Ultra-leftists Make Strategic Adjustments After Deng Died

The ultra-leftists, in terms of their numbers, do not possess significant power. Neither do they have an efficient means of exerting influence on the actual policy-making process of the economic reform and open-door policies. The trend of recent ultra-leftist activities, however, points to some noticeable adjustment measures being taken on their part.

As has been well known, China's reform is just stepping into a critical stage, where it faces all sorts of inevitable social conflicts which arise as the result of lacking a comprehensive approach to reform the entire system. The needed political reform is still a tabooed area. The lack of vision by the post-Deng leaders is confounded with many uncertainties over the transition of power.   All of this presents an excellent opportunity for the ultra-leftists to launch counterattacks on reforms.

As a result, they are changing tactics, moving from previous attacks on reform guidelines to a new strategy of picking on specific problems, which are both difficult to resolve and considered important by the public. By doing this, the ultra-left hopes to win public support and sympathy and then enlarge its influence so as to finally alter the direction of China's policy-making.

The recent publishing of the third "Ten Thousand Word Letter" is an example of the ultra-left's new tactics. Instead of launching direct attacks on the general guidelines of reform, they concentrate criticisms on specific problems emerging from the reform of state-owned enterprises, meanwhile proposing their own package for restoration of these state-owned enterprises by a return to the planned economy model of the Mao era, which included more government administrative control. They may not only command both public attention and sympathy by doing this, but also avoid suspicion that their real motives are anti-reformist.   In addition, the current drift of the reform of state-run enterprises provides the ultra-leftists with great political opportunity.

Political Resources of the Ultra-leftists

Although the ultra-leftists are not many in number, their influence on China's political arena can hardly be underestimated. What the ultra-leftists hold onto is still basically Mao Zedong's theory of class struggle, and they push the communist leaders in power for both a tightened control over all of China's economic, social, and cultural sectors and a hold on the development of China's foreign relationships. There is nothing said about China's market economy in their theories. The current communist leaders already have done away with these theories of orthodox communism as a basis for policy-making.

Thus, the leaders in Beijing may share with the ultra-left an anti-west ideological stand, especially they are still very much in the shadow of Tiananmen and the Soviet disintegration. But the ultra-leftist policy agenda does not appeal to the top leaders of China because it will not solve any of the problems that China is facing in social and economic development.

But between downfall of communism and the ultra-leftist return to the Maoist control, the latter is still a much better option to the leaders in Beijing. This is why the ultra-leftists have constantly found their supporters within the Communist Party, and especially among those who either lost their power or were marginalized in the reform.

The fact that the three "Ten Thousand Word Letters" could widely spread without any open criticism from party leaders is an example of their influence. The party press showed a clear ultra-left tendency in recent years, and the increased anti-liberal shift in the areas of the press and of ideology since last year is another example of this left trend. All this accounts for the fact that the ultra-leftists' influence within the party cannot be underestimated.

Utilizing the Difficulty of the State Enterprises

Since 1995, China's leaders have escalated the reform process in the area of state-run enterprises. A series of measures have been taken in the restructuring and merging of the state-owned enterprises which have been suffering great losses. In the implementation of these measures, many enterprises have gone bankrupt. Some have had to stop manufacturing, while others have had to close half of their operations. Some factories have postponed workers' salaries while others simply are not able to pay at all.

As a result, some workers are taking to the streets in

strikes, and others have even taken over government buildings. A great number of laid-off workers in the manufacturing industry have to live on an extremely small amount of social welfare which cannot support their families.

Furthermore, the government's job-creating or re-hiring projects have run into all sorts of problems, leaving the majority of laid-off workers still unemployed. Meanwhile, the state's social welfare policies meant to alleviate the social pressure are still not in place, therefore, the social crisis continues to worsen. This social crisis began to surface in the form of an increase in criminal activities, which is interrupting the peaceful lives of the citizens all over the country, leading to unprecedented social disorder in cities like Beijing.

The communist decision makers, who, reluctant to encourage private economic development, cannot come up with valid measures to tackle the reform problems of the state-owned enterprises, still hold on to the principle of a state-dominated economy. This near-sighted position reflects the lack of conformity among China's decision makers and will lead to the impossibility of a timely relief of laid-off workers from their difficulties.

It is under this circumstance that the ultra-leftists' Third "Ten Thousand Word Letter" came out with a proposal, which, although not really a valid method, does comply with the general principles of the communist leadership and which even presents a "new" way of thinking. The ultra-leftists are capable of exerting considerable impact with their views and initiatives after the death of Deng Xiaoping, which is a critical period when China is at crossroads for its development.

Until now, ultra-leftist theories have not reached the public, nor do China's communist leaders allow the proliferation of these thoughts for fear of public turmoil. But the ultra-leftists will resort to every possible means to create influence on both China's leaders and the society at large. The actual fact is that, among the communist leaders, excepting the determined reformers, those in the middle and those slightly toward the left are very vulnerable to the ultra-leftists' impact.

Last Chance for Regaining Communist Paradise

Due to the deepening of the reform process in recent years, the tensions and conflicts within the system are reaching to a breaking point. Some fundamental questions are no longer avoidable: whether to pursue a private economy or state-ownership economic development, whether to give more freedom or to reduce freedom, whether or not to adopt democracy, and whether or not to merge with the global economy so as to realize economic globalization. These are crucial questions that need to be answered.

When Deng Xiaoping was still alive, these issues could not be questioned. Deng's reform on the one hand has brought about prosperous economic development in China; on the other hand many problems and new conflicts have also resulted from the reform. According to the ultra-leftists, the main objective of Deng's reform is to take the route toward capitalism. Therefore, after Deng's death, contradictions begin to surface and could evolve into political confrontations within the governance system.

Before the real political clashes take place, however, political struggles in China are always first reflected in arguments over ideology and theory. There is no doubt that this is an excellent opportunity for the ultra-leftists to aggrandize their power.

Based on the status quo, it is impossible and unnecessary for the reformists to strike first against the ultra-leftists due to the fact that Deng's reformist camp already has won both popular support and the dominant political position. Therefore, it is very probable that the ultra-leftists will attack the reform policies first. Strategically speaking, they cannot win popular support if they attack the general reform principle, hence it is very possible that they will attack the reform policies first by picking on specific problems, especially when the reforms encounter substantial difficulties.

The problems resulting from the current reform of state-owned enterprises present a good excuse for the ultra-leftists to attack. By taking advantage of this vulnerability in the reform process and based on what they have already achieved, they will further attacks on reform.

This is indeed a valid strategy on their part. The current leaders of the Chinese Communist Party will be forced to state their positions concerning the ultra-leftists' attacks on specific issues of the reform. They have to respond to the ultra-leftists in order to show the Chinese public that they are the ones in control. If these communist leaders, especially Jiang Zemin, support Deng's reformist route, they will become targets of more ultra-leftist attacks. But in light of the political realities in China, one should believe that Jiang Zemin probably will hold on to Deng's reform policies, due to the fact that Jiang's consolidation of his supreme political position was accomplished through his support of and siding with Deng's reformist line.

Hence, Jiang's renunciation of Deng's reform policies would mean much the same thing as a self-renunciation, which would shake his own political foundation. If Jiang does not appear firm enough or expresses second thoughts about Deng's reform principles, the senior statesmen in Deng's reformist camp will come out to criticize him. This may well create chances for Zhao Ziyang's re-entrance into China's political arena, a scenario Jiang would do all he can to prevent from occurring. All this will decide Jiang's position in support of Deng's reforms and in opposition to the ultra-leftists' restoration proposal.

Despite this expected result, the ultra-leftists will still launch attacks on the problems of policy-making first. They will, in the name of opposing liberalism, provoke clashes in ideology and in policy propositions. Deng's death indeed presents a very good opportunity, which may be a once-and-for-all chance, so there is no reason that they will give up. In view of both their resources within the Communist Party and in society at large, the ultra-leftists should be able to create their own platform. They may even have a bigger impact on the direction of China's political evolution if they have a leader and large-scale coordinating capability, which is something remains to be seen.

Possible Disruption Before the 15th Party Congress?

The ultra-leftists, judging by their recent activities, will never accept their doomed destiny, rather, they will engage themselves in a series of attacks on Deng's reform policies so as to enlarge their political leeway, taking advantage of the communist power restructuring after Deng's death. To achieve their objective, the ultra-leftists probably will take the following specific steps:

I. They will take advantage of the papers and magazines they control to heighten their ultra-leftist tone in criticizing problems arising from the current reform movement. They will pick on one or a few points and gradually proceed to attack the general principles of the reform. They will raise a great fuss especially about the reform of state-owned enterprises so as to hold the general reform principle accountable for all problems.

II. They will further promote the propaganda of nationalism. In order to reduce and eventually stop China's open-door policies, they will, by encouraging and taking advantage of the narrow-minded nationalistic fever in China, try to hurt China's foreign relations, the status of which is an important factor in the success of reforms and open-door policies, creating the impression of international hostility toward China, which will intensify China's sense of crisis and isolation.

III. They will deliberately create friction within the Communist Party so as to apply pressure on Jiang Zemin, forcing him on the one hand to take backward steps in reforms by making a fuss over the problems and the difficult situation of the reform, and on the other hand supporting his turn to the left by utilizing the political conflicts between Jiang and other reform-minded leaders.

IV. They will produce theories both old and new to attack the
furthering of the reform process. They will constantly
employ the "Ten Thousand Word Letter" format to
aggrandize their influence, and they expect their influence
to spread abroad.

Deng's reform and open-door principles, at least up to
now, are still dominant in the policy domains, but in reality,
there are still numerous anti-reform propositions yet to be
unleashed for open dispute. In fact, such dispute in the ruling
circles about reform has always existed, only Deng's
overwhelming power was able to keep the ultra-leftists'
influence at bay when he was still alive. Obviously, his death
made the difference in this regard.

Therefore, if the ultra-leftists, headed by Deng Liqun,
start a campaign against reform by the commencement of the
Fifteenth Congress of CCP, attacking specific policies of the
reform, a restructuring of power among different political
factions in the party surely will take place. Considering some
of Jiang's actions last year when Deng was still around,
including his reiteration of the importance of "talking politics"
(jiang zheng zhi), aimed at appeasing the ultra-left, we may
tentatively conclude that the so-called "Jiang core" is still to a
large extent subject to the influence of the ultra-leftists. Apart
from the factor of Deng's death, the more important reason for
this is the nature of the communist political system, which
lends so much legitimacy and leverages to this small group.

Conclusion

The sufferings that the ultra-leftists have inflicted upon
the Chinese people have been enormous, but far from falling
out of power as in former USSR or Eastern European
countries, the ultra-leftists as die-hard communists are still
alive and active in today's China. The primary reason for their
existence lies in the political system where the communists
monopolize all political power. Thus, the only way to do
away with the ultra-leftists as well as their potential threat to
China's progress is to reform the political system.

The ultra-leftists, if they get out of control in the post-Deng era, will inevitably create economic chaos as well as political turmoil because their proposed policies imply reversing many of the reform policies introduced in the last two decades. Their unchecked ascendance means that China is in great risk of a national catastrophe. Needless to say, they are a major obstacle of China's democratization.

To prevent the ultra-left crisis from turning into a national catastrophe, Chinese democrats should form a coalition with all groups that support the continuation of reform policies. At least, in the areas of ideology and political theories, Chinese liberal intellectuals should start publicly campaigning against the ultra-leftists and create their own platform in the process. It is apparent that the political defeat of China's ultra-leftists is extremely vital to China's future, for this would determine whether China is able to transform itself peacefully into a constitutional democracy. A thorough reform of the existing political system would entail first of all controlling and minimizing the ultra-left's room to maneuver, and then eliminating its hold on the system by opening up to democratic processes.

THE POWER STRUGGLE IN THE CHINESE
COMMUNIST PARTY
China Strategic Review, Vol.II, no.4 (July/August 1997)

Writing about the factional infighting among China's ruling elite is always risky. Aside from the obvious difficulties—too many rumors and little reliable data—the fluidity of political alliances at the top adds to the complexity of the issue. The importance of the issue cannot be underestimated, especially when the post-Deng era is unfolding where profound socio-economic transformation parallels the rise of a new generation of leadership. Thus, understanding China's political trends requires insight into the grouping and re-grouping of factions among the Chinese leadership.

This paper attempts to understand the current power struggles within the Chinese Communist Party (CCP) as embedded in the larger context of China's changing social structure. In other words, the question of who is up and who is down at the top is not my primary concern, rather the focus of this study is to explain how larger social changes, such as the emergence of interest groups and the changing relationship between different political forces, may have impacted the evolution of elite factions and how factional infighting may be a reflection of these social changes.

I base the above conception on the following observations. First, China's economic reform has considerably divided Chinese society through corruption within the state system and the emergence of distinct interests in the market economy. And the unitary system commanded by the party apparatus is being dismantled in the process.[3] With the post-

---

[3] This process has been documented by several studies from a number of angles. Among others, see Kate Xiao Zhou, *How the Farmers Changed China: Power of the People* (Westview Press, 1996); Bih-jaw Lin and James T. Myers, eds., *Forces for Change in Contemporary China* (University of South Carolina Press, 1993); David Goodman and Beverley Hopper, eds., *China's Quiet Revolution: New Interactions Between State and Society* (New York: St. Martin's Press, 1994); and Wei Ting, *"Zhong gong zheng jing*

Deng era ascending rapidly on the horizon, factional infights are becoming increasingly entangled with the entrenched interests of Chinese society. It becomes impossible to understand one without the other.

Second, the strongman era of Chinese politics ended with the death of the paramount leader Deng Xiaoping who, as a revolutionary veteran, had a solid power base in the three key sections of the regime (executive, military, and party branches). In contrast, the new generation of leaders is mostly made up of technocrats who probably will never be able to fill the power vacuum left by Deng.[4] This condition will necessarily provide ample opportunities for those who are outside the ruling clique to influence the central decision-making processes.[5]

Third, perhaps because of the above reasons, the factional infighting is less deadly than in the Mao and Deng eras. Compromises are easier to reach, making the lethal struggles similar to the past more unlikely. However, the reduced risk will likely increase the frequency of factional engagement if not outright showdowns. Thus, the post-Deng political order is subject more and more to constant negotiations among faction leaders, which will provide more opportunities for interest groups to participate in the decision-making process.[6]

---

zhuanxing qi zhong quanli yu chanquan de guanxi" (The relationship between power and property rights in the present political and economic transition period in mainland China), *Zhongguo dalu yanjiu* (mainland China studies), Vol. 36, No. 10 (1993), 29-37.

[4] For Jiang's weaknesses in comparison to the previous CCP leaders, see Wang Shaoguang et al, *Jiang Zemin mianlin de tiaozhan* (challenges faced by Jiang Zemin) (Hong Kong: Ming Jing, 1996).

[5] The partial pluralisation of the decision making began in Deng's era when the CCP stressed that decision making should be scientific. See Carol Lee Hamrin and Suisheng Zhao, eds., *Decision-Making in Deng's China: Perspectives from Insiders* (New York: East Gate Books, 1995); Lowell Dittmer, "China's Informal Politics", *The China Journal*, No. 34 (July 1995).

[6] Tsai Wei, "*zhong gong de juece moshi ji xingwei*" (China's decision-making and behavioral patterns), *zhong gong yan jiu* (studies on Chinese communism), Vol. 31. No. 4 (April 1997), 99-111.

In short, the power struggle among the CCP leadership, if the above is taken into consideration, is expected to be more discernible, as well as reflective of the mapping of political forces and interest groups. In this sense, the interactions between the ruling clique and microsocial changes may play a significant role in changing China's political landscape in the post-Deng era.

Factions Embedded in Emerging Interest Groups[7]

Unlike the leaders at the time of the civil war who derived political power from the barrel of a gun, the present leaders may have to represent China's current political forces, in order to enhance their political power.[8] The emergence of interests has compounded a number of profound changes in Chinese society in the last two decades.

First, the ideological control in Mao's era was seriously undermined in the reform era, and few in China took communist indoctrination seriously. A moral vacuum was followed by the national drive to get rich. This get-rich mentality legitimizes new rules that recognize material interests of groups and individuals.[9] People no longer fear to

---

[7] While conceptual tools such as interest division inevitably risk over-simplifying present Chinese society, defining the post-Deng elite factions in terms of their connectedness to interests is very useful in substantiating the nature of the factions.

[8] The interaction between central leadership and group interests is in a formative stage, and the principle-agent model in social science is hardly applicable here. Hence the choice of terms like "loose coupling" or "embeddedness" to denote the connectedness of the two spheres.

[9] Much of the early discussion on the moral decline in China surrounded the topic of "san xin wei ji" (crisis of three beliefs). But in recent years the issue has been taken up by many academicians, who have produced a number of books on the subject in the fields of history, philosophy, and ethics. Among others, see He Huaihong, *Liang xin lun* (on conscience) (Shanghai: Sanlian, 1994); Zhao Tingyang, *Lun ke neng de shenghuo* (on the possibilities of life) (Beijing: Sanlian, 1994); Wan Junren, *Lun li xue xin lun* (on new ethics) (Beijing: Zhongguo qingnian chuban she, 1994); Wang Haiming, *Xunqiu xin daode* (in search of new morality) (Beijing:

speak their minds in private and among friends and relatives. In community and organizational life, increasingly what matters most are perceived interests.

Even top leaders like Zhao Ziyang tended to recognize the emergence of differentiated interests as a new condition born out of economic reforms.[10] For instance, the central and local conflict of interests was well recognized in national politics as early as the 1980s, and the phenomenon of "fief economy" or "local economic lords" (di fang zhu hou) has been widely recognized in both academic and policy circles in China.[11] Meanwhile, the sector interests became more assertive, too.[12] The younger leaders at all levels of government were produced in the reform process and born into the intricate networks woven and consolidated by emerging interests in different social spheres.[13]

Indeed, the economic reform restored much of economic life to the ordinary citizens, who became increasingly assertive of their rights to advance their material well-being.

---

huaxia chuban she, 1994). And for a more recent review on how the CCP policies failed to reverse the moral decline, see Lu Jing, "Zhonggong jingshen wenming jianshe dian ping" (on CCP's building of spiritual civilization), Zhong gong yan jiu (studies on Chinese communism monthly), Vol 31, No. 5 (Taiwan: May, 1997), 54-67.

[10] In fact, Zhao Ziyang, while promoting the theory of the primitive stage of socialism during and after the CCP's Thirteenth Congress, had given many internal speeches on the need to "handle well different interests" (chu li hao ge zhong li yi zhi jian de guanxi). See Chen Yizi, Shi nian gaige yu ba jiu min yun (ten years of reform and democratic movement in 1989), (Taiwan, 1990).

[11] The term "fief economy" often appeared on Chinese official press. The People's Daily published a commentary on the issue on August 8, 1989. For studies by Chinese scholars on the center-local conflict, see the combined issues No. 1 and 2 of the journal, Dangdai zhongguo yanjiu (modern China studies) (Total No. 46 & 47, 1995), which focuses exclusively on the issue.

[12] Chien-min Chao, "T'iao-t'iao versus K'uai-k'uai: A Perennial dispute Between the Central and Local Governments in Mainland China," in Bih-jaw Lin and James T. Myers, eds., Forces for Change in Contemporary China (University of South Carolina Press, 1993), 158-170.

[13] Tsai Wei, op. cit.

This amounts to pressures from the bottom up to accelerate the formation of interest groups. Thus, no matter how latent they were, factions at various levels of government became more and more entangled with a deep structure formed by interests. Jiang Zemin and his colleagues are no match for Deng Xiaoping, who was able to throw his weight around in elite circles, balancing the different interests. In fact, Deng's unchallenged authority served to check factional infighting.

Deng's death certainly provided opportunities for China's diversified interests to renegotiate an order. Under these circumstances, factional infights are likely to be coupled (however loosely) with the rivalry among interest groups vying for gains in their respective spheres of influence. The following analysis would not qualify the CCP as actually representing these social categories, but as the CCP is the omnipotent institution in China, these social groups will inevitably find their voice within the party system. The following is a rough characterization of China's emerging interests. It would not be surprising if they function as formative political forces in China's political arena down the road,

- THE LOCALS. China's move to a market economy entails a dismantling of its previous system of a planned economy. As a result, the locals free from the control of central planning exert more power and initiative in making decisions about their own affairs. The tax system also favors the locals, whose financial power threatens to surpass the central government's in the late 1990s. Thus, local authorities had a strong interest in the continuation of the open door and reform policies and in keeping the Beijing's paws out of their territories.[14]

---

[14] *Dangdai zhongguo yanjiu* (Total No. 46 & 47, 1995); Chien-min Chao, *op. cit.* For a more recent and focused case study on the Chinese county government, see Marc Blecher and Vivienne Shue, *Tethered Deer: Government and Economy in a Chinese County* (Stanford University Press, 1996).

- THE LEFTISTS. The orthodox Marxists, or leftists, whose golden days during Mao's era have passed, still hold onto the communist apparatus. Though their power in policy making was restricted during Deng's reign, their influence in the ideology remains strong. In the post-Deng era, they would like to represent those who are victimized by market reforms. They use the problems of reform as a rallying mechanism to resist what they call "the capitalist take-over of China." Their appeal to the distraught state-sector workers and to the impoverished rural population was reported in the western media, but their weakness is that no one, even among the disadvantaged population, would like to return to the Maoist era when state control and repression were prevalent.[15]

- THE STATE-SECTOR WORKERS. They occupy the majority of the urban population in China. The inefficiency of the state sector and an unequal tax structure have made most of the state enterprises unsustainable. With the state budget further constrained and state subsidies dwindling, their fate is sealed. Between bankruptcy and further privatization, these enterprises have relatively few choices. But the workers in those failing enterprises, long envied for their job security and state benefits, have seen their "iron rice bowl" (*tie fan wan*) being smashed by the onslaught of market competition. The unemployment and under-employment among the state workers creates high tension in Chinese society. Their plight puts pressure on market reform, but raises popular demand for political reform, which would ensure their political and economic rights. Social injustice and corruption tend to be the focal point of their grievances.[16]

---

[15] Drew Liu, "The Emergence of the Ultra-Left in Post-Deng China," *China Strategic Review*, Vol. 2, No. 2 (March/April, 1997), 41-56.

[16] Ye Zhangmei, "*Dalu guoyou qiye de gaige yu kunjing*" (reforms and difficulties of state-owned enterprises on the Chinese mainland),

- PEASANTS AND FARMERS. The economic reforms have raised the living standard considerably for most people. But a large disparity has appeared between different regions and between the rich and the poor. Corruption has taken a heavy toll on the disadvantaged, leading to widespread grievances against local officials and about privileges enjoyed by urban residents. The system of residence registration (*hukou zhidu*) and the state-enforced one-child policy are also flash points.[17]

- THE MILITARY. This is the group that has suffered the most severely in terms of social status during the reform era. In Mao's era, most political and economic resources went into this sector, upon whose support Mao's power became predominant. During the Cultural Revolution, the army was dispatched to civilian quarters to take control of the entire country. But in Deng's era, the military sector was forced to stand on the side, while economic development took center stage. Deng's foreign policy was based on the assumption that peace and development are the major themes of the world. But the military skillfully used the Tiananmen crisis (1989) and the Taiwan issue to get back to the center stage of policy-making. The military's chief concern is maintaining territorial integrity and preventing social disintegration, a task that entails the rapid modernization of Chinese defense forces.[18]

Zhongguo dalu yanjiu (mainland China studies), Vol. 40, No. 3 (March 1997), 66-82.

[17] The dynamics of rural change is well-documented in Kate Xiao Zhou, *How the Farmers Changed China: Power of the People* (Westview Press, 1996). For a brief overview of rural grassroots elections, see X. Drew Liu, "A Harbinger of Democracy: Grassroots Elections in Rural China," *The China Strategic Review*, Vol. 2, No. 3 (Many/June, 1997), 50-75. As for the rural problems, a piece is published in the same issue of the *CSR* analyzing the major grievances of Chinese farmers.

[18] For an overview on the PLA's position in the decision-making process, see Carol Lee Hamrin and Suisheng Zhao, *op. cit.*; and Harlan W. Jencks,

- THE OFFICIALS/BUREAUCRATS. They work in different branches of the Chinese government at all levels and have a serious problem of corruption. Market opportunities afford them new avenues to unaccountable personal wealth and power, a fact deeply resented by the Chinese public. In general, the Chinese officials have formed a close alliance with the new merchant class, and some of them have turned into official-entrepreneurs. Because of their vested interests, they generally support continued economic liberalization, but take a very conservative stand on labor and political reform.[19]

- THE REFORMERS AND LIBERAL INTELLECTUALS. Not entirely free from corruption, they tend to differentiate themselves from corrupt officials by taking more liberal attitudes towards political reform. Their interests are not in maintaining the status quo, but in progressing with reform so as to overcome the contradictions in the current socio-economic system. But

---

"The Party and the PLA in 1990-91" in Bih-jaw Lin and James T. Myers, eds., *Forces for Change in Contemporary China* (University of South Carolina Press, 1993). The PLA missile test near Taiwan in March 1996 was widely regarded as an indicator that the PLA had strengthened its hand in the regime's policy-making process. For this, see Cai Wei, "*Zhonggong dui tai zhengce de juece zuzhi yu guocheng*" (Beijing's Taiwan policy: the decision-making structure and process), *Zhongguo dalu yanjiu* (mainland China studies), Vol. 40, No. 5 (May 1997), 36-58; in the English language, the book edited by Michael Pillsbury contains valuable and up-to-date data about the new generation of PLA generals, their vision and strategic thinking for the future; see Michael Pillsbury, ed., *Chinese Views of Future Warfare* (Washington, DC: National Defense University Press, 1997).

[19] The officials/bureaucrats have formed in their respective jurisdictions well-coordinated networks that serve the interests of their members. See Wei Ding, *op. cit.*; Lu Jing, "*Zhong gong jiguan dang zuzhi zhuangkuang fenxi*" (PRC officials and party organizations), *Zhong gong yanjiu* (studies on Chinese communism), Vol. 31, No. 2 (February 1997), 37-50; also Marc Blecher and Vivienne Shue, *op. cit.*

they are deeply divided in policy options coupling economic and political reforms. Some are more conservative than others. They do share a common ground in their belief that China cannot turn back to the old communist system, and that democracy (however it is defined and however remote it may appear) is an inevitable result of China's modernization.[20]

• ENTREPRENEURS IN THE PRIVATE SECTOR. The rise of the private sector is the major force in China's economic growth. Politically, it is regarded as the arena where a middle class will emerge in time. Though the private entrepreneurs have not grown powerful enough to present their own political voice, their pervasiveness in the Chinese economic scene makes them a vital force. They have formed intricate networks and alliances among themselves and with corrupt officials for the benefit of mutual interests.[21]

It should be stressed that the above categorization only serves analytical purposes. A static view would risk over-simplifying the fluidity of these groups' boundaries, not to mention their interrelatedness on some issues. However, the macro-mapping of these interests will have an inevitable and

---

[20] Of course, I do not think this is a cohesive and uniform group in the regime. Rather, my argument for lumping them together is based on the fact that they have a high vested interest in continuing to push reforms forward and in opposing a return to the orthodox communist system, thus, among them, some are more conservative than others. For the more conservative end, see Youzhuo Li, "Will Neo-Conservatism Dominate Post-Deng China?", *The China Strategic Review*, Vol. 2, No. 2 (March/April, 1997), 31-40; as for the more liberal views by intellectuals and policy researchers inside China, they frequently appear in the journals of *Du shu* (reading), a monthly published in Beijing, and *Er shi yi shiji* (the twenty-first century), a bi-monthly published in Hong Kong.

[21] Xueye Yang, *Zhongguo fuxing de dongli: siying jingji ruhe zaisheng zhuangda* (capitalizing communism: the rise of private economy in China) (Hong Kong: Mingjing, forthcoming).

profound impact on the formation and processes of factional infighting in elite Chinese circles.

The Restructuring of the Post-Deng Factions Is Inevitable[22]

The reality in China today is that negative aspects of Deng's reforms and open door policy, such as serious corruption, social injustice, income disparity, unemployment (especially in the state sector), regional differences, losses in state-run enterprises, moral decline, growing crime rates, and failures in the banking industry, have generated heated debates in general and within the party specifically. This will have a profound impact on the restructuring of elite factions.

Some factions think the reforms have proceeded too fast, while others think they have gone too slowly. But most are unsatisfied with the status quo. This general mood of discontent provides those within the party who are not satisfied with Jiang Zemin with enough reasons and opportunities to challenge his authority after Deng. Both the conservative and liberal wings of the Chinese Communist Party are readying themselves to challenge the status quo. Such a challenge would encompass both policy issues and power distribution among the factions.

The political struggle for power in the Fifteenth Congress began even before Deng passed away, but it was mostly covert. Deng died more than half a year before the party congress scheduled for the fall of 1997, and personnel matters were not yet decided. Therefore, there was plenty of time for factions to shape the coming party congress and the personnel re-arrangement, reflecting any shifts of power inside the party.

However, the consensus among the top party leaders was that, for the first half of 1997, the central task of the CCP was

---

[22] Unless otherwise cited, the sources of the data used heretofore in this paper are provided by a number of CSI research associates from China. The author made his best effort to judge the data and use caution with them.

to prepare for the return of Hong Kong and insure a smooth handover on July 1. If the political struggles within the party had affected the handover, the CCP elite would have been viewed as national criminals by the Chinese public. Any group that initiated an open political challenge during this sensitive time would have been sanctioned by all the others. Under such circumstances, all political struggle was restrained.

In fact, even after the handover, whoever initiated the political struggle would have taken the risk of appearing to "damage party unity." As a result, the power struggle within the party remains covert and restrained, as no one wants to face inevitable political failure. The subtlety and delicacy of the political situation in Beijing favored the incumbent leadership structure headed by Jiang Zemin, but this delicate situation crashed with two developments in late July 1997. One was the crisis with state-sector workers whose public protests endangered China's stability. The other was the convening of party elite at Beidaihe, the seaside resort town, when policy and personnel matters entered into substantive debate. This meeting is the symbolic occasion for factional showdowns, the results of which determine the new structure for the factional make-up at the Fifteenth Party Congress.

As a result of these circumstances, the Fifteenth Party Congress will be a watershed event for the post-Deng factions, and, moreover, a restructuring of the elite factions seems inevitable. But to me, the more important question remains to be: To what extent will this new round of power struggle compound the political needs of the emerging interest groups? Or will it reflect the recent changes of the larger structure that are rapidly unfolding in China?

Jiang Zemin and the New Generation of Leadership

According to Deng's personnel arrangement of the last eight years, Jiang Zemin is at the core of the collective leadership of the third generation. This was clearly a compromise enforced by the crisis in 1989. The design of a "core" and "collective" was aimed at maintaining leadership stability. The "core" functioned as a public relations image for the world as well as the Chinese population to see; the implication being that, if there is one in charge, then constant speculations about the government leadership will be prevented. The "collective," on the other hand, was an internal arrangement to ensure the sharing of power among the third generation of leaders.

When Deng was alive, even if many leaders were not satisfied with the arrangement, they could not alter his decision or challenge his authority. Thus, there were no major changes in the personnel structure of the leadership during the Fourteenth Congress. The death of Deng made it possible for the leftists and the liberals to demand more power-sharing, although it is hard to say what their chances were for success in this endeavor. The alliance of Jiang Zemin and Li Peng was created on the basis of a shared sense of threat to the CCP political leadership from liberal forces within or outside the party system, because these forces, if united, will be very powerful and could easily win support from the West as well as the Chinese public.

Since the June Fourth Massacre of 1989, the regime has done its utmost in suppressing liberals and the democracy movement, marginalizing or forcing into silence those officials who are sympathetic to the students' cause. Leaders, such as Zhao Ziyang and Wan Li, were actually responsible for enforcing reforms and the open door policy and are strong supporters of Deng's policy line. Like Deng, they favor faster and more aggressive reform measures and are not satisfied with the conservative posturing of Jiang Zemin. Although silenced publicly, within the party apparatus, they can exert more powerful influence than the leftists and the Jiang Zemin faction can. The source of their power comes from the vested interests growing out of Deng's reform policies.

The local governments would like to maintain the status quo, in which they have the leverage to bargain against the center. The general policy they desire is the further softening of restrictions imposed by the center. Economic power at the local levels will turn into political power against the central government if the interests of the local government are seriously undermined.

Ironically, even the managerial class in the state enterprises would oppose any change of policy direction, in spite of the plight of this sector. Unlike the workers, they do not fear impending unemployment or loss of benefits. On the one hand, they use the workers' plight to gain political loans from the state, but on the other hand, they continue to expand their independence from the state in the name of reversing losses. Now they are ironically getting the benefits of both ends.

At present, these vested interests appear to be somewhat inactive, waiting to see what Jiang will do. With a strong internal network, a cooperative challenge from these interests is strong enough to overthrow Jiang Zemin if he is unable to satisfy them. Moreover, Jiang has a number of weaknesses which make him vulnerable to attacks from both the leftist and liberal factions.

First Jiang, with the help of Deng Xiaoping, promoted his trusted followers in order to maintain control, but his basis of power in the party remains weak. Under the present circumstances, with the support of Deng Xiaoping, he has become the "legitimate" heir of Deng and the nominal head of the party, the executive branch, and the military branch. But in China, nominal power and real power are often not at all compatible. His nominal positions technically make him a political strongman like Deng Xiaoping. However, he is not even close to holding the real power status of Deng. In fact, it is still unclear whether Jiang's leadership is taken seriously by the remaining old guard and the elite circles of the younger generation. A major reason people do not listen to him is the lack of any significant achievement since his inauguration as Party General Secretary eight years ago.

Up to now, Jiang has done nothing in the reform and open door process that can be considered his own remarkable success. In addition, while Deng was on his tour of southern China in 1992, he openly criticized Jiang Zemin and Li Peng in his speeches. Deng thought that Jiang and Li had brought reform and the open door policy to a halt and he had to take this non-institutional way to push Jiang and Li to continue reforms. These speeches exposed the public to the divergence between Jiang and Deng in the handling of reform and shaped a conservative image for Jiang Zemin. For all of Jiang's expressed support for reform, it is very difficult for Jiang to change this conservative image, something that downsizes his leadership capacity within the elite circles.

Another source of weakness can be found in Jiang's relationship with the Chinese military. An important factor of every CCP leader's power base has been support from the Chinese military. Mao Zedong and Deng Xiaoping both commanded the CCP's military forces and were successful and popular commanders. In contrast, Jiang has neither held a leadership position in the military nor had any war experience or personal ties within the military. Therefore, although he is legally the commander in chief, he cannot command or control the military as Deng did. His actual influence in the military is only nominal.

In short, the death of Deng left a more or less level playing field on which potential leaders of China compete with one another to appease the interest groups that have emerged as the result of Deng's reform process. Though Jiang occupies a more favorable position than his competitors, his power is far from being consolidated. The left can still challenge Jiang on issues concerning the erosion of the party monopoly on power, the crisis of state-owned enterprises, unemployment, and other problems in China. However, if Jiang does too much to appease the leftists, the reform-minded wings with vested interests of reform policies can threaten Jiang with their strong power base. In the power play in Beijing, in order to secure his leadership position Jiang has to change his conservative image and cement his relationship with the military.

Attacks Left and Right after Deng's Death

In these circumstances, it is almost inevitable that the leftists will utilize the plight of the workers and popular resentment of social injustice to advance their position. Since the death of Deng, the leftists within the party launched the first attacks on Jiang's authority. Though leftists within the party are in a weak position to impact the policy-making process, they have considerable influence in society and within the party as a result of their control over many propaganda instruments and the media. With such social clout, if the left won the support of the unemployed workers, the political situation could become very volatile.

The political struggle among the factions actually began as an intellectual debate. In 1996, Liu Ji edited a book entitled *Talk with the General Secretary*. In February 1997, the pro-left journal *Middle Stream* published an article by Hong Yuxing entitled "What Kind of Book Is This?", attacking the book and criticizing its presentation of guiding principles opposite of the resolutions of the sixth session of the party congress.[23] The article also indirectly criticized Liu Ji, the vice-president of the Chinese Academy of Social Sciences, for supporting such a problematic book.[24]

There have been other similar events, such as the so-called third "*Wan yan shu*" (ten-thousand-word letter) entitled "Several Theoretical and Policy Issues Concerning the Dominant Status of State Ownership" published in the name of the special commentator of *Current Thought*. Another was

---

[23] The journal *Middle Stream* emerged after the June Fourth Incident, providing the theoretical grounds for the extreme left within the party who opposed reforms and the open door policy. Ironically, people paid more attention to the criticism of *Talk with the General Secretary* than to the book itself. The incident indicated the beginning of the open political power struggle among factions for dominance in the post-Deng era.

[24] For a more detailed review of the incident, see Xiaoxian Zhang, "The Ultra-leftists' First Move after Deng: the Internal Power Struggle surrounding the Book *Talking With the General Secretary*," *The China Strategic Review*, Vol. 2, No. 3 (May/June, 1997), 87-96.

a series of critiques of the book, *Talk with the General Secretary*, published in the third and fourth issues of the 1997 edition of the *Pursuit of Truth*, another pro-left journal. These articles openly criticized Liu Ji and the party secretary Li Youwei. The fifth issue continued the attack against Li Youwei.[25]

In addition to the fierce conflict between the leftists and the liberal-leaning incumbent leaders, there are also unreported conflicts between the liberal faction and conservative-leaning incumbent leaders. This conflict was first reflected in the effort to overthrow Ding Guan'gen, initiated by the liberal camp.

Ding Guan'gen is the representative of the conservative incumbents in the party and the orthodox ideology of the CCP. He has been in charge of political propaganda in the party since 1992. After Deng's well-reported tour in the South in the spring of 1992, the political guidelines for the Chinese Communist Party have been to continue economic reform in order to achieve rapid economic growth. This indirectly promoted the expansion of civil liberties for many common people, and the intellectuals also began to push the envelope again for more freedom in research and publication.

However, from 1995 to 1996, under Ding's management, the CCP agencies in charge of ideology suddenly tightened control over politics, the press, academic research, publication, and ideology. At the end of 1996 and the beginning of 1997, the tightened ideological control led to the massive censorship of newspapers, journals, and periodicals. The intellectuals were very discontent with such tightened controls. They regarded Ding as a major conservative among the CCP leaders in office, and feared that the conservative forces in power might reverse the general trend towards greater reform and openness.

---

[25] The surfacing of these papers was reported in the western press, but more comprehensive coverage, including the actual texts of these papers, appeared in several of Hong Kong's journals. See related reports in *Kai fang* (the open magazine), *Zheng ming* (*Cheng Ming* monthly) and *Qian shao* (the front-line magazine) from March through July.

In fact, Ding Guan'gen has followed the orders of Jiang Zemin and Li Peng, who reportedly will promote Ding's standing in the party hierarchy further in the coming Fifteenth Party Congress. But for the liberal wing in the party, this is too much. The liberal wing of the CCP has formed an alliance with the liberal intellectuals outside the party system, and has launched an attack on Ding personally to prevent him from gaining more power in the party system.[26]

Because the participants in the "Down with Ding" campaign are primarily famous veteran intellectuals in the party and some liberal political figures that do not hold an office, this campaign has strongly influenced the party and intellectuals. The campaign also reflects the strong discontent of the liberals in the party and intellectuals regarding the tightened control over politics and ideology. The reality of intellectual freedom, not the historical background of a politician, is the true issue here.

These political attacks from both the left and the right have generated political pressures that have forced Jiang to reveal his political line. If Jiang refused to counter-attack the leftists, the reform-minded leaders in the party would think that Jiang was moving to the left and going to change Deng's reform and open door policy, which would push the incumbent reformers and non-incumbent liberal intellectuals and party elements to form an alliance to resist his conservative turn. To circumvent such difficulties, Jiang broke his silence on his policy preferences after Deng's death and struck back on the attack from the left when he gave a

---

[26] The excuse for attacking Ding seems to be trivial. It starts from digging up Ding's past. Some presented the proof that Ding used to be a member of the "Three Youth League," the major youth organization controlled by KMT before it withdrew to Taiwan. In the 1940s, Ding reportedly once represented the KMT in negotiations with the CCP-led student organization. Later, of course, he joined the communist party, but hid this part of his background. With this problematic history, such a person is not qualified to be a top leader in the CCP. Related reports also appeared in the Hong Kong media's, See, among others, *Qian shao* (the front-line magazine) (July 1997), 14-15.

lengthy speech at the Party School on May 29, 1997. He reiterated Deng's reform and open door policy and stated that he supported further reforms. This is the first time Jiang openly parted paths with the leftists since his arrival in Beijing in 1989.[27]

The Fifteenth Party Congress

The death of Deng Xiaoping indicated the beginning of the re-adjustment of alliances among different political factions and forces of the party. For those incumbent leaders, the most important thing is to maintain their power and interests in the power re-distribution. They want the interests of their factions to be expressed in the coming Fifteenth Party Congress, not sacrificed. At present, the various factions in the offices within the party can be divided into the following groups:[28]

- the Shanghai faction, headed by Jiang Zemin and Zhu Rongji; the major players are Wu Bangguo, Huang Ju, and Xu Kuangdi;
- the bureaucracy of the State Council headed by Li Peng;
- the NPC and the legislative branch headed by Qiao Shi;
- the local-power faction headed by Li Ruihuan;
- the military;

---

[27] Jiang's earlier political shrewdness in cruising through the CCP system is documented; see He Ping, *Jiang Zemin de quanli zhi lu* (Jiang Zemin's road to power) (Hong Kong: Mingjing, 1977).

[28] Here I have excluded the new entrepreneurs from the private sector as a contending interest group because their role has been so pervasive and opportunistic in the system. Politically, they try to be very cautious and they stay connected with all the political forces/interests favoring continued reforms. Thus, they function more as lubricants in China's dense and complex network system while developing allies among official elements for individual business interests. Their quiet way of working in the system is documented. See Xueye Yang, *Zhongguo fuxing de dongli: siying jingji ruhe zaisheng zhuangda* (capitalizing communism: the rise of private economy in China) (Hong Kong: Mingjing, forthcoming).

- the liberals consisting of the pro-Zhao Ziyang group with Tian Jiyun as the key player;

Of these factions, the Shanghai gang holds the most advantageous position and faces the greatest challenges. Normally, Jiang would have no problem consolidating or enlarging his power in the Fifteenth Party Congress if he firmly adhered to Deng's reforms. The liberals and pro-Zhao Ziyang group, now allied with Qiao Shi, have been the rivals of Jiang Zemin. Thus, the first concern of Jiang Zemin is the threat of the reinstatement of Zhao Ziyang; Jiang has done his best to prevent this scenario from occurring by keeping an eye on the pro-Zhao group.

Strategy and Maneuvering

It should be reiterated that the post-Deng factions are still in the formative process and that the Fifteenth Party Congress will be a watershed event for their .restructuring and reorganizing, hence the long-term impact on China's political development. The following is a preliminary assessment of the factional development based on the sketchy data that are available. There is no sense in assuming that the nature of the factions is clear-cut, because there is still significant uncertainty about their future development.

The faction headed by Qiao Shi, while adhering to Deng's reform and open policy, is working hard to gain the support of the pro-reform veteran leaders such as Yang Shangkun, Wan Li, and Bo Yibo. If they succeed in doing so, they are likely to keep their power and position beyond the Fifteenth Congress. This group does not have big problems with the locals or the powerful military. Its chief enemy is Jiang Zemin's intention to keep it out of the central power structure. Their apparent alliance with the pro-Zhao group as represented by Tian Jiyun may strengthen their liberal image, but will also further strain their relationship with the Shanghai gang. Qiao Shi's personal leadership may be an important variable for the rise and fall of this faction. Qiao was recently rumored to be in poor health and lacking the will to lead.

The   local-power group is primarily headed by Li Ruihuan, a key figure in the coming Fifteenth Congress. It appears that Li will not find it difficult to retain the group's power because Jiang Zemin and the Shanghai gang will need his and his faction's support to consolidate their own power. However, the local power group will demand further reforms to strengthen local power and protect local interests after the Fifteenth Party Congress. If Jiang Zemin does not accept this condition, the local-power group will not support him in the power struggle.

The military faction most probably will be grasped by Zhang Wannian, a potential military strongman in China. He is now the vice-chairman of the Central Military Commission. The veterans Liu Huaqing and Zhang Zheng will retire but remain influential in the military. Recently, Jiang Zemin has been making efforts to secure his power in the military, and it seems that military supports him, although he does not have controlling power over the military. The competition between Zhang Wannian and Chi Haotian is an important variable and perhaps the biggest headache for Jiang Zemin. A blunder or a divided military brass will considerably weaken Jiang's hand in the military and his following within this group. But one thing is certain. The military will have increasing influence on the policy of the party after the Fifteenth Party Congress.

The bureaucracy of the state council headed by Li Peng is very likely to lose its power in the Fifteenth Party Congress. The major reason for this loss is that Li Peng's term will expire next year. According to the Chinese Constitution, he may not be re-elected to the position of premier. He must turnover his position to the new premier in the session of the National People's Congress next spring. The personnel arrangement in the State Council made by Li Peng will greatly change after Li leaves his position.   The new premier will make a new personnel arrangement in the State Council according to his own plan. Even though Li Peng can keep a high position in the party, he cannot interfere with the new arrangement. Of course, Li will re-arrange his followers and demand that the new premier keep many people in their positions in the State Council. Regardless, it is most likely that Li's faction will lose its power either during or after the Fifteenth Party Congress. But if Qiao Shi steps down from the chairmanship of the NPC, Li may make a comeback by replacing him.

The pro-Zhao Ziyang group is the major force against which Jiang Zemin is on guard. If the pro-Zhao faction is able to align with the local power groups and the liberals as well as win the support of the veterans of the party, they will be able to hold on to their future potential to make a comeback. Otherwise, they will lose their influence.

Considering the current the political situation and political forces within the party, it is very likely that various factions of the party will be able to retain some power-sharing, for this outcome will ensure the world and the Chinese people of political stability and the perpetuation of Deng's reform policies. The changes most likely to occur are in Li Peng's faction and the pro-Zhao Ziyang faction. These two groups will probably lose power, although they will reject this reality and continue to struggle to retain their political power and influence. The only chance for the survival of the pro-Zhao group is a renewed alliance with the pro-Hu Yaobang group.[29]

Because Qiao Shi and Hu Jintao, who have past connections with the pro-Hu Yaobang Communist League, are still members of the Standing Committee of the CCP Central

---

[29] After 1986 when Hu was deprived of his position, the pro-Hu and pro-Zhao groups became rivals as the pro-Hu group accused Zhao of attacking Hu from behind at a crucial moment. Now, however, the pro-Hu groups connected with the Central Communist league are very young and still in office. They have considerable political influence. The power basis of Jiang Zemin within the party apparatus is said to be not even close to that of the pro-Hu group. Therefore, after Jiang came to power, he gradually enrolled some pro-Hu leaders and promoted pro-Hu leaders and to suppress the pro-Zhao group. Every faction desires the support of the pro-Hu group.

Committee, it is crucial for Jiang to win their support if he wishes to consolidate his own power and prevent Zhao's reinstatement. Under such circumstances, the coming Fifteenth Party Congress presents opportunities for the pro-Hu group to further expand its influence.

The Era of the Shanghai Gang?

The factions most likely to increase their power are the Shanghai gang, the local-power group, and the military. The Shanghai gang, as the most powerful of all the factions, holds the most advantageous position in the power struggle of the party congress because of Jiang Zemin's position. If a person from the Shanghai gang becomes premier, the Shanghai gang and its business interests will control Chinese politics. At that time, the Shanghai gang can control both the party system and the government.

Other factions will make efforts to prevent the ascendance of the Shanghai gang by endorsing someone from another faction for the position of premier. However, despite the resistance from other factions, it is very likely that someone from the Shanghai gang will be the next premier. At present, the most appealing and likely candidate is Zhu Rongji. Whether Zhu can finally grasp the premier position is dependent on the degree to which the local-power group supports him. For many years, Zhu has been the economic czar of China and has enlarged the government's central authority at the expense of local interests and powers. The policy based on the interests of the center and Shanghai has generated a great deal of discontent with him among local leaders. Recently, Zhu made efforts to appease those local interests and has given them preferential treatment regarding state policy in an attempt to win support in his bid for the position of premier.[30] In short, the Shanghai gang has had no

---

[30] Zhu reportedly gave a speech to this effect on May 20, 1997 at Qing Hua University.

problem enlarging its power. The question is to what degree it can continue to do so.

The Rise of Local Powers

The local-power group is a strong force within the party. It claims the support of the liberals within the party. With the progressing economic reform in China, local autonomy is increasing. The power base of the local officials has been greatly enlarged.[31] However, the rise of local power has not reached the extent that local leaders dare to act independently of central policy. The central government still has effective control over the localities. For instance, the center can still override the local officials by sending their own officials to localities. However, local power is expanding, particularly in some of the provinces with rapid economic development, raising the significance of local interests.[32]

Considering the economic development in China, the continued shift of power from the center to the localities is one condition for sustained economic growth. Otherwise, there is no local incentive. In order to increase local power, it is necessary to appoint some leaders with local backgrounds as key members of the central government in the Fifteenth Party Congress. It is necessary to appoint leaders who have experience in local work as vice-premiers and to other key positions. The primary representative of the local-power group in the central government is Li Ruihuan. Considering the imperative of maintaining political stability after Deng, the

---

[31] The locals are especially noted for their growing financial power relative to the center; see Xiaozhu Liu, "*Cong zhongguo dalu caizheng tizhi de yanbian kan zhuhou jingji de xingcheng*" (the emergence of the fief economy based on the evolution of China's budgetary system), *Zhongguo dalu* (mainland China monthly), Vol. 25, No. 7 (September 1992),53-56; and Ma Jun, "*Zhongyang yu difang caizheng guanxi de gaige*" (fiscal reform on the center-local relationship), *Dangdai zhongguo yanjiu* (modern China studies), Total No. 46 & 47 (No. 1 & 2, 1995), 118-133.

[32] *Dangdai zhongguo yanjiu* (Total No. 46 & 47, 1995); Chien-min Chao, *op. cit.* (1993), 158-170; and Marc Blecher and Vivienne Shue, *op. cit.*

Fifteenth Party Congress presents a good opportunity for the local-power group to increase its influence.

Their power enlargement will be reflected in two aspects. One is that the policies made in the party congress will embody local interests. The other is that the appointment of personnel will take local leaders into consideration. The party or government leaders originally from localities, such as Zhao Ziyang, are more likely to consider local interests when making policies, while the leaders without any local background, such as Li Peng, will focus on central interests. The local power group wants one of its representatives to be the next premier, but if it cannot achieve this it will arrange to support someone who cares about local interests to be the new premier.

The Ambition of the Military

Now that Deng Xiaoping has died, Jiang must win the support of the military if he wants to consolidate his power status. In return, the military can take advantage of this opportunity to expand its political power and influence. Because most current political leaders have no past relations with the military, they will be very careful to avoid interfering in military affairs. Jiang Zemin, as the chairman of the Central Military Commission, is the only leader who can interact with the military with nominal authority. This is a political advantage that other leaders do not have. But if Jiang wants to use the military to raise his own political power status, he must raise the political status of the military in return.

Because reform in China causes many problems and because society is already unstable, the military must continue to be the last resort for the consolidation of the CCP regime. The expansion of the military's political power can be realized by absorbing more military officers into the CCP Central Committee, assigning more military officers to be top CCP leaders, and enrolling more people with military backgrounds in the civil government and party affairs.

Conclusion: The Role of Chinese Democrats

As long as there are political struggles within the CCP, the division of the party into factions is inevitable. Because of the lack of transparency in the CCP's system, these struggles are often hidden by political subterfuge. With the coming of the Fifteenth Party Congress, the intensity and complexity of these struggles are likely to increase because of the changing political and social context developed after Deng's death. The emerging interest groups will pull the CCP factions in different directions. The alliances between the Chinese interest groups and CCP factions will undoubtedly accelerate the disintegration of the CCP regime, paving the way for instituting democratic mechanisms (e.g., checks and balances, division of government) in China's political system.

The recent reforms, particularly those that unfolded in 1996 and 1997 in the state sector, have placed China at a crossroads in terms of its political evolution. If such reforms are a success, the primary economic forces in China will be subject to market forces, no longer to be directed by the party. The so-called working class will be fragmented and will no longer belong to the state, but rather to domestic and foreign capital. As a result, they will not listen to the party.

The rising entrepreneurial class will be able to dominate the Chinese economy and gradually will be able to phase out the party-state ownership structure. This outcome is by no means acceptable to the leftists of the party, of course. For them, such an outcome means the annihilation of the CCP and all it stands for. This may well be the case, but it does not naturally imply the arrival of democracy.

For the Chinese democrats, the road is still a long one. The evolution of internal party factions is a factor to bear in mind, but not a source for building democracy. Democracy has to be won by the people and is therefore only capable of success from the people's power. Under the current circumstances, the most under-represented populations within the party system are urban laborers and rural peasants. As the leftists further lose their grip on power, the Chinese democrats should step into the void and campaign for the ordinary men and women whose democratic rights so far have been denied by a regime that claims to represent their interests but has already been bought by China's nouveau riche.

QUESTIONING THE PROSPECT OF
POLITICAL REFORM IN CHINA
China Strategic Review, Vol.II, no.5 (September/October 1997)

After the death of Deng Xiaoping in February of this year, the call for political reforms from the Chinese Communist Party (CCP) suddenly grew resonant among Chinese liberal intellectuals and policy circles. However, the intentions of the party leaders in this regard were unclear. At first, Jiang Zemin raised the issue of political reform during the memorial service for Deng. Then, Jiang discussed political reform again on May 29 in his speech to the Central Party School. The Chinese leaders Qiao Shi and Li Ruihuan also championed political reforms on different occasions, discussing at least nominally the development of democracy in China.

These references made by the Chinese leaders found their way to the foreign press. Western scholars and media began to note possible reform measures to promote democracy in China, giving considerable credit to the grass-roots elections in China. However, people both inside and outside China were uncertain about what kind of political reform program the CCP leaders actually desired to undertake and waited impatiently to learn the answer from the Fifteenth Party Congress.

Political Reform or Political "Muddling Through?"

If the Chinese leadership is sincere in pushing for political reform that may end many of the ills, such as corruption, of the governmental system, we would expect them to have a vision and a comprehensive program that would embrace this vision. But both were absent in the CCP Congress in spite of the promises made by Jiang himself on a number of occasions after Deng's death.

However, the pressures for political reform exist both inside and outside the Chinese governing system, both from the liberal   sectors and the international community. These pressures account for the fact that political reform as a state policy made some advancements during the Fifteenth Congress of the CCP. The increasing number of elections at basic levels has strong support from local communities in rural areas. The CCP apparatus has more or less lost control of its grassroots branches in the rural areas due to the dysfunction of these grassroots organizations. However, rural grassroots elections do not present an immediate threat to the power of the central CCP elite. On the contrary, these elections will help maintain local order and general social stability, which is a high priority on the agenda of the CCP leadership.

The revision of the Civil Prosecution Procedure Law is now moving towards greater compatibility with western legal systems. These are reforms of profound and far-reaching effect, even though they may not change the behavior of the system in the short run. They add to the Chinese efforts to build a system of government based on the rule of law, which will mean an increase in civil liberties in China. The role of the National People's Congress at both the central and local levels has expanded. The legislative and oversight functions of the NPC have especially been enhanced. This reflects the growing demand for power-sharing by local and various other interest groups in China. The CCP regime, however, is too rigid and much too controlled by the center to allow these interest groups to participate in policy-making processes, but the NPC may provide an avenue for localities and interest groups to advance their own interests in policy matters.

With regard to current issues of popular concern, such as an institutional design for popular political participation, the establishment of a system of government that responds to the need for public services, and an effective check on corruption, there was little or no progress during the CCP Congress. Without new initiatives in these areas, the future of political reform is not very optimistic.

However, the progress of economic reform in China makes political reform an urgent issue. Without further political reform, the current political problems of rampant corruption, popular discontent, a lack of transparency and accountability, social injustice, and the official abuse of power, will continue to develop and multiply, creating a bottleneck for future economic reform.

It was hoped that the Fifteenth Party Congress would specify a long-term plan to promote substantial political reform in China, which would ultimately lead to the democratization of China. Jiang Zemin's work report at the Fifteenth Party Congress included an individual chapter on political reform. However, upon careful examination, this chapter is simply a summarization of old clichés of related rhetoric. Compared with Jiang's explanation of Deng's economic reforms, the chapter on political reform is very unimpressive. However, this important document may set the tone for the lagging or lack of the regime's political reform for the time being.

Indeed, all the so-called political reform measures proposed at the Fifteenth Party Congress originated in earlier economic reforms, barely able to take on the fundamental communist political system.[33] These measures focus on the restructuring of bureaucratic organizations and the strengthening of the role of the National People's Congress on the condition that CCP's monopoly on political power is not affected. Other reform measures reiterated for the occasion included adopting a cooperative system of multiple democratic parties, which really has no meaning for moving

---

[33] The main goals for CCP political reform were spelt out as:
To develop democracy with Chinese characteristics
Enhance the legal system
Enforce the separation of government and enterprise
Reduce and simplify bureaucracy
Perfect democratic monitoring systems
Maintain stability and unity.
  These goals are more abstract than being capable of producing specific policy measures to reform the system. Without specific measures, the CCP Congress affirmed political reform nominally, but failed to give it substantive meaning.

towards a multi-party system. The only significant step to reforming the system is the formal commitment to undertaking free elections at grass-roots levels. But this is an ad hoc recognition of local development rather than an initiative by the center.

The bottom line advanced at the Fifteenth Party Congress is that political reform must be able to strengthen the vigor of the CCP-controlled government, which is the cornerstone of the Chinese socialist political system. Under such an arrangement, the CCP aims to maintain the one party rule, to increase its legitimacy and social stability, and to motivate the people to produce more and better goods.

Uncertain Political Future

According to the party's proposed plans for political reform, the Chinese Communist Party is not likely to make significant progress in the near future. The proposed political reform represents a compromise between the conservatives and reformers within the party, and therefore has little substantive merit.

Lacking a basic framework, any progress in political reform at the present stage is at best the result of the balance of power among various forces and factions in China. Qiao Shi's presence as a Standing Committee member and chairman of the National People's Congress was a significant political check and a necessary precondition for the emergence of an institutionalized system of checks and balances in the future. His retirement will adversely affect a driving force among the elite circles to build Chinese rule of law, which would be one important aspect of political reforms in China. The usurpation of Qiao Shi's position by Li Peng annuls this precondition. It remains to be seen whether Tian Jiyun, NPC's vice president, and Wei Jianxing will be able to aggressively push for the rule of law.

If small factions in the party want to have their voices heard in a more open political system, they must form a coalition and ally themselves with the local powers.

Unfortunately, this is very difficult at present. As a result, the future of political reform in China is plagued with many difficulties, especially in its top-down style. The reformers have the upper hand in economic reform, but have failed to make any breakthroughs in political reform. The general trend of policy after the Fifteenth Party Congress will be a dual-track policy: loosening economic controls but tightening political controls.

Because the Jiang-Li faction survived the Fifteenth Party Congress and achieved dominant control of the regime, the policy of the Chinese party and government after the Fifteenth Party Congress will follow the path set by Jiang and Li at the Fourteenth Party Congress. Ideological control will be tightened and political dissidents will continue to be prosecuted. Free deliberations and democratic decision making will continue to be suppressed. China's entire political scene will remain oppressive. The political reforms themselves will continue to concentrate on the reform of the administrative system and adjusting administrative organizations.

Thus, after the Fifteenth Party Congress, the basic policy of the Jiang-Li regime will be to further broaden and deepen economic reforms but take a very conservative position on political reform. But a point will be reached when the regime can no longer sustain the increasing disparity between polity and economy. Then true political reform will be forced onto the agenda of the Chinese leadership.

A HARBINGER OF DEMOCRACY:
GRASSROOT ELECTIONS IN RURAL CHINA
China Strategic Review, Vol.II, no.3 (May/June 1997)

As with economic reform, China's efforts in reforming its political institutions were initiated first in the rural areas. They originated in the early 1980s as a spontaneous creation of the peasants, only to be adopted by the regime later. Though its development has been uneven in China, the introduction of the direct election of village-level officials since 1988 represents a major institutional break-through. In Guangdong and Yunnan Provinces, for instance, such elections have not been formally adopted at all. But in other areas, there are in total 931,716 elected village committees (*cunmin weiyuanhui*) and four million elected village officials. All of which are elected by the direct ballots of 600 million peasants.

There is no doubt that the scale and scope of these grassroots elections have entered a threshold, and their impact on China's general political development in the post-Deng era should not be underestimated. This article stands as a preliminary attempt to make sense of China's political development, first briefly analyzing the political, social, and economic conditions in the late 1980s that may have accounted for the emergence of the rural grassroots elections. The evolutionary process of the rural elections in the last ten years will be reviewed noting its major characteristics. The article concludes with a summary of the general implications that these elections hold for China's democratization processes in the post-Deng era.

Political Origins

It took enormous efforts to establish a legal system for village elections and years to put them into practice, but, despite all the hardships and obstacles, the achievements of the past ten years are quite significant. One might wonder how and why this step toward democracy in China was taken in the first place. How, in a society dominated by the communist party, can such political reform be successfully implemented in the rural areas?

The answer lies partly in the general direction of politics in China since the Cultural Revolution. In fact, beyond the rural villages, China as a whole has gradually begun to build democratic and legal systems. The change comes from both the Chinese elite and the public's rethinking decades of PRC history. The Chinese public, having suffered most from the Maoist dictatorship, would not allow this kind of repressive control to be repeated in the Deng era. That repressive system brought China to the brink of economic collapse and social revolution in the late 1970s. In addition, Chinese intellectuals started to dismantle communism as both an ideology and social system. They have continued to do so systematically and comprehensively, even in the wake of political persecution after 1989.

The commune system of the 1960s devastated the population in the countryside. In villages, the old communist control mechanism of class differentiation could no longer function, and its intimidation effect was lost to the rural population. With the disintegration of the collective system, the CCP had to substitute another system in order to maintain basic order in the rural areas. In the 1980s, the CCP leadership attempted to revamp the party's control in the rural areas, but failed to achieve any results. Thus, with the old governing system gone, only the form of self-elected village committees proved to be acceptable to the rural population to handle matters of tax collection and grassroots law and order in the countryside.

As for the post-Mao Chinese leaders, many (including Deng Xiaoping himself) had suffered personally during the ten years of the Cultural Revolution, which they believe was caused by a political system characterized by the "rule of man" (*ren zhi*). To save the CCP's power and to ensure that there would not be another Cultural Revolution, they believed that China had to terminate the old rule of man and adopt rule of law (*fa zhi*).

The move to rule of laws is an indication of both the political will and forces within the communist system that would like to move China towards democracy. As in the former Soviet Union under Yeltsin, the kind of democratic forces also exist in the Chinese communist system in concurrence with economic reforms. To them, democratization is the only viable road for China's modernization. In this light, the village elections at grassroots levels were supported by many Chinese officials at various levels, though many did so for political purposes.

On November 24, 1987, the fifth session of the Sixth National Peoples' Congress (NPC) Standing Committee passed the *Organization Act for the Village Committees in the People's Republic of China*[34] with 113 "yes" votes, 1 "no," and 6 abstentions; the act going into effect on June 1, 1988. Since the first draft in 1984, it had taken four years and more than forty revisions to come into being as law. The birth of this act is the inevitable product of the social, political, and economic changes in China's rural areas in the reform era.

The Engine of Economic Reform

It is very difficult to explain the development of rural grassroots elections without looking at the great transformations caused by China's economic reforms in the villages. The economic reforms in the rural areas deeply transformed economic relations, social structure, and political relations, setting the economic, social, and political foundations for village elections. Some of these transformations are highlighted here.

- The system of rural family responsibility replaced the collective system, allowing peasants more of a voice in production and marketing processes. Now, they respond more and more to the market than to the

---

[34] *Zhonghua Renmin Gongheguo Cunmin Weiyuanhui zuzhi fa (shixing)*.

state's planning. As soon as they were given limited economic rights, they implemented a political system that would protect their newly gained economic rights. The village election system was in fact spontaneously instituted by peasants in many villages to guarantee that their economic rights would not be taken away by governmental officials.

- Rural families now have control over production and distribution. More complicated economic relations call for a new governing system to respond to these new challenges. In the past, the state controlled everything from production to distribution under a command economy. Peasants had to plead with officials for greater distribution from state and local governments. Now this system is reversed. State and local governments have to solicit taxes from peasants. While it is impossible for the state to restore the command economy, officials have to settle for a feasible system. The elected village committee is proving to be the only viable means for the government officials to collect taxes and regulate the new economic relationship between the state and peasants.

- Since 1978, the social structure in rural villages has gradually changed. Most obviously, the peasants live in a society where traveling and hunting for jobs is less restricted. In a sense, the strict residence registration system (*hukou zhidu*) was undermined by a rural population that searched for new employment opportunities in the booming coastal regions. New enterprises created by the peasants are growing rapidly throughout China. As a result, the new generation of rural youth can pursue many different professions instead of being tied to working in agriculture.

The transformations in villages also generated many new problems, such as social and financial instability and tense relations between the cadres and the masses. Different from their parents' generation, the peasants of the last ten years live in a more complex world where conflicting interests among different groups need to be balanced. The only way to solve these problems is to permit democratic grassroots participation. As the old form of governance no longer kept order, the villagers embraced the new democratic village committees to work for a negotiated order among the different interests in the community.

Early Development: 1988-89

Ten years has already past since the formal election of village committees began. However, in dealing with a vast rural area of 900 hundred million people, changes in the regulations of democratic elections were very unevenly implemented across different regions. From 1988 to the present, some provinces, such as Fujian, have already entered their fourth election terms, while another eighteen provinces, autonomous regions, and municipalities have finished their third round of elections. Last June, Guangxi and Hainan provinces abolished village work offices and switched to directly elected village committees for the first time. Only Guangdong and Yunnan maintain the old system without elections.

In the first phase (1988-1989), only a few provinces carried out legislation on village elections. In some provinces, the elections were widespread. After the *Organization Act for Village Committee* was promulgated, the Ministry of Civil Affairs also issued several memos on the act's implementation, calling for all provinces to study, advertise, and implement it. During this period, the provincial congresses in Fujian, Zhejiang, Gansu, Hubei, and Hunan respectively, passed the operational regulations on the implementation of the act in their provinces, detailing how to pursue the elections. These provinces are considered the pioneers in undertaking this reform through provincial legislation.

For example, on September 2, 1988, the Fujian province passed the regulation on the implementation of the act, and was the first province to do so. The election regulations included provisions that the head, the deputy-head, and other members of the village committee were to be directly elected by villagers over eighteen years old in a competitive and anonymous way. The preliminary candidates for the committee positions must be nominated with the concurrence of no less than five people. Then, the formal candidates can be selected according to the opinion of the majority of villagers. There must be at least one more candidate than there are positions to be elected. If the head of the committee cannot be determined after two rounds of elections, a one to one election is permitted in following elections.[35]

On November 28, 1988, Zhejiang province passed regulations on implementing the act mandating competitive elections. The candidate must be nominated with the concurrence of at least ten villagers or nominated by a group of villagers. The final candidates are decided according to the village's majority opinion and after deliberations and consultations. The list of candidates generated through the above process must be publicized five days ahead of the election day.[36]

In summary, the elections of village committees are generally competitive, and there should be one or two more candidates than there are positions to be elected. Candidates can be nominated jointly by villagers, a small group of villagers, or an election leading group. The final candidates are chosen through the process of deliberation and

---

[35] Zhongguo Minzhengbu Jiceng Zhengquansi (Bureau of grassroots governments of ministry of civil affairs) (eds), *Zhonghua Renmin Gongheguo Cunmin Weiyuanhui Youguan Fagui ji Ziliao Huibian* (Compilation of laws, regulations, and documents on village committees in PRC), Beijing, 1994, 23.
[36] *Ibid*, 25.

consultation then selected according to the opinions of the majority of villagers.

In 1988, a total of 1,093 villages were chosen as sites for experimental elections. In Hunan, the experiments first pursued in 343 villages spread through twenty-eight towns. Several months later, village elections were carried out experimentally in 200 towns and communes. Shandong and Henan provinces had detailed plans for the experimental elections. Based on these experiments, from the second half of 1988 to 1989, a total of fourteen provinces, autonomous regions, and municipalities undertook direct village elections in all their rural areas. In 1988, the local governments of Tieling City of Liaoning Provinces, Qingang County of Heilongjiang Province, and Xiangcheng County created rules for the village election campaign. The local government of Nanping City of Fujian Province also encouraged elections, although there were no consistent regulations for it.

Two Case Studies of Peasant Political Pressure

The passing of provincial regulations was one thing, but implementing them was quite another task because of the resistance of the local government officials. They did not like the competitive ballots, which took the selection of candidates out of their control. They preferred the elections to be a matter of show with the candidates still assigned by the party. Thus, the early local competitive ballots were adopted as a result of bottom-up pressure from the peasants. Here, two cases describe the initial peasant reactions to the new law as well as the common act of seizing political opportunity to demand democratic rights.[37] Their enthusiasm in embracing the elections surprised many officials and fueled the rapid spread of elections in the rural areas.

---

[37]Both cases are taken from the book published by Zhongguo shehui chubanshe, *Zhongguo Nongcun Cunmin Weiyuanhui Huanjie Xuanju Zhidu* (The system of Change of Office and Election in China's Rural Village Committees), Beijing, 1994, 78-79.

The election campaign in Tieling City of Laoning Province emerged in the democratic election of village cadres according to the *Organization Regulations of Village Committees.* In the Village of Hu within the administrative district of Tieling City, Li Chunbao, together with several other villagers, wrote to leaders of Tiefa Town, the region in which Hu was located. In the letter, he said he wanted to run for the head of the village using his family property as collateral. The leaders of Tiefa Town and Tieling City agreed with his self-recommendation and used the village as a democratic experiment. In the end, the former head of the village still won the election with a minor advantage.

But the word about the election in Hu spread to other villages. Peasants from nearby villages soon demanded similar rights. Kaiyuan Town decided to allow villagers to run election campaigns for the head of the village and used Xiaosuntai Village as an experiment. The leaders of Tieling City thought that this practice was a very useful attempt to strengthen governance at the village level in spite of complaints from many of the grassroots party operatives. Because of the peasants' firm demands, it was later decided that competitive ballots should be spread to all villages under the city's jurisdiction.

The rural election campaign in the Nanping City jurisdiction of Fujian Province also implemented the *Organization Regulations of Village Committees* in 1988. That year, in Tiantou Village, Luxia Commune, more than thirty villagers jointly recommended Chen Jinman, Luo Shuicai, and three other individuals as village leaders and demanded the reformation of the present village committee which had been appointed by the party. They wrote an open letter to the election working group saying: "The working manners of some village leaders in the past few years cannot be tolerated any more. We are faced with a serious problem. But reform brings hope and the election of a village committee to our village. In order to improve our village's situation, we solemnly recommend Chen Jinman and four other comrades as our new village leaders."

Meanwhile, the five nominees also drafted a three-year work plan and posted it at the village committee headquarters for the villagers to critique. They also put down 8,000 RMB yuan as a trust fund or guarantee for their promise (3,000 RMB from the candidate for village head, 2,000 from the candidate for deputy, and 1,000 from each candidate for committee member). This event incited strong reactions from local conservative officials, who argued that this was premature democracy and would lead to chaos. They were quoted as saying "If others follow suit and whoever wants to be a cadre can run for office, there will no longer be any order." They insisted that local authorities should not compromise but prohibit such actions from villagers. However, faced with strong pressure from the peasants, the Nanping City government backed away, and the five candidates were all elected. During this phase, villages in more than twenty counties held experimental village election campaigns. [38]

The methods in which peasants run their elections varies with the region the election is held in. In Tieling, the candidates must register with the village election group, and then prepare plans for governing the village to be presented in a speech to all the villagers. In Qingang County of Heilongjiang, the candidates are selected in preliminary elections and then prepare a plan on how to govern the village. Some villages in Nanping City of Fujian Province grade the lectures of candidates, and only those who score

---

[38] In Tieling City District of Liaoning Province, 876 villages allowed their villagers to run for village head voluntarily. That is 44% of the total village committee. In Jingang County of Heilongjiang Province, 933 persons were nominated through villagers recommendation or self-recommendation; 680 persons gave election speeches; 159 incumbent village heads run for re-election successfully, 71% of total village heads. The newly elected heads were 66 persons, 29% of the total. Of the elected village heads, 83 persons had technical knowledge in some fields, 37% of the total. The average age of village heads is 34.5.

well can be formal candidates. No matter what the specific mechanisms of the election campaign are, all candidates must show the villagers their plans on the governance of the village. In order to prevent speakers from borrowing ideas from the candidates before them, villagers often keep all the candidates together in a separate area from where the speeches are given. Thus, candidates cannot listen to the speeches of their competitors. They are taken to the meeting of villagers one after anther in a random order determined by a lottery. Although there is no debate between the candidates, the villagers know the arguments of each nominee and are free to question them. The ballot also has blanks for villagers to write in new candidates they deem appropriate. Thus, underground competition operates alongside open campaigns in the elections.

During this first phase, China went through the political shock of the 1989 democratic movement, which created an unfavorable atmosphere for reformers to push for the village level elections. Despite a lack of experience and the haunting influence of the June 4th Incident, the peasant population never stopped increasing the pressure to have the new democratic changes fully implemented according to the law. Their enthusiastic participation in the political process as it effects their lives has surprised everyone. Particularly in the aforementioned localities, free and competitive elections were not suppressed. The village election, although not widely practiced outside of rural areas, has opened the door for political participation and spread like a wildfire to the hundreds of millions of peasants in the last ten years.

Gaining Momentum: 1990-93

The second phase in the development of village elections, from 1990 to 1993 saw the experience of the model self-governing villages spread across the country. In order not to allow this process to fall out of the existing control mechanism, the leaders in Beijing decided it would be better to go along with the popular opinion. Most provincial legislatures came up with regulations regarding the elections. The trend of village elections swept throughout the rural areas of the country.

In 1990, *The 19th Instructive of the CCP Central Committee* required every county to choose several villages as model self-governing villages. The Ministry of Civil Affairs issued a directive on the creation of model villages across the whole country, demanding that provinces, prefectures, counties, and towns set up model villages and use them to spread village elections and establish village representative systems. In the whole country, a total of fifty-nine counties and numerous towns and villages were identified as models because of their successful village self-governing systems. These model villages greatly pushed forward the provincial legislation regarding village elections and put village legislation into practice.

From 1990 to 1993, provincial legislation was widely enacted. There were sixteen provinces which passed regulations regarding the implementation of the act.[39] During this period, the legislation was relatively formal and complete in that state policies and local experience were incorporated into legal regulations. In December 1990, Fujian Province enacted the first operational law regarding the election of village committees, which had specific and explicit regulations. On September 24, 1993, the fifth session of the eighth Congress of Fujian Province revised the regulations with regard to village elections. Fujian Province is more advanced in terms of legislation on village elections than other

---

[39] The dates of legislation in different provinces are listed as follows: on August 20, 1990, Hebei Province; September 21, 1990, Heilongjiang Province; November 3, 1990, Qinghai Province; December 28, 1990, Shaanxi Province; January 29, 1991, Tianjing Municipality; May 12, 1991, Shanxi Province; May 28,1991, Sichuang Province; July 13, 1991, Jilin Province; August 31, 1991, Xinjiang Autonomous Region; May 10, 1992, Shandong Province; August 25, 1992 Henan Province; October 30, 1992 Inner-Mongolia Autonomous Region; December 19, 1992, Anhui Province; December 26, 1993 Tibet Autonomous Region. (*Zhongguo Nongcun*...1994, 42)

provinces. October 27, 1992, Jiangsu Province passed *"Some Regulations on Village Elections Work"* in the seventh session of the Peoples' Congress of the province. Other provinces also have specific regulations defining village election protocol, of which Xinjing, Inner-Mongolia, Shangdong, Henan, and Sichuan listed the regulations in separate chapters and sections. All provinces, except Tibet, have stipulations on the competitive elections in their legislation.

In 1990, Qinghai, Hebei, Shandong, Guangxi, Xinjiang, Shanxi, and Shanghai conducted their village elections together with their elections at town and county levels. By the end of 1992, twenty-six provincial level units had been through the first round of direct elections of village committees. [40]

However, the village elections conducted in the vast rural area during this phase were considerably different from each other. The legislation was different among provinces and even among different cities and counties within a single province. The speed of elections varied from region to region. In addition, the notions of how to organize village elections were divergent among the government leaders in different areas.

At first, there were multiple ways to be nominated for office in the different regions. In the local legislation of twenty-two provinces, autonomous regions, and municipalities, all except Hebei Province had specific regulations on the nomination of candidates. In these regulations, Shaanxi, Shandong, Hunan, and Gansu required

---

[40] In 1991, in some provinces, the three year term of village committees expired, and thus the second round of village elections were conducted three years after 1988. From 1991-1992, these elections occurred in the villages of Fujian, Liaoning, Jilin, and Beijing. In 1992, in Jiangsu, Shandong, Hunan, Hubei, Zhejiang, Sichuan, Qinghai, Gansu, Ningxia, Yunnan, and Guizhou, the second round of village elections were planned. In 1993, the villages of Shanxi, Hunan, Xinjiang, and Shanghai began the second-round village elections after 1988. In Heilongjiang, the third-round village elections also began. By that time, village elections were carried out in the whole country.

that candidates be nominated by a small group of villagers or concurrently by individual villagers. But there were no regulations on how many villagers could jointly nominate a candidate.[41]

Shown in the above various stipulations, the nomination processes in different regions of the country are far from unified. The divergences are even more striking in the following descriptions of the various types of nomination procedures at the basic levels:

I. Direct nomination by villagers, in which villagers nominate their candidates by themselves. This type of nomination can take three different forms.

Villagers can nominate candidates independently. This is common in the villages of Hequ Town, Shanxi Province. This practice encourages villagers to nominate without restrictions. Everyone has the right to nominate a candidate without discrimination. The candidates are finally selected through a vote.[42] The candidates nominated in this way are more likely to be successfully elected to the village committee. Villagers can also jointly nominate candidates.

---

[41] Heilongjiang, Fujian, and Shaanxi stipulated that the candidates for the Village Committee must be nominated jointly by no less than five villagers; in Ningxia Autonomous Region, the candidates, according to the regulations, must be nominated jointly by no less than twenty villagers; in the other thirteen provinces, autonomous regions, and municipalities, including Tianjin, Inner Mongolia, Liaoning, Jilin, Jiangsu, Zhejiang, Anhui, Henan, Hubei, Sichuan, Guizhou, Qinghai, and Xinjiang, it is stipulated that candidates for the village committees must be nominated jointly by the villagers who have political rights of citizens. In Tianjin, Shanxi, Jilin, Heilongjiang, Jiangsu, Henan, Sichuan, Linxia, and Xinjiang, the local laws stipulate that candidates also can be nominated by the local Chinese Communist Party committee or by other people's societies at the grass-roots levels. In Ningxia, it is stipulated that the town government or party committee can nominate candidates after consultation with villagers. In Heilongjiang and Henan provinces, the villagers are also allowed to recommend themselves as candidates.
[42] *Zhongguo Nongcun*...1994,42

Self-recommendation is the third method by which a candidate can be nominated. This form is common particularly in those places where election campaigns are permitted. Villagers are encouraged to register and recommend themselves as candidates. In Shenliu Village, Raomiao Town, Linfen City, and Shanxi Province, the incumbent head of the village committee was nominated by self-recommendation and successfully elected in the second round of village elections. He was formerly self-employed and owned his own small business. When the village election campaign began, he decided to run for the head of the village committee and succeeded in the end.[43]

II. Candidates are nominated by villagers indirectly. In this process, some villagers represent others to nominate candidates for the election. Through this experience, villagers have developed three forms of indirect nomination.

Candidates can be nominated by a small group of villagers or through a village congress system. The third form is nomination by representatives of the families of the village. This form is taken in the villages where village congress do not exist, and it is inconvenient to summon the all villagers together. In this practice, every family send a representative to the meeting for nomination of candidates for the village committee.

III. Candidates are nominated by organizations. The specific forms of this kind of nomination also vary. A small group of village leaders or the party committee can nominate candidates. The town government can put up a nominee for election. Any combination of the above can also serve as a method of nomination. For example, the villagers' nomination is combined with the party committee's nomination. Candidates can be nominated by villagers independently or jointly, or by the recommendations of party committee in the village or of other social organizations. In some villages,

---

[43] *ibid.*

candidates can be nominated by a small group of villagers small group, by a village party committee, and by the town government at the same time. This model is a mixture of nomination directly by villagers and by official organizations, that has been used in Luokou Town, Zixin City, and Hunan Province. In some villages, candidates are nominated at a joint meeting presented by villagers representatives, villager small group heads, party members, and village cadres. This model is also a mixture of direct nomination by villagers and nomination by organizations.

Although the regulations on nomination are not unequivocally fair nationally, the mistakes can be corrected in the process of an election. For example, in Daqiuzhuang Village, Fanshan County, Hainan Province, in the 1991 village election, villagers did not agree that a woman was officially nominated as one of the four final candidates. After the government cadres had done persuasion work, the villagers allowed the woman to be in the list of final candidates. However, the woman still lost the election, held by anonymous vote, to another candidate.[44]

Similarly, in some villages, the formal candidates for village head were defeated by individuals not on the election ballot. The peasants call this type of election result a "village head jumping from the ballot box." In Donggu Village, Nucheng County, Hunan Province, an organization nominated the younger brother of the secretary of the village party committee as a candidate for village head, but he was defeated by a person who was not a candidate for the position in the election.[45]

Some villagers do not openly demonstrate their attitudes towards the candidates nominated by organizations, while others firmly resist this unfair practice. In Dawa Village, Chengguan Town, Datong County, Qinghai Province, the villagers were regarded as very passive and tolerant. The former village head Ji Cenfu worked hard and had a good

---

[44] *ibid, 38.*
[45] *ibid, 91.*

performance record, but his work manner was very brutal and simple, far from democratic. In the village election, he was nominated by an organization as one candidate for village head. In the election, twenty-seven family representatives abstained, almost forty-seven percent of the total seventy-nine representatives, invalidating the vote invalid. In the second election, government officials went to the election meeting and attempted to persuade villagers to choose Ji Cenfu considering his good work. The masses still rejected the recommendation. In the third election, Ji Cenfu was excluded from the list of candidates, and seven other candidates recommended by villagers were nominated and successfully elected by at least seventy-three votes, and one got seventy-seven votes.

In contrast to the nomination process, the voting process is relatively uniform in the rural areas. The list of final candidates is generally publicized five days before the election, as shown in the regulations in Heilongjiang, Liaoning, Inner Mongolia, Shandong, Anhui, and Gansu provinces; the list is published three days before the election in some provinces, such as Jilin, Ningxia, Henan, and Jiangsu provinces and Chongqing Municipality. In some provinces, there are no specific regulations regarding the time for publishing the candidate list, but it is done before the election day. In some places, the list is shown publicly only one day before the election. The concern is that if the list is published several days before the election, some people might mobilize support through lobbying and family ties.

In the process of voting, village residents who work outside the village become a problem. There are specific regulations regarding this issue in Liaoning, Inner Mongolia, Tianjin, Shandong, Henan, Hunan, Jiangsu, Gansu, Xinjiang. Those people who are working out of the village or cannot vote for other reasons can delegate their voting rights to others. But one person can at most represent only three persons in the voting. In some places, it voting for others is not allowed in order to minimize the influence of family ties.

In the two villages of Xinlang Town, Jiahe County, and Hunan Province, people away from the village can ask their family members or relatives to vote for them. Village election groups and villagers both consider delegate voting seriously. For example, Lei Jinheng, a peasant of Tiangantou Village, Yuanjia Town, Jiahe County, Hunan Province, wrote to his uncle and his wife at home and asked them to vote for him and his parents shortly after he received the letter on voting from the village. Similarly, Peng Shesheng, a peasant in Linangtang Village of the same town, shortly after he got the letter from the village, wrote back a letter from Guangxi explaining that he could not go home to participate in the voting because he was too busy, but he asked his father to vote for him and his wife. In some villages with a considerable number of people out of the village, voting for others even without their written delegation is not uncommon. Voting during this phase has no secret ballot.

The major improvement in village elections in this phase is that election campaigns are becoming more common and more intense. The election campaigns during the first-round village elections were intense only in a few places. In the second-round village election three years later, more villagers realized the importance of the village elections, and thus candidates competed intensely for positions at different levels. For example, in Huangshen Village, Qiaotou Town, Benxi City, Liaoning province, the former village head Huan Xiyuan, constrained by the traditional conception of election, neither voted for himself nor actively made efforts to win votes from others in the nomination process. As a result, he was defeated in the election. After the election, he appealed to higher government offices and complained that canvassing a vote for himself would be corrupt behavior. He was convinced of the importance of self-recommendation after talking with government cadres at higher levels. Another case involved an election dispute occurring in Shuikou Village, Dongshi Town, Zixing City, Hunan Province. In the village election, the candidates were selected by the town government, while

most villagers were kept in the dark. The list of candidates
was publicized only one day before election. The secretary of
the Communist League at the village Chao Guohong and his
colleague in the League Liu Xiaoyun thought that the elections
were non-democratic and unfair, and in particular that the
candidates for village head were not competent at all.   To
protest the election and attempt to invalidate it, they put up
white slogans in each of the twenty small village groups,
totaling seventy-four banners, some of which read:

- All villages should take action immediately to reform
  the election system !
- Struggle for the four modernization in our village!
- Practice election, and oppose dictatorship election !
- In order to develop the local economy, we must
  change our leadership !
- Down with the bureaucracy, Give back our civil
  rights !

Later their actions were regarded as illegal by the city.
Although their efforts were aborted, this reflected that non-
democratic elections formally controlled by the party
operatives were resisted by common villagers. In some places,
the competition among candidates was so intense that only
after several rounds of voting could the winner be
determined.   In some villages, villagers rode their bikes
following the moving ballot box to prevent cheating.

Between 1990 and 1993, appeals by peasants with respect
to village elections greatly increased, demonstrating that
villagers were seriously concerned with the quality of village
elections. However, open election campaigns, though very
common in some places, were relatively rare overall in the
country.   In addition, most election campaigns used
traditional means to develop interpersonal relationships, for
example, advertising candidates through chatting and family
visits, giving people cigarettes or tea and asking them to vote
for certain candidates, inviting people to campaign dinners to

win their support, buying votes with money, or mobilizing support through family ties.   All these actions were very common in those places without open competition.   When candidates do not have forums and opportunities to give speeches and show people their plans for governing the village, they must resort to traditional instruments to enhance their competitive advantages in village elections.

The second improvement in the village election process in this phase was the high voter turnout, reflecting the high interest of villagers in the elections.[46]

In Baodi City of Hebei Province, there were two nationally famous incidents: the Yong Cheng Incident and the Yi County Incident. More than sixty peasants from the village of Yong Cheng went to Beijing and complained to the Discipline Committee of the CCP that the village party secretary chose the candidates for the village committee regardless of popular opinion. When people were voting, the candidates followed the ballot box and forced voters to write the ballot in their presence. The town government did not take this problem very seriously and thus mishandled it. As a result, several hundred discontented villagers surrounded the town government offices and caused some disorder. In the end, the Central Discipline Committee and the Ministry of Civil Affairs sent officials there to resolve the dispute.

In Xigusi Village of Yi County, an unfair village election was investigated three times by the "Talk on Hot Topics"

---

[46] There are 410,923 villagers who are entitled to vote in Lishu County, Jilin Province. In total 387,359 people voted in their village elections. The turnout ratio was 94.3%. In Zixin City, Hunan Province, 156,507 of the total 164,675 qualified voters voted in their village elections. The turnout ratio was 95%. In Xiaoshan City of Zhejiang Province, the turnout ration was 95.5%, and in 45% of other villages, the turnout was 100%. In Tongxiang County, Zhejiang Province, 391,246 of 450,839 villagers voted in the election, with a turnout rate of 96.4%; 277,642 went to the voting stations in person, about 70.96% of the total voters, and the delegated vote was 67,627, about 17.29% of total votes. Moving votes were 45977, about 11.75% of total votes. The people who vote at the voting stations in person increased by 1.6% compared with the previous village election. (*Ibid*, 91)

program of China Central TV and was reported in its program. After that, the Bureau of Civil Affairs of Hebei Province sent officials to the village and re-organized village elections.[47]

The second phase was a period of broadening the village self-governing system. This democratic system finally extended to every village of the country. Many villages which had two rounds of village elections felt that village elections must be taken seriously. Peasants paid much more attention to village elections than to elections for representatives to the Town or County People's Congress.

Consolidation: 1994-1997

Since 1994, the village elections in China have moved to a new stage of standardization and institutionalization. On February 27, 1995, the Ministry of Civil Affairs distributed a directive on *Further Strengthening the Work Related to the Village Committee,* demanding that work on village elections should be taken very seriously as a central issue of rural areas. Every province should have uniform organizations and plans. From 1995 to 1996, village elections were conducted in twenty-four provinces, autonomous regions, and municipalities.[48]

During this phase, the overall quality of the village elections has greatly improved. The major indicators for the improvement are that:

---

[47] For records on cases, see *1995-1996 Niandu Quanguo Cunweihui Huanjie Xuanju Ziliao* (Documents on Village Committee Election in 1995-96), Beijing, 1997.

[48] The election was the third round after 1988 in sixteen provinces, autonomous regions, and municipalities, including Laioning, Jilin, Beijing, Sichuan, Jiangsu, Hunan, Guizhou, Shanxi, Hebei, Ningxia, Qinghai, Hubei, Xinjiang, Xizang, Shanghai, and Zhejiang. It was the second round elections in Tianjin, Gansu, Yunnan, Zhejiang, Henan, Jiangxi, Anhui, and Shaanxi provinces. In Fujian and Heilongjiang provinces, village elections had already entered their fourth round after 1988. In the above provinces, having finished village elections, the terms of election were unified.

- The village elections are much better organized than before;
- uniform plans have been made to detail election procedures
- officials are trained to handle elections according to standard procedures
- provincial organs specify a uniform election time.

There were official directives from the provincial government regarding the village elections, in Henan, Anhui, Gansu, Beijing, Tianjin, Shandong, Liaoning, Xinjiang, Ningxia, and Hunan, to plan village elections in their provinces. Some provincial governments also set up small leading groups for the village elections in the provinces. For example, leading groups were set up at four levels of province, town, prefecture (city), and county. In Jiangsu, there are specific regulations regarding the budget for village elections in the documents of the provincial working office. It was stipulated that the budget for the village election be decided by the standard of five cents per capita, coming from the county government budget. At the town level, the budget level is ten cents per capita. The costs for village elections are budgeted at the government's expense at the same level where the election occurs.[49] In other provinces, it is only stipulated that the budget for village elections be decided by the county, city, or town government.

In Henan, Sichuan, Ningxia, Hunan, Gansu, Jiangsu, and Anhui provinces, there were some regulations on the inspection and reviewing process of village elections. Resistance from local officials is still present. In Yejiping Town, Zhaodong County of Hunan Province, the town party committee issued a document to appoint the village head rather than elect him or her, on the excuse that family influence was too strong and the village committee was disintegrating. After the problem was exposed, most people

---

[49] *1995-1996 Niandu.*

were so upset that they appealed to higher levels governments. During the process of inspection and review sponsored by the Hunan Party Committee, the illegal behavior of the town officials was punished, and the village election was conducted successfully.

With the further advancement of village elections, the election methods, procedures, and institutions are all fundamentally improved. Village elections are rooted in basic levels and involve the interests of a vast peasant population. Therefore, it is easy to motivate their enthusiasm to participate in this democratic process.   If a problem, such as the suppression of the peasants' right to vote existed, they might collectively appeal to a higher level of government.   The peasants' active participation, combined with the efforts of some sympathetic government officials at different levels, pushed forward the work to improve the quality of village elections.

The Achievements of the Last Ten Years

.The improvements in this consolidation period can be summarized in the five following observations.

(1) The nomination of preliminary candidates is done through the *hai xian* system, that is, preliminary candidates are generated through a preliminary election, in which everyone has the right to nominate candidates and be a candidate. This is a revolutionary change in the nomination system. In the village elections, the nomination of preliminary candidates for the village committee is a question of whether or not villagers enjoy complete election rights, because the right of nomination is a precondition for the election rights of every voter. If voters only have voting rights without the right to nominate a leader, election rights are truncated to a considerable degree. At the beginning of the village election system, candidates were nominated jointly by many groups, and under some circumstances by the governments at different levels. This nomination system was opposed by the peasants because they thought it was unfair and lacked

transparency. To solve the problems associated with the old nomination system, Lishu County of Jilin Province, advanced the *hai xian* system, which was strongly supported by peasants. In the *hai xian* system, every voter can write a name on a piece of blank paper as a recommended candidate for each position of the village committee, then those names are tallied. The preliminary candidates are selected according to the number of votes they get. This mechanism is so considerably open and transparent that nobody can manipulate it behind the scenes. Therefore, voters believe it is fair. In the village elections of 1995, thirty percent of the villages chose to use the *hai xian* system. With time, this method spread to other villages as a way to generate preliminary candidates for the village committee.

(2) Final candidates were selected through a preliminary election, which increases the transparency and democracy of the process in determining the final candidates. In the early stages of the electoral process, final candidates were generally determined by the small village election group. This method was criticized by many villagers, who though it was unfair because the selection of final candidates was made by the leaders without any public consultation. Therefore, in many places, final candidates were also selected through a preliminary election by all villagers. Because the final candidates are determined strictly by the number of votes cast in the *hai xian* system, villagers have a direct influence on the selection of the final candidates. In some villages, the final candidates are chosen by the representatives of the villagers through anonymous voting, allowing these representatives to make the final decision. Both methods are relatively open. The candidates enjoy respect and credibility among the people and are welcomed by them.

(3) Election campaigns were spread to many rural areas. In many provinces, after the final candidates were selected, particularly the two candidates for village head, they generally had opportunities to tell villagers their work plans if elected. Villagers also were very active in asking them

questions, with the candidates answered them directly. The open competition among candidates not only increased the mutual understanding between voters and candidates, but also forced candidates to remember their promises and make an effort at fulfilling them.

(4) The secret ballot was set up, replacing the traditional way of voting in front of other people and further protecting the democratic rights of villages. The setup of the secret ballot box not only improved the election procedures, but also revolutionized the peasants' concept of elections. The conventional idea was that a democratic election just meant voting without external intervention. But people learned that family ties could influence the outcome of the vote, even controlling elections if the voting process was not private, but that voters can freely make a choice if they vote in the secret voting box. In the village elections after 1994 in the counties of Jilin, Gansu, Sichuan, Hunan, Jiangxi, Jiangsu, Anhui, Ningxia, and Henan, secret voting boxes were set up in all major voting stations. Voters entered the voting box one by one. This was a breakthrough in the history of China's election system.

(5) The development of the absentee ballot is very significant. The peasants who work or do business out of the village can still vote if they cannot come home to participate in the elections. This absentee ballot began to replace delegate voting. Since the reform and open-door policy began, the productivity in rural areas has greatly improved. Many laborers, tired of agricultural work, went to cities and stayed there for years if they could find jobs there. The outflow of village peasants caused difficulties for village elections. Local governments basically adopted two ways to deal with the problem: ask villagers to come home to participate in elections or permit them to delegate their voting rights through legal procedures. Delegate voting maintains a high turnout rate, but the villagers out of the village still cannot fulfill their voting rights according to their own wills. In a 1996 village election in Qindong County, Henyang City, of Hunan

Province, a system of absentee ballots was invented in which more than 10,000 votes were received of the total 430,000 votes cast. This was the first time the "absentee ballot" system was used in the history of Chinese elections.

Lessons to Be Learned

Without a doubt, direct elections have proven that China is suitable for democracy. It follows that the direct elections of the past twenty years raise several questions and issues regarding the common thinking about China and democracy.

These elections show that it is possible to implement democracy in rural areas where unenlightened and illiterate peasants do not have a complete understanding of democracy.

The places where rural democracy performed well are not necessarily economically advanced areas. Because China has not waited for a middle class to emerge prior to democratization, these elections show exception to the idea that advanced economic development equals democracy. Inland China where the economy is fairly poor could have a higher quality of democracy than in economically advanced areas.

While democracy based on abstract ideas does have limited appeal to the Chinese public, once combined with a real situation and the ability to protection its rights, democracy can have an enormous appeal to the Chinese public. In China, democratic change must be combined with people's concrete interests.

The rural democracy inherent in the direct election of village cadres is an inevitable result of rural social development. Therefore, the progress toward democracy is a need demonstrated in the development of the social and economic life of rural people. China's democratic changes must be organically integrated with the economic reform still unfolding in China. They should be an inevitable part of the economic reform process, without which the economic reform will fail.

Finally, democratic reform can succeed only with strong popular support. While the resistance for democratic change is strong, such bottom-up pressure for change combined with reformers at the top has the best chance at success. Ultimately, democracy has to be fought for and then gained by Chinese citizens, though reformers at the top could greatly accelerate and smooth out the process.

Problems and Prospects

In spite of the impressive achievements mentioned above, there are also many difficulties for the further development of rural democracy. First of all, the specific regulations in the legal system regarding village elections are still inadequate. This reflects the general weakness of the rule of law in China. There is a conspicuous lack of training for the election officials, whose mistakes often retard democratic change.

Second, peasants are still relatively new to the elections and the democratic institutions are still recent. It will take time for the electoral system to firmly take root and then expand to higher levels of the government.

Third, the corruption of the officials and the election processes threaten the long term development of democracy in the countryside. If government corruption unites with the Chinese Mafia and family clan organizations, the goal of fair and open elections may be greatly undermined.

Fourth, in order for the grassroots election system to be fully consolidated, a democratic, constitutional framework is necessary to guarantee peasants their rights. With many of the constitutional rights (e.g., free speech, free association) still suspended, Chinese peasants are allowed to practice their rights only in restricted areas. Thus, Chinese rural society has a long and tough way to go before realizing full democracy.

In short, the last ten years has been historic in regard to villagers' self-governance. For the first time in Chinese history, new democratic governing mechanisms have replaced traditional public administration in Chinese rural areas. Peasants have become increasingly familiar with elections and will raise more demands to improve the quality of village elections. All these factors will establish a solid foundation for the further improvement of rural democracy in the future. Through democratic ways, the old generation of rural cadres is replaced by a new generation. Those cadres directly elected by the people will understand better that power is from the people, will value this power, and use it more appropriately. In addition, some of the elected village cadres have already joined the People's Congresses at higher levels and will inevitably influence the construction of democracy construction at higher levels.

Village leaders are directly elected by villagers. People now have channels to express their opinions. The elected cadres will serve the interests of people, which will contribute to the stability of vast rural areas in China. More people and government officials at different levels will accept the conclusion that the development of democracy and rule by law in rural areas will not lead to social disturbance, but to social stability. Furthermore with Chinese political, economic, and cultural conditions becoming mature, Chinese people, including some officials, will have a greater willingness to institute democracy at higher levels. In particular, city people will have greater motivation to demand that they have the same rights as the peasants do.

The vast rural areas are the best places to experiment with democratic reform. The self-governance in villages provides an excellent rehearsal space for democracy at the town, county, and even higher levels. As the wind of democracy blows through the rest of China, and as officials at rural grassroots levels become more adapt at the democratization process, a democratic consensus will build up. China will move towards a constitutional democracy with confidence.

ABOUT THE AUTHOR

X. Drew Liu, writer and scholar, is a co-founder and director of the China Strategic Institute, a think tank in Washington DC promoting China's peaceful transition to a democratic and modern nation through research and public education. He is editor of *Issue Brief* newsletter, *Issue Papers on China*, and *China Strategic Review* journal.

Like many of his generation growing up in China during the Cultural Revolution (1966-76), Mr. Liu had a wide range of experiences in Chinese society, working in factories and countryside before he reached the age of 21. He received a B.A. degree from Beijing Foreign Languages Institute in 1982, a M.A. degree from Foreign Affairs College (Beijing) in 1985, and a Ph.D. in sociology from University of Arizona in 1995.